ECONOMIC HISTORY

GERMANY'S COMEBACK IN THE WORLD MARKET

EUROPE

GERMANY'S COMEBACK IN THE WORLD MARKET

The German 'miracle' explained by the Bonn Minister for Economics

ERHARD LUDWIG

Translated from the German

Routledge
Taylor & Francis Group

LONDON AND NEW YORK

First published in 1954

Published in 2006 by
Routledge
2 Park Square, Milton Park, Abingdon, Oxfordshire, OX14 4RN
711 Third Avenue, New York, NY 10017

First issued in paperback 2014

Routledge is an imprint of the Taylor & Francis Group, an informa business

British Library Cataloguing in Publication Data
A CIP catalogue record for this book
is available from the British Library

Germany's Comeback in the World Market
ISBN 0-415-38201-7 (volume)
ISBN 0-415-37907-5 (subset)
ISBN 0-415-28619-0 (set)

ISBN 978-1-138-86519-8 (pbk)
ISBN 978-0-415-38201-4 (hbk)

Routledge Library Editions: Economic History

GERMANY'S COMEBACK
IN THE WORLD MARKET

Professor Ludwig Erhard, Federal Minister for Economics

GERMANY'S COMEBACK
IN THE WORLD MARKET

BY PROFESSOR
LUDWIG ERHARD
Minister for Economics in the German Federal Republic

WITH THE ASSISTANCE OF
DR. von MALTZAN

Edited by Dr. Herbert Gross
Translated by W. H. Johnston, B.A.

LONDON
GEORGE ALLEN & UNWIN LTD
RUSKIN HOUSE MUSEUM STREET

Translated from the German
DEUTSCHLANDS RÜCKKEHR ZUM WELTMARKT
(Econ Verlag, 1953)

First published in English 1954

PREFACE TO THE ENGLISH EDITION

THIS book, at once a factual report and a confession of faith, was written for German readers. Yet it may be of interest to foreign readers also, and particularly to those in English-speaking countries. This is not only because these countries take a traditional interest in general economic events, or because they have a particularly lively understanding of problems of economic policy. Apart from such considerations the United States, Great Britain, Canada and the other Commonwealth countries are closely concerned with the Federal Republic's return to world markets and with the scope, methods and objectives of this comeback.

The United States have placed at our disposal $3·5 milliards in the form of G.A.R.I.O.A. (Government and Relief in Occupied Areas) and of aid given under the European Recovery Programme and Mutual Security. In this way the first foundation was laid for our reconstruction in the economic and in other fields. After a study of this book American readers will be able to judge whether the American aid helped the Federal Republic to help itself—as was the original intention. They will be able to see how this was done and what remains to be done to make the Federal Republic into an economically sound and socially stable country, firmly integrated into the trading community of the free world. They will find that the views on economic policy outlined in this work largely agree with their own views on the significance of the free play of economic forces, of fair competition, and of a world market freed from artificial barriers.

British readers, in view of the similarity existing between the economic and export structures of their country and of the Federal Republic, may experience anxiety at the rapid increase of our foreign trade from 1947 to 1952. But the figures relating to this increase also show its limitations. During the first postwar years we were totally eliminated from world markets, both as buyers and as sellers. The starting point for most figures is that of 1947. It is abnormally low and consequently gives a distorted comparison with other countries whose foreign trade began again immediately war ended. And even in 1952 we were far from having recovered our earlier share in world trade. The Reich in 1938 accounted for 9·4 % of world turnover, and thus ranked third after the United States and Great Britain;

in 1952 the Federal Republic in whose territory the greater part of Germany's economic strength was concentrated—this was even before it was invigorated by the entry of refugees and the transfer of undertakings from the East—accounted for 5·4 % and thus was fifth after France and Canada as well as the United States and Britain. Moreover, this book shows that a number of factors favouring our foreign trade during the years of rapid expansion have since lost in importance. Our foreign trade has now reached the stage of consolidation which other countries reached some years earlier.

More than two-thirds of our foreign trade turnover takes place with the European Payments Union. No reader from the sterling area will fail to note the importance for the development of our foreign trade resulting from the link established between the E.P.U. and the sterling area. It was the establishment of this link which enabled the Federal Republic to effect multilateral settlements with wide regions overseas, and thus to increase the exchange of goods with these regions on which it has to rely so largely for its imports and exports.

This book is also a confession of faith—faith in the policy of a free exchange of international goods, in healthy competition among the producers and traders of all countries, and in the increase of productivity through the international division of labour. It accepts wholeheartedly every international action directed to these objectives. More perhaps than any other economy the German one has had to experience the economic and supra-economic consequences of an economic and trading policy subjected to the extremes of nationalism, autarky and Government control. We have learnt the lesson; and if the basic principles of a liberal economic policy are championed in the following pages with a vigour possibly startling to foreign readers, the reason must be sought in the special circumstances of our recent economic history. I personally am profoundly convinced of the validity of these principles; but in bringing out this book I have been far from desiring to read the world lessons on world economic policy. Yet I believe that the candid description of the way in which our foreign trade was reconstructed—a description anxious to record the occasional weaknesses and blunders as well as the successes of this period—may constitute a modest contribution to the joint labours of the nations in building up a healthy world economy.

My thanks are due to all collaborators in this work, particularly to Herr Herbert Gross.   LUDWIG ERHARD

CONTENTS

Preface to the English Edition   *page* 5

Introduction   13

I. THE FEDERAL REPUBLIC'S RETURN TO
   WORLD MARKETS   19
   *The Stages in Detail—From Emergency Imports to
   Liberalisation—World Trade Policy—From the Dollar
   Gap to the Deutsche Mark Gap—The Initial Vacuum—
   Away from Nationalism—Instruments of Free Trade—
   How Do We Stand Today?—The Statistical Picture—
   High Exports to Europe—High Imports from Overseas—
   The Political Foundation of our Foreign Trade—An
   Integrated Trade Policy—Problems of Competence—
   Tariffs as Instruments of Trade Policy.*

II. OUR FOREIGN TRADE AGAINST THE
    BACKGROUND OF POST-WAR EUROPE   38
    *High Production—Inadequate Total Exports—The
    German Vacuum—Structural Changes in Europe.*

III. TOWARDS POLITICAL INDEPENDENCE   45
     *Are We a Disturbing Element in World Markets?—The
     Occupation Statute.*

IV. INTERNAL LIBERATION   49
    *Lack of an Economic Order—Post-1918–Post-1945—
    First Beginnings. German Authorities—German Plans—
    West German Initiative—Frustration All Round—Plans
    in the British Zone—OFICOMEX—O.M.G.U.S.—
    Frustration—Exports and Calories—The History of
    J.E.I.A.—J.E.I.A. No. 1—Raw Materials Shortage—
    The First J.E.I.A. Agreements—First Agreement with
    Belgium—Monopoly Prices—The Dollar Clause—The
    Currency Reform of 1948—The 30-cent Rate—Foreign
    Trade Procedure—Step by Step—Relaxing—A Closer
    Network of Agreements.*

V. AMERICAN ECONOMIC AID   91
   *G.A.R.I.O.A. and E.R.P.—Imports Financed by
   American Aid—The Counterpart Funds—Equal Partner-
   ship.*

8   CONTENTS

VI.   WORK IN THE INTEGRATION OF EUROPE   97
      *Stages in the Integration of Europe—Bilateralist Begin-
      nings—Dollars for Exports to Europe—The Little
      Marshall Plan—Western Germany's Debtor Position—
      Multilateral Drawing Rights—The E.P.U. from mid-
      1950—Germany's Experience—Ending Liberalisation in
      Western Germany—The Course of Liberalisation—The
      Federal Republic's Part in Liberalisation—Effects on
      Different Branches of the German Economy—Trade
      Agreements with E.P.U. Countries—Italy—Capital
      Investment— France—Benelux—Scandinavia—Portugal
      and Spain—Jugoslavia.*

VII. OUR PARTNERSHIP WITH THE STERLING
      AREA   134
      Opportunities Offered within the Sterling System—India.

VIII. THE FUTURE OF EUROPEAN INTEGRA-
      TION   145
      *The Dynamics of Integration—Limited Unions—Trade
      Problems of the Limited Groups—Agrarian Union.*

IX.   OPENINGS IN LATIN AMERICA   155
      *Europe and Latin America. Findings of a United Nations
      Report—Market Changes—German Treaties with Cen-
      tral and South America—Development Plans—Colombia
      —Dollar Markets in Latin America—Venezuela.*

X.   DOLLAR MARKETS—LARGE BUT DIFFI-
      CULT   176
      Tariff Problems—The Dollar Gap.

XI.   OPENINGS IN THE MIDDLE AND FAR
      EAST   183
      Egypt—The Far East—Japan.

XII. LOSSES AND POTENTIALITIES IN EAST-
      ERN EUROPE   191

XIII. RETURN TO A LIBERAL TARIFF POLICY   197
      *The Federal Republic's New Tariff—Our Part in
      Brussels—Entrance into G.A.T.T.—The Search for
      Further Tariff Reductions—The Benelux Plan at Torquay
      —The Pflimlin Plan—The Ohlin Plan.*

XIV. CHANGES IN IMPORT AND EXPORT
PROCEDURE 215

*Removal of Import Supervision—Promotion of Exports
—J.E.I.A. No. 4 and No. 10—J.E.I.A. No. 29—
More Relaxations—Raw Materials Credit—Tredefina
—Reciprocal Transactions—Export Promotion.*

XV. IMPORTS AS AN INSTRUMENT OF EXPORT
POLICY. SOME THOUGHTS ON THE WAY 229

*Problems of Foreign Capital—Increasing Imports—
Better Prices—Transit Business—Prospects for Raw
Material Prices—Trade Policy at the Parting of the Ways.*

XVI. MACHINERY FOR ENCOURAGING FOREIGN
TRADE 235

*Information Services—Looking into the Future—Dis-
semination of Information—German Chambers of Foreign
Trade—Fairs and Exhibitions—The Significance of the
Machinery Adopted—The Foundation: Setting up Estab-
lishments Abroad—The Instrument: Patents and Trade-
Marks—Exports of German Films.*

XVII. SETTLEMENT OF FOREIGN DEBTS 251

*The London Debt Agreement—Course of the Negotiations
—The Federal Republic's Debt Service—Prospects—
O.E.E.C. Obligations.*

XVIII. ENTRANCE INTO WORLD FINANCE 258

The World Bank and the International Monetary Fund.

XIX. LOOKING AHEAD 263

*Ensuring Most-Favoured-Nation Treatment—Convert-
ible Currencies—Visible Trade Surpluses—A Dynamic
Trade Policy—Overseas Transactions.*

Editor's Postscript 271

Index 273

ILLUSTRATIONS

Professor Ludwig Erhard, Federal Minister for
Economics   *Frontispiece*

Arrival of the first German Trade Delegation under
Dr. von Maltzan at Rio de Janeiro   *facing page* 144

Professor Erhard in conversation with the American
Secretary of Commerce, Mr. Charles Sawyer,
Washington, July, 1951   145

The Turkish Ambassador, Mr. Ayasly, calling on
the Federal Minister of Economics, in connection
with the German-Turkish economic talks, 1952   160

The Argentinian Foreign Minister, Sr. Remorino,
signing the German-Argentinian Trade Treaty,
summer, 1950   160

The German delegation at the Torquay Conference, September, 1951   161

Dr. van Scherpenberg with Mr. Nehru of the Indian
Foreign Office during the German-Indian Trade
Treaty negotiations at New Delhi, October, 1952 192

German-Pakistan Trade Treaty negotiations,
Karachi, September, 1950   192

Dr. Reinhardt, and Mr. Triantaphyllis in conversation during the German-Greek Trade Treaty
negotiations, 1953   193

Mr. Ushiba and Dr. Strack, heads of the delegations,
signing the German-Japanese Trade Treaty, 1953   193

THE PSYCHOLOGICAL FOUNDATIONS
OF A HEALTHY FOREIGN TRADE

FOR Germany foreign trade is something more than a matter of figures, however impressive. Its existence also testifies to our readiness and capacity for harmonious co-operation with the rest of the world in merging markets on the basis of a division of labour. Our exports signify that we are producers and suppliers; our imports, that we are customers and partners of other nations. This may appear self-evident; but it was not always so. There was a time when politicians thought that they were acting in the national interest if they erected a nationalist wall around the country and replaced imports by a domestic production which was artificially protected and also made artificially more expensive; they preached national autarky, and aimed at a closed economy. Behind a screen of distorted rates of exchange and currency regulations they pursued power politics and the formation of national blocs. They destroyed world trade, and with it the international foundations of mutual trust. Merchants were replaced by bureaucrats in a Ministry of Foreign Trade; in their wake followed rearmament, restrictionism and finally destruction.

History thus shows that there are many different ways of handling overseas trade. It can be stimulated or restricted. It can be caused to atrophy by promoting autarky, by currency restrictions and by a closed economy generally—a game of beggar-my-neighbour worked by closing other countries' export openings. There follows a chain reaction of retaliatory measures by former suppliers. The final result is the co-existence of a number of hermetically closed groups in which production is pursued regardless of cost, accompanied by so-called full employment and inflation. The standard of living declines, while the distortions attending this kind of dubious co-existence are intensified. In Germany we had to experience all this personally and to drain the dregs until the spring of 1948.

The alternative is a policy of stimulating foreign trade. This aims at an international division of labour, which works by exchanging the national specialties against those of the rest, thus contributing to the prosperity of all. This is the way we have chosen since the war; and we have pursued it the more resolutely and successfully in proportion as we regained control of our economic policy. We have thus contributed to strengthen free trade all over the world. We are continuing to open our own markets, and we are finding a corresponding readiness to open outlets abroad. The merchant has replaced the bureaucrat; in our trading policy we are reviving the pioneer spirit in opening markets, a spirit operative also in our engineers and merchants, ever eager to discover fresh fields.

Foreign trade thus reacquires a philosophy of its own, reflecting the lofty idea that a free community of interests exists among the markets and merchants of the world. It is based, not on the pseudo-dynamism of economic nationalism, but on the knowledge that we serve our real national interests better in proportion as our ideas and the shape of our economy become internationalised.

In this sense foreign trade affects not only the experts concerned, but all of us. An understanding of foreign trade thus becomes a pillar of the basic economic knowledge which in our age of large-scale economics is everybody's business. Foreign trade is not the specialty of the minority engaged upon it; it is a general condition essential to the economic and social order in which we live.

German economic policy and German private enterprise today have two main tasks: to effect the closest contact with the rest of the world on a basis of the division of labour and to relax social tensions through a genuine partnership between the two sides of industry and in other fields. The result will be a homogeneous economic policy based on the test of competition and of service at home as well as abroad. This also implies a contribution calculated to strengthen our economic and social order and to consolidate the economic links within the western community. We thus become part of a greater whole which will increase our prosperity the more we can increase its own by adopting a policy of all-round free trade.

A glance at the map explains our position. With about 50 million inhabitants the Federal Republic lives on a narrow strip of land between the Elbe and the Rhine. This strip is viable only if it is the workshop of the world, with a maximum export of machinery and consumption goods. It is to our advantage that these goods, as well as our technical knowledge and talents, are liked, and indeed required, abroad. Our own productive efficiency in turn is increased the more the world markets afford us a chance to adopt mass production methods. Germany was always a workshop of Europe. We were, and continue to be, the great furnishers of equipment for European industry; today we are in process of establishing new connections with more distant overseas regions where a new epoch of mechanised production of raw materials and of general industrialisation is beginning. An expanding foreign trade is accompanied by new pioneer work in economic development. This pioneer work implies exacting tasks as well as promising openings for every industrial country. It is thus as partners that we enter, together with others, upon a new process of world-wide economic growth.

Wide prospects are opening, and an optimistic note appears to be appropriate. Once again trade policy and a spirit of mercantile and industrial pioneering are going hand in hand; we are exchanging growing opportunities abroad against corresponding openings at home. Nor could it well be otherwise. Our mechanical, electrical and vehicle industries, the tool and cutlery industries of Remscheid and Solingen, our consumption goods industry and our heavy chemical industry must all look upon the world as a large-scale market if they are to combine specialisation with the mass production needed for maximum efficiency. We possess no preferential markets or colonial empires. Our foreign trade, and with it our existence, are guaranteed only by the efficiency of our merchants and by the effectiveness of a trade policy affording protection against unreasonable import barriers and discriminations.

Our world-wide contacts are not confined to the exchange of goods. A new merchant fleet is building, and our balance of payments is strengthened by various services, beginning with patents and licences and the supply of technical information, and including the tourist trade. On the other side of the ledger there are payments abroad for patents, capital services, etc. Our dealings with other countries, if duly liberalised, contain as many and as complicated contacts as those between Bavaria and Württemberg and other States of the Federal Republic.

If our trade policy is to be successful, every German should have a sound knowledge about the nature of foreign trade, a knowledge which must be active and must be reflected in the actions of the individual, in the way in which every Swiss knows that his country lives on the tourist trade. For Germany the trade nexus with other countries is pre-eminently a source of personal freedom and general prosperity. As early as 1952 our turnover of trade was equal to DM.33 milliards, and contributed materially to stimulating world trade. Accordingly what matters is not only that individuals shall appreciate the significance of foreign trade, but also that they shall grasp the manifold advantages accruing to other countries from our return to the world market. It is arguable that an understanding of the nature of foreign trade and of international economic relations forms the real crown of an economic education. This understanding can form the root of a toleration which appreciates the needs of other parties; toleration leading to a genuine balance of interests. An autarkic or nationalistic policy aims at narrow advantages at the expense of other nations, and leads to a dead end, whereas a policy of free world trade identifies the national interests with those of a multiplicity of other countries. It does not abuse its machinery in order to lock others out, but employs it as a key to open many gates.

A special point affecting our position lies in the fact that we must aim at trade with every other country. Even the most ambitious regionalism would be inadequate. Even the smallest and most remote market is an indispensable item in our foreign economic policy; a one-sided discrimination can bring us no gain, since we are bound to lose by the disadvantages caused to other countries by such a policy.

Unconditional most-favoured-nation treatment, convertible currencies, the abandonment of quotas and of artificial rates of exchange—these are the theoretical and practical foundations of a world trade policy required by a highly specialised industrial and exporting country like Western Germany. We share these requirements with many other industrial countries, both in Europe and overseas. For this reason the new ideas for international co-operation as developed in the Havana Charter or the General Agreement on Tariffs and Trade, in the idea of European integration, in the International Monetary Fund and in the World Bank, are particularly relevant to the interests of our trade policy and of our industrialists. In this sense, since the foundation of the Federal Republic, we have become an element of co-operation rather than of interference in world trade. The brief history of our economic policy since the end of the war has been dominated by this spirit; it will have to remain alive and vigorous in every German if the stage we have reached is to be maintained and is to become the starting point towards further fruitful contacts in the system of world trade. The general line is clear, and is marked by the successes of these last years. It is outlined in the following pages, and it points towards a promising future.

2

CHAPTER I

THE FEDERAL REPUBLIC'S RETURN TO WORLD MARKETS

THE course of our return to world markets since 1945 has been full of changes. In judging of it, much depends on the point of view and on the temperament of the observer. A valid yardstick is frequently wanting, and comparisons with other countries and periods are apt to be deceptive. If one confines one's view to the last three years, one can fittingly speak of the sensational development of our foreign trade and refer to the current turnover of over DM.33 milliards. In that case it will be difficult to convince our worried competitors abroad of the fact that our share in world trade continues to be below the pre-war level, and that there is hardly a country among whose suppliers we play the part we had before the war. It will be necessary to stress the advantage gained by other countries whose foreign trade could develop with virtually no restraints since 1945. At the same time we shall have to convince German sceptics of the fact that our trade policy did find it possible, despite a number of obstacles, to harmonise the impulses governing the German market economy with similarly powerful impulses at work elsewhere. It will further be relevant to point to the carefully planned network of trade and payments agreements and to our participation in the new international organs in which we have been enabled to co-operate.

Every answer, however, would raise new questions. Our average foreign trade since 1945, for instance, would produce disappointing figures. Resentments going back to the early years of the Occupation would be reawakened. A confused picture would result, a picture containing the first difficult attempts at co-operation, and the simultaneous conflicts between the Occupying Powers and the earliest official organs of our foreign trade. All the difficult stages leading from the trade autonomy of the different Zones by way of the Joint Export and Import Agency and culminating in full national autonomy, would be resuscitated. At the same time changes on the Allied side would become apparent, beginning with Mr. Byrnes's Stuttgart speech in 1946, and gradually overcoming the Morgenthau spirit and other negative factors.

Awkward distortions in the structure of German trade would also become visible, e.g. the elimination of our Eastern trade, and the so-called 'dollar gap' in the exchange of goods. Nor must the fact be disregarded that the Russian Zone has analogously lost most of its Western trade. The partition of Germany has intensified the Eastern Zone's Eastward trade in a similar way to that in which the Federal Republic has intensified its Western trade, with two-edged consequences for both parts.

We ought consistently to regard our foreign trade within the framework of European developments generally. Our successes and failures frequently do no more than reflect the general European position, the fate of which we share and partly determine. The difficulties and opportunities which our own overseas trade experiences occur in a similar form in the foreign trade policy of other European countries. To give one example only, the change in the relation between the prices of raw materials and of finished goods since the war applies to all industrial countries; it handicaps their balance of payments and their standard of living as it does with us; at the same time it also offers chances for exporting machinery and capital goods and opens a new phase in developing foreign countries. In this way new future possibilities arise for a prudent and elastic trade policy. The world market of these years accordingly appears as a field full of obstacles but also of chances; as a field also for the initiative by which economic statesmanship and men of business are bound together. Adaptation and initiative are thus placed in a continually varying relationship. Many of the advantages we enjoy may have been windfalls; yet something also depended on the beneficiary. It is true that the Federal Republic was a latecomer to world markets. The speed and intensity of this return are all the more astonishing; so also are the opportunities which it was granted and the skill with which it simultaneously made its own opportunities.

The Stages in Detail

A meaningful development of the Federal Republic's foreign trade became possible only with the currency reform of June, 1948. This date is certainly of far greater significance than that of the dissolution of J.E.I.A., or of the return to the Republic of freedom in conducting trade policy.

It was the initiation of the market economy that awakened entrepreneurial impulses. The worker became ready to work, the trader to sell, and the economy in general to produce. In this way alone the conditions making possible a genuine foreign trade were provided.

Hitherto there had been a premium on stagnation. Foreign trade moved languidly in a framework provided by Allied instructions. Goods were lacking; there was a universal cry for supplies; yet the economic impulse was wanting. Until the currency reform our economy was like a prisoners-of-war camp; the inmates were partly kept by the Allies (through the Category A imports) which were paid for by the Allied taxpayers. The imports laid down in the directives were designed to prevent catastrophes, famine and disease, but they were not intended to promote any economic initiative. Any exports permitted from this camp, particularly of raw materials, did not agree with the economic interests of the inmates, who were compelled to supply them; at best the proceeds diminished the costs accruing to the Allies. So far as Western Germany was concerned, these exports merely diminished our stock of raw materials and injured the prospects of our output. The retention of controls over goods and prices (originally introduced to maintain a controlled economy during the war) crowned the folly of those years by a total paralysis.

From Emergency Imports to Liberalisation

On the other hand the barriers fell with striking speed as soon as the prisoners' camp was given a working currency and economic order, was enabled to work productively, and to pass on profitable economic impulses to foreign countries. The imports of Category A were replaced by valuable openings for other nations. Neighbouring countries in particular had found the German vacuum from 1948-9 to be a dangerous obstacle to their own recovery. The new impulses provided by German imports and the re-emergence of German sources of supply rapidly created fruitful reciprocal relations, and helped to break the Allied fetters sooner than people had originally dared to hope. The necessary evil of German imports under Category A was eventually replaced by the 90% liberalisation of the spring of 1953, and by kindred measures applied by the Government to the satisfaction of all. The dramatic change in our import policy from a restrictionism working through currency regulation to a dynamic liberalisation provided a practical example of the way in which a free-market economy can pull itself up by the bootstraps of its own import requirements and fit itself into the world market.

World Trade Policy

The distinction between this system and autarky, e.g. of the Schachtian type, thus becomes obvious. During the thirties the rates of exchange were deliberately distorted and ended in a system of currency rationing and restricted imports. A variety of planned imports were used to stimulate exports in accordance with a State plan, but were not intended to replace State controls in the export trade. Since 1948, on the other hand, we have been pursuing a policy not of deliberate import barriers, but of deliberate liberalisation. Admittedly there have been setbacks, but they were due to foreign rather than to domestic obstacles. Our quota with the E.P.U. was originally too small. We stopped because others wanted it so, whereas in reality we wished, and for the most compelling reasons, to import more. For us the stop of 1951 was not a welcome instrument for a new autarky; it was a stimulus causing us to forge a key to unlock the German import market with the help of our trading partners. Thus from the start our import policy was meant to utilise the impulses inherent in our market policy so as to provide export openings to other countries.

From the Dollar Gap to the Deutsche Mark Gap

Import nationalism leads to a proliferation of currency controls. On the other hand the German import drive from 1948 onwards contributed to overcome the shortage of foreign currencies, and promised eventually to end currency control altogether. The changes which have occurred in our balance of payments and our currency position since 1952 are visible stages in this direction: first we had the dollar gap, and now we have already reached the Deutsche Mark gap. Presumably this development is due primarily to the fact that from the beginning the exchange rate of the Deutsche Mark was a genuine one, and largely agreed with the true purchasing power parity. In competing with other countries we are not hampered by an over-valuation of the Deutsche Mark and no foreigner can charge us with using an artificial rate of exchange.

Admittedly, we had to rely on dollar help in the beginning. Without this assistance we would never have been able to give our economy a smooth start. It was not as it had been after the First World War, when the banks and thousands of firms were immediately able to raise credit privately. The gulf between the German currency area and the rest of the world was profound and clear cut. Thus it came about that a multitude of private channels of credit leading abroad had to be replaced by the Marshall Plan, by Allied advances, and by European Payments Union credit quotas. Dollar assistance, which was concentrated upon a few obvious points which impressed the layman and possibly at first frightened our creditors, proved, however, to be inadequate for an industrial nation of nearly 50 million people. Today the position is radically different.

The advance of German exports was favoured by structural factors, which also made it easier to overcome the shortage of foreign currencies. Most of our output contains a high labour content, i.e. we add substantial values of our own to the raw materials we utilise. At the same time our industrial production has always contained a large percentage of exports. Alternatively, we can say that relatively small imports of raw materials can provide the basis for a high volume of industrial exports. Our consumption, on the other hand, as opposed to our production, is strongly dependent on imports. Accordingly we gave a maximum freedom to import raw materials while deciding that imports of food-stuffs would be liberalised only to a moderate degree. There followed an immediate and somewhat dynamic supply of raw materials for industry. Moreover, since capital goods are among our most important exports, and since these require fewer imports of raw materials than does, for instance, the textile industry, it followed that these vigorous imports of raw materials rapidly led to a large-scale and valuable output of goods for export. The more we liberalised, the more we strengthened the raw materials basis of the German exporting industry, whereas hitherto raw materials had formed the chief bottleneck. It was therefore not surprising that the dollar gap of the first years changed fairly rapidly into the Deutsche Mark gap which is today threatening to hamper our trade with virtually every soft currency country.

The Initial Vacuum

Special factors, like the Korean boom, the accumulated world need for every kind of German goods and our structural specialisation in capital goods helped to stimu-late our exports. At first we encountered in the markets a vacuum which our competitors could not adequately fill despite their earlier start. Frequently we utilised for our exports the impulses coming from the world markets, very much in the way in which we allowed other coun-tries to benefit by the impulses originating from our import needs.

'The period of rapid expansion and unhampered entry into the "vacuum" resulting from a virtually insatiable and world-wide demand, particularly during the Korea boom, has evidently come to an end.'* This indicates that the existence of the Deutsche Mark gap does not reflect the normalisation of our foreign trade any more than the dollar gap did previously. The first task for German trade policy was not to strive after some preconceived normal state or structural condition; the contacts with world markets had become far too loose for such an ambition. The proper function of our trade policy at first could only be to effect the widest and best correlation between German impulses and those operating in the world markets, and thus to effect a mutual stimulation of trade which, at the same time, fostered our rapid return to the markets of the world. And indeed nobody at home could see or plan in advance the scope and direction within the national economy which the impulses resulting from a market economy ought to have. What mattered was that the initiative of private enterprise and of workers should be set free, while the consumer decided what goods were to be produced. And similarly in foreign trade the first objective was to remove the barriers restricting trade.

Away from Nationalism

It was not the case that the State wanted either to export or to import; it was the multitude of consumers, at home and abroad, and their agents in the market place, the merchants and entrepreneurs, who sought to determine the course of business. There resulted a large volume of trade, spread over a vast range of goods and over a wide range of regions. In this way the real function of our trade policy since 1948–9 began to emerge, a function inherent in the nature of a market economy. The objective was a maximum division of labour embracing all the markets of the world. Trade barriers were now no longer erected: they were abolished. The trade policy of economic nationalism seeks to convert foreign trade into artificially controlled domestic sales. It tends towards the throttling of world trade; its instruments are protectionism, foreign exchange control and, in the end,

* Ferdinand von Bismarck-Osten and Theodor D. Zottschew, on 'German foreign trade as a part of the development of world trade.' *Weltwirtschaftliches Archiv*, vol. 69, no. 2.

the control of the entire economy. Federal German trade policy, on the other hand, aimed at the abolition of these interferences. It wants to increase world trade, not to diminish it. Accordingly it seeks to extend a market economy to economic relations beyond the State frontiers, which it does not identify with economic frontiers. A genuine market economy cannot stop short at the national frontiers: it tends to abolish its own frontiers and thus provides powerful inducements to others to reciprocate. A market economy cannot flourish as an island in a sea of controlled economies. It is always striving to establish contact with other such economies.

Instruments of Free Trade

In this sense our trade policy has assumed a new shape; at the same time its instruments have undergone a rapid change. In matters of administration, liberalisation was the object; in foreign negotiations the objective was to establish trade agreements of the classical type. Naturally the different stages often reveal the inevitable contrast between objectives and reality. The transition towards long-term treaties of trade, navigation and friendship and their adaptation to the special requirements arising from case to case, is still a matter of the future. Admittedly, the network of our payments and trade agreements has meanwhile become fairly close; yet at the same time it is beginning to assume the character of an intermediate stage designed to lead towards the classical commercial treaty. Our payments and trade agreements represent an inevitable phase of adaptation, a phase embodying a great deal of effective German initiative. Yet they represent a preliminary stage resulting inevitably from the exchange controls employed by our trade partners. The original objective was to obtain promises to supply; today the objective is to obtain promises to import. Originally the duration of these agreements was restricted to a few months, and this is still the case with certain difficult countries. But with the consolidation of the international payments position and with the development of the E.P.U., longer currencies are beginning to predominate. The trade and payments agreements were chiefly designed to ensure that, despite our partners' shortage of foreign moneys, trade should reach a maximum volume, the greatest possible freedom being given to the initiative of traders within the existing framework.

The limitations of these agreements are, however, becoming clear. Today we are compelled forcibly to fit into them our long-term capital development business. Thus new problems arise, e.g. the priority given to the export and later servicing of capital goods, at the expense of consumer goods exports. These exports of capital goods thus imply the need for a new contractual framework, and for convertibility. Within the E.P.U., too, changes, ultimately implying convertibility, are becoming necessary. The outlines of a network of classical long-term trade agreements are beginning to emerge, as exemplified in the agreement with Cuba (spring, 1953) and in others. But this implies that the barriers resulting from non-convertibility must be abolished; trade policy will again have to aim at establishing a wide legal framework while leaving the actual work of trading in the world markets to private initiative.

How Do We Stand Today?

The general picture today can be described as follows. The period of active and intelligent adaptation effected through the exchange of impulses is virtually ended; foreign trade and trade policy are entering a new pioneer phase. At the same time, numerous new avenues are becoming apparent. Trade treaties have to be relieved of the burden of currency and clearing questions; i.e. convertibility must be established. The future of our foreign trade is tied to the promotion of a world-wide expansion of trade, in which there is no place for emergency measures like clearing agreements: this is the real way to clear the road for international development. The success of our trade policy hitherto has lain in the fact that it managed to adapt itself so quickly and reached so rapidly the limits permitted by the methods in use until now. Thus it is compelled by its own success to look to new methods for preserving and promoting our foreign trade.

The Statistical Picture

Seen in this light, the figures of our export trade until 1952 represent an intermediate stage in a dynamic process which raises a number of new problems precisely because it has already overcome so many earlier ones.

One example is furnished by the regional structure of our foreign trade.

REGIONAL STRUCTURE OF FOREIGN TRADE
(per cent)

	Federal Area				Average 1935–1937 Reich
	1949	1950	1951	1952	
IMPORTS					
Europe	39·0	54·9	46·6	51·8	59·1
of which Eastern Europe*	4·1	2·5	1·5	1·4	10·2
Overseas	61·0	45·1	53·4	48·2	40·9
of which U.S.A. and Canada	37·1	15·6	19·9	18·7	6·8
Central and South America	7·0	7·8	9·7	8·8	14·3
Africa	5·5	9·1	7·4	8·8	6·9
Asia	7·0	9·3	12·9	10·2	11·3
Australia	2·4	3·1	3·2	1·7	1·3
EXPORTS					
Europe	83·2	75·8	67·9	70·0	71·0
of which Eastern Europe*	3·8	3·8	1·8	1·2	9·2
Overseas	16·8	24·4	32·1	30·0	29·0
of which U.S.A. and Canada	4·7	5·7	7·5	6·8	4·2
Central and South America	3·1	7·9	10·8	10·3	10·6
Africa	3·2	3·4	4·4	4·6	3·3
Asia	4·1	5·4	7·3	7·1	10·0
Australia	1·1	1·4	1·9	1·1	0·8

* i.e. Albania, Bulgaria, Czechoslovakia, Hungary, Poland, Roumania.

BALANCE OF TRADE IN E.P.U. AREA
(in millions of dollars and % of total trade)

	Federal Area						1936 Reich	
	1950		1951		1952			
	Value	%	Value	%	Value	%	Value	%
Imports	1,870·0	69·2	2,110·9	60·3	2,414·1	62·6	1,009·5	54·4
Exports	1,495·6	75·5	2,531·2	72·9	2,909·8	72·1	1,177·2	61·2
Balance	— 374·4		+420·3		+495·7		+167·7	

High Exports to Europe

Today Europe has reached its pre-war share in our exports; about 70% of them go to European countries. On the one hand, this reflects our traditionally close connection with highly industrialised countries which we supply with machinery, spares, tools and consumption goods. But on the other hand, the predominance of Europe in our exports is accompanied by a dwindling of the European share in world trade as a whole. In 1938 this share was 52%; in 1951 it was no more than 41%. What may at first appear as a return to normalcy contains in fact the danger that we may miss our connection with overseas trade which today, with the growing importance of countries supplying raw materials, is particularly vigorous. The element of improvisation in our return to world markets appears here in a strong light. We began by resuming trade with neighbouring countries, and later entered the European market through the wide gates of the E.P.U. and the Organisation for European Economic Co-operation. What was much less easy was to reconstruct our overseas branches or to get a footing in the difficult dollar market. The process involved large changes within our European exports. Our exports to Eastern Europe which, from 1935 to 1937, amounted to 9·2% for the Reich, shrank to 1·2% in 1952. While our exports to Europe as a whole cover 70% of our entire exports, this total thus masks substantial losses in our Eastern business, as well as missed opportunities overseas. Within the European Marshall Plan countries, we are far from having reached our pre-war share in imports. In several countries, e.g. Denmark, Great Britain, Greece, Italy and Jugoslavia, the share of our imports is lower by a half, or even two-thirds, than before the war. In view of the dwindling importance of Europe within the total of world trade, the high percentage which European business forms within our exports can only be interpreted as signifying that we did succeed in quickly reaching the easy objective, but have still to display our initiative in the expanding overseas markets. This view is confirmed by the fact that the other European countries sustained losses in their share of world trade which were much lower than those experienced by the Federal Republic. Moreover, the advantage gained by the other European industrial countries between 1945 and 1948-9 and the growing volume of the trade between the colonial Powers and their empires or overseas currency areas, have constituted a further handicap for ourselves. To this extent the diminution in the part played by Europe within our total exports (from 83·2% in 1949 to 70% in 1952) can be treated as an advantage. Similarly a further decline of our European exports, if accompanied by an increase in the total volume of our trade, could be taken as a sign that we were successfully expanding our overseas business.

High Imports from Overseas

In our imports, on the other hand, overseas countries continue to play an important part, a part further structurally increased by the loss of our imports from Eastern Europe. Great as has been the value of the Marshall Plan as an instrument of reconstruction, it has nevertheless implied a handicap increasing our debts and burdening our trade relations. To stimulate dollar-saving imports will consequently be an important task of our future trade policy; its counterpart will be a fostering of our overseas exports, particularly of those going to underdeveloped countries.

At present we have a heavy, unfavourable balance in our trade with the dollar area, while we have a growing favourable balance with the E.P.U. area and with those countries with which we have clearing agreements. Our favourable balances within the E.P.U. area are only partially convertible into dollars, and compel us to effect high export surpluses elsewhere, which in fact is what has happened in the clearing countries in Europe and overseas outside the E.P.U. The entire problem of saving dollars is contained in these facts. Problems of capital exports outside the clearing and of increased imports from the E.P.U. area are also involved. At the same time it becomes apparent how great is our interest in seeing that our soft currency partners achieve convertibility.

DEVELOPMENT OF OUR FOREIGN TRADE BY PAYMENTS AREAS
(in millions of dollars)

	1950	1951	1952
Total Imports	2,703·7	3,503·0	3,853·9
Exports	1,980·5	3,473·0	4,037·4
Balance	—723·2	—30·0	+183·5
Of which free dollar area			
Imports	595·9	875·2	890·7
Exports	240·2	379·9	450·7
Balance	—355·7	—495·3	—440·0
E.P.U. area			
Imports	1,869·9	2,110·9	2,414·5
Exports	1,495·6	2,532·1	2,909·8
Balance	—374·3	+421·2	+495·3
Sterling area			
Imports	447·4	603·8	584·7
Exports	205·4	509·5	512·0
Balance	—242·0	—94·4	—72·7
Other E.P.U. countries			
Imports	1,422·5	1,507·1	1,829·7
Exports	1,290·1	2,022·6	2,397·7
Balance	—132·4	+515·5	+568·0
Other Clearing countries			
Imports	234·2	516·9	548·7
Exports	238·8	553·7	668·1
Balance	+4·6	+36·8	+119·4

Any strengthening of our visible trade within the E.P.U. and the sterling area and with the other clearing countries would serve to diminish the structural dollar gap in our trade. At the same time tendencies to concentrate our visible trade upon certain given areas (which would diminish the country's ability to fit itself into world markets on the basis of a division of labour) could be prevented only if such a policy culminated in the all-round convertibility of currencies.

DEVELOPMENT OF THE FEDERAL REPUBLIC'S VISIBLE
TRADE
(in millions of dollars)

	Total	Imports, of which			Exports	Exports as % of Imports
		Self-financed	Financed by E.R.P.	Financed by G.A.R.I.O.A.		
1947	843*	—	—	—	315*	37·4
1948	1,554*	748	—	806*	698*	44·9
1949	2,237	1,085	580	572*	1,128	50·4
1950	2,704	2,223	303	178	1,981	73·3
1951	3,503	3,075	416	12	3,474	99·2
1952	3,854	3,740	114	—	4,037	104·7

* From Allied sources.

High Exports of Capital Goods

Other problems result from the growing part played by our exports of capital goods, which threaten unduly to reduce our exports of consumption goods.

Unquestionably capital goods play the major part within the world trade in industrial finished goods, the reason being that the world is in a phase of general economic expansion. Admittedly the world turnover will in any case probably fall structurally, but this process will be intensified if the international effort in exporting to under-developed countries is forced with excessive zeal into the framework of the existing trading and payments agreements without financial methods being found to assist the export of capital goods. In our trade with overseas clearing countries in particular, the practice exists of setting off certain import quotas against each other, their total amount being determined by the availability of foreign exchange. The different countries are anxious to purchase machinery and neglect consumption goods. Should it prove possible, however, to eliminate capital goods, by means of special financial transactions, from the current trade and payments system, or alternatively to increase the foreign exchange available to our trade partners by means of a vigorous importing policy, then it may be practicable to increase our exports of consumption goods—a category for which a market still exists despite the tendencies towards industrialisation at work overseas.

ANALYSIS OF EXPORTS OF FINISHED GOODS

		Exports of finished goods in	of which			
			Select capital goods*		Select consumption goods†	
		$ 1,000	In $1,000	%	In $ 1,000	%
Monthly Average	1936	88,425	24,667	27·9	13,635	15·4
Monthly Average	1951	211,595	76,892	36·3	26,439	12·5
Monthly Average	1952	252,780	121,072	47·9	26,788	10·5
4th Quarter	1951	704,567	273,018	38·8	85,243	12·1
1st Quarter	1952	706,533	305,527	43·2	81,394	11·5
2nd Quarter	1952	742,174	347,138	46·8	82,551	11·1
3rd Quarter	1952	762,129	374,305	49·1	74,878	9·8
4th Quarter	1952	822,518	425,891	51·8	82,635	10·0

* Based on exports of machinery, electrical goods, ships and vehicles, as shown in the export statistics. (These categories contain mainly capital goods.)
† Based on exports of textiles, paper, printed goods, leather goods, glass and pottery, as shown in the foreign trade statistics.

The Political Foundations of our Foreign Trade

These facts and figures indicate that our trade policy is as yet in a relatively early stage. To fulfil its tasks, our exporters and trade delegations need that freedom of action which they are only slowly recovering, which they lack in dealings with the East, and which even in the conclusion of classical trade agreements is subject to Allied sanction. The Occupation Statute of 1949 granted us merely conditional liberty of movement and negotiation in trade policy; full independence will not be reached until the European Defence Community treaties enter into force. Moreover, the machinery serving our trade policy has only recently been reconstructed. It cost endless trouble merely to set up Section V (External Economy) of the Federal Ministry of Economics. Admittedly, a number of trained officials who had formerly administered our trade policy could be reinstalled, and within a few years an efficient and technically skilled apparatus dealing with a multitude of countries and goods was set up. Together with the Trade Policy Section of the Foreign Office, this body today represents the brains of the Federal Republic's economic policy. But here too we are threatened with the phenomenon observed in so many spheres of our economy: the living on our own fat, and the absence of suitable recruits, or indeed of any adequate reservoir of experts—developments which become all the graver as the existing officials are removed by age or other factors. There is further wanting a healthy balance, both in the existing and in the future staff, as between the officials and the business community. The difference is striking in the financial and other rewards which await the high qualities demanded by our trade policy on the one hand, and the earnings of private industry on the other. This contrast has an unsettling effect. It is not surprising that able young men should yield to the allurements of private enterprise and that the difficult tasks of trade policy should rest on the shoulders of a small minority. For a reward which, measured against their responsibilities, is quite inadequate, these men have to smooth the way which leads private overseas traders to prosperity.

An Integrated Trade Policy?

The course of foreign trade reveals with particular clearness whether an integrated economic policy is in existence. A genuine market economy implies a maximum number of contacts with the world economy, and a maximum growth of imports and exports. A nationalist economy on the other hand generally adopts a beggar-my-neighbour policy; it tries artificially to replace imports by domestic production, and to gain an advantage by ruining the trade of other countries. Admittedly there is such a thing as an excessive forcing of exports, which ruins production at home. Today the art of fashioning a soundly integrated economic policy consists in avoiding the extremes of protectionism and of Manchester free trade, while maintaining a market

policy based on the division of labour. But this requires a
policy secured against log-rolling on the one hand, and
against an imprecise delimitation of functions on the other.
In all countries it is agreed that trade policy belongs to the
Ministry of Economics, which with us means the Federal
Ministry of Economics, to which the Trade Policy Section
of the Foreign Office has recently been joined. This is the
natural authority for the administrative work needed to
establish our economic contacts with the rest of the world in
so far as such work can be effected through economic policy.
This implies essentially freedom of action in establishing
tariffs (particularly in lowering or reducing protective ones)
and in sanctioning imports and exports within the framework
of the different trade and payments agreements.

Problems of Competence

Accordingly, our foreign trade policy demands a clear
delimitation of competences. This applies particularly to our
endeavours to find the correct place for our foreign trade
policy regarding foodstuffs. If this were lacking, interferences
would arise which could injure our economy all the more
severely since they would intensify the Deutsche Mark gap
and would cause people abroad to rumour that we were
suffering from the American disease, i.e. that we were not
importing enough. Ultimately the problem can be solved
only by treating industry and agriculture as a whole, which
today can no longer be done, as in Bismarck's time, by one
side throwing the ball to another, i.e. by an all-round
agreement to raise tariffs. The solution must be one resting
on the all-round fostering of the national income, of production and of consumption. The import problem thus is
not a simple matter of clear alternatives. As an example we
can take milk marketing. Industry and agriculture join in
promoting the use of fresh milk, e.g. by works canteens and
by milk bars; the consumption of milk in the Federal Republic
is still well below the average of other countries. In this way
German farmers are given a demonstration of the way in
which common tasks unite the interests of agriculture and of
industry.

As the consumption of fresh milk increases, the amount available for making butter, cheese, etc., diminishes, and it becomes at once more essential and politically easier to lower the barriers for imports of butter and cheese from Denmark, Sweden, the Netherlands, etc. Similar expansionist solutions could be applied to eggs, fruit, vegetables, meat, etc. In view of the dynamic growth of production, scientific skill, personality and consumption in this industrial age, any measures which take from one merely to allow the other to produce or to sell are universally felt to be out of date. A dynamic conception of a market economy has room for all, at home and abroad. The competent ministries are well aware of these facts, and consistently aim at a synthesis between these factors. Accordingly the Federal Ministry of Agriculture annually draws up an export and supply plan to conform with the enactments covering its new sphere of activities, the trade policy aspects of which are agreed with the competent Ministries.

Similar questions of competence arise in connection with tariffs. In most countries it is agreed that Ministries of Finance are concerned only with the financial administration of tariffs or in appropriate cases with assessing the amount to be raised by tariffs; the tariff proper is regarded as an instrument of economic and trade policy in most countries, particularly the economically advanced ones. Its structure and severity or otherwise concerns the Departments dealing with economics and foreign trade. This sort of division of labour as between the protective and the financial aspects of tariffs is a more or less organic growth arising out of nineteenth- and twentieth-century tariff policy.

Tariffs as Instruments of Trade Policy

In the case of protective tariffs, the fiscal yield is a by-product which cannot be allowed to determine these tariffs; their reduction is accordingly a matter for trade policy. Before the war the Reich Ministry of Economics dealt with tariff policy, this being regarded as the most important instrument of economic and of price policy, while the Reich Ministry of Finance dealt with financial tariffs and with administrative and legislative points. The Reich Ministry of Finance never thought of challenging the right of the Ministry of Economics to determine the level of protective tariffs. After the war, and even before the Federal Republic came into being, the division of spheres was much as before the war, so far as the German authorities had a share in tariff policy. After that date the same principle was at first followed; a Cabinet resolution of October 11, 1949, charged the Federal Ministry of Economics with the preparation of tariff reforms.

These are largely questions of organisation, and we have touched on them at this introductory stage because they show how many obstacles, at home and abroad, can stand in the way of a clear and successful trade policy.

Since early in 1953, the implementing of our trade policy abroad has reverted to the Foreign Office, where it is dealt with in the Trade Policy Section under Freiherr von Maltzan. Internal trade policy, i.e. its relations with the German economy, is handled in the Ministry of Economics Section for Foreign Trade under Herr Hermann Reinhardt.

During the first years the object of trade policy was chiefly concentrated on building up an internal organisation and in turning the ideas of German industrialists and others in the direction of foreign trade. Now that we have a Foreign Office, it has become appropriate to revert to the earlier division of functions. Accordingly, large powers have been given to the Foreign Office, powers necessary in view of its function in negotiating trade treaties. In this way a working connection is established between our foreign trade and our diplomatic and other external relations. Hence it was that Herr von Maltzan and a number of his staff were transferred early in 1953 from the Ministry of Economics to the Foreign Office. As the measures taken internally for the promotion of exports become less important, the initiative in trade policy falls again into the field of foreign relations which have their natural place in the Foreign Office.

CHAPTER II

OUR FOREIGN TRADE AGAINST THE BACKGROUND OF POST-WAR EUROPE

THE successes, difficulties and unsolved problems encountered by our trade policy must be seen against the background of the post-war economic position of Europe if they are to be properly appreciated. Many German problems merely reflect analogous changes and preoccupations in Europe. Europe, for instance, was able to increase its production long before the Federal Republic. The absence of German exports until 1949, on the other hand, exacerbated the difficulties of Europe's export trade. The lack of German supplies increased the dollar gap—partly because imports of machinery, etc., from the United States were correspondingly increased, and partly because the German market was closed to a number of export goods. The partition of Europe into East and West and the inadequacy of the contacts between Western Europe and the world overseas are difficulties shared by the Federal Republic and should promote an understanding for Germany's problems. It may, therefore, be useful to provide a cross-section through the post-war development of Europe. Sources exist in the shape of the O.E.E.C. reports published in Paris and those of the E.C.E. published in Geneva. For technical reasons the following description is based on the latter.*

High Production

The chief result of post-war developments in Europe probably lies in the fact that, although production has successfully been increased, the balances of payments in the different countries and the integration of Europe as a single market leave much to be desired. Production overcame

---

* Economic Commission for Europe, Economic Survey of Europe for 1949, 1950, 1951. (Geneva, 1950–1–2.) See also Economic Survey of Europe since the war, Geneva, 1953, and the E.C.E. Quarterly Economic Bulletin for Europe.

the destruction caused by the war with great rapidity; but this development was in each case the outcome of a policy pursued in *different* countries, and was based on existing capacity. The nationalist impulse emanating from the investments and from the economic policy of the different countries accordingly had different effects abroad. The sum of these individual developments was not fully reflected in foreign trade, where distortions arose which demanded high dollar subventions. The deterioration in the terms of trade as compared with the pre-war rate was a further obstacle, since raw materials and foodstuffs became correspondingly dearer in Europe. To maintain a volume of imports at the 1938 level, exports would have had to be increased, according to E.C.E. estimates, by 80%. (The E.C.E. assumes a long-term unfavourable relation in the prices of raw materials and finished goods.)

The growth of production in the different countries and the collapse of the international payments system are two aspects of the same thing. The increase in the production in many countries of Europe and abroad was at once the cause and the effect of this collapse. The European payments crisis was further intensified by the loss of foreign investments sustained by the European countries with the result that a larger proportion of imports has had to be covered by current exports. The nature of the structural crisis affecting Europe is most clearly seen in the changes undergone by Western European imports as compared with the pre-war period.

COURSE OF WEST EUROPEAN IMPORTS BY REGIONS
(in millions of dollars at 1948 prices)

	1938	1948	1950	1951
Dollar area	5,200	6,200	4,900	6,700
Overseas sterling area	4,400	3,950	4,300	4,400
European possessions	2,150	2,050	2,350	2,200
Latin America				
outside dollar area	2,100	2,000	1,700	1,400
Other overseas areas	2,400	1,250	1,800	1,800
Eastern Europe	3,150	1,150	1,000	850
Total	19,400	16,600	16,050	17,350

By 1951 the pre-war volume of imports had not been reached, and actual imports had been radically shifted in favour of the dollar area at the expense of Eastern Europe and of the independent overseas areas; imports from the colonial areas were barely maintained. The decline of imports from Eastern Europe (by about three-quarters) and from Latin America and other independent overseas areas (by between a quarter and a third) shows how great has been the change in Europe's position in the world economy. The conflict between East and West destroyed the East European sources, and the war, as well as the doubtful view taken of Western Europe during the first years after it, induced Latin America and other overseas countries to turn away from the production of goods formerly destined primarily for the European market. An outlet was found either in production for the United States, or in a vigorous and autarkic industrialisation; meanwhile Europe had to draw its most urgent needs from the dollar area without being able to pay for them. It is significant that the import of foodstuffs by the six leading countries of Western Europe from non-dollar areas during 1949–51 fell by about a third, while those from the dollar area increased by over a half. For raw materials a decline in total imports was recorded, since for these goods the dollar area did not provide an alternative source.

WESTERN EUROPEAN EXPORTS TO OTHER AREAS
(in millions of dollars at 1948 prices)

Destination	1938	1948	1950	1951
Dollar area	2,000	1,700	2,750	3,300
Overseas sterling area	2,650	3,350	4,450	4,650
Attached area	950	1,300	2,000	2,300
Non-dollar Latin America	1,200	1,000	1,350	1,650
Eastern Europe	1,600	800	750	700
Other overseas areas	1,600	950	1,350	1,550
Total	10,000	9,100	12,650	14,150

Inadequate Total Exports

Compared with before the war, exports show a considerable expansion in volume—about 40%. Yet this increase evidently did not suffice to make good the losses in the invisible items in the balance of payment, e.g. in the yield of overseas investments. Most important of all, the exports to the dollar area, considerable as they were, failed to close the dollar gap; the balance of payments as between the United States and Western Europe showed a dollar surplus of over $3·5 milliards in 1951 and 1952; in practice this sum had to be found in the shape of American dollar aid, which was met by the American taxpayer.

The tardy return of Western Germany to the world markets undoubtedly intensified these European difficulties, a point stressed by the E.C.E. The absence of Western Germany, for example, intensified Europe's dependence on imports of American industrial goods. Europe's total exports overseas, too, were hampered by the Federal Republic's late emergence. Even before the war Germany was the chief European supplier of machinery to overseas countries; and when this source failed, the other European industrial countries were unable to make good this loss. After 1948, however, German machinery and capital goods flowed first into the Western European vacuum, while playing a negligible part in overseas trade.

The German Vacuum

The E.C.E. has been particularly eloquent in deploring the lack of German supplies in overseas trade, and there can be no doubt that this helped to increase Europe's dollar gap. According to the E.C.E. Western Germany's absence from overseas markets until 1951–2 had a number of causes. First, Germany before the war had had a bigger trade with Eastern Europe, so that a considerable redeployment was required before entering on overseas business. A second cause presumably lay in the fact that most of the Federal Republic's imports were covered by the Marshall Plan, etc., and by American military payments in the country. The E.C.E. prints an interesting table illustrating this point.

WESTERN GERMANY'S SOURCES OF FOREIGN AID
(in millions of dollars)

Source	1948	1949	1950	1951
Civilian supplies from U.S. and U.K.	884	536	178	12
Marshall Plan	142	420	303	416
American military expenditure	—	43	50	87
Total	1,026	999	531	515
Above as % of total overseas imports	94	69	41	27

According to the E.C.E. this aid enabled Western Germany at first to neglect its overseas business; but it assumes that the growing strength of Western Germany's payments position in Europe will eventually induce the country to concentrate more strongly on its overseas markets.

It may be doubted whether dollar aid did in fact act as a soporific on our initiative. Naturally, our trade policy and our exporters followed the line of least resistance, which meant that they began by exploiting the openings in the neighbouring European countries, which had always been their most important markets. It was only after the European openings had reverted to normal that the far more difficult overseas trade became attractive.

Structural Changes in Europe

All in all, the structural changes in Europe's position within world trade as a whole have turned out to be greater than was originally assumed. The view that all that was needed was to prime the pumps of production and to ensure financial stability at home to allow Europe to recover its place in multilateral world trade has proved to be mistaken. For one thing, it was not entirely a simple matter to show the courage needed for a return to financial stability, and some of the Western European countries have shown neither the courage nor the energy to this day. This fact alone demonstrates how deep are the structural difficulties against which a remedy was sought in the opiates of a latent or open inflation. The internal difficulties, e.g. of France and of Great Britain, led to exchange controls and to limitations of output which further dislocated the development of world trade.

Attempts made hitherto to cure Europe's troubles have proved relatively unsuccessful because the intensity of the disease was not fully appreciated. The terms of trade have radically changed; moreover, the world demand for consumption goods and for certain other finished goods supplied by Europe has become less intense. Consequently the different areas must not only look for different markets; they must also supply different goods if they wish gradually to approach a new equilibrium. The foundations of a new balance in payments and in the exchange of goods must be provided, and this in turn requires new forms of co-operation of the sort emerging in some of the contemporary plans for integration. According to the E.C.E. the main task is to increase imports to the dollar area, to increase the output of foodstuffs and raw materials outside the dollar area, to diminish American exports to Western Europe and overseas, and to develop vigorously Europe's overseas contacts in general. On the E.C.E.'s view the increase in the production of raw materials and foodstuffs outside the dollar area would be the most useful contribution for restoring European payments to a healthy state. The measures taken within Europe towards creating an integrated market are welcome as far as they go; but they do not go very far. Nationalism has not yet been really abolished, and there is no real freedom of movement in Europe for either labour or capital. The liberalisation of trade by itself is a relatively small step towards the structural regeneration of Europe; moreover, this process has suffered many reverses. And further—a point specially stressed at the end of the last E.C.E. report—the danger of a regional autarky inherent in the plans for the integration of Europe must not be under-estimated. The real objective is to establish an interdependence between Europe and the overseas areas; and the ultimate objective of the integration of Europe is to cut out dead wood and promote efficiency, not to create a closed economy for its own sake. But these aims imply a general economic expansion.

The problems and the trend of European development thus show a substantial resemblance to those encountered by Western Germany on its return to the world market. Europe and the Federal Republic alike—if we are to draw the logical conclusion from the E.C.E. Report—must never forget the importance of overseas trade as a deliberate means to save and to earn dollars—a truth which remains even when full weight has been given to the importance of integration. In each case trade policy must get ready for large-scale developments requiring capital exports and a liberal importing policy.

The problem of Western Europe is a part of the European problem. Historically Germany has always been closely interwoven with Europe, and consequently any increase in the output of Western Germany benefits the total production of Europe. The vigorous part played by the Federal Republic in the post-war organs of European integration was an important preparation for the next stages on which all the European industrial countries are now getting ready to enter.

CHAPTER III

TOWARDS POLITICAL INDEPENDENCE

'TRADE policy is one part of the State's total policy; it is consequently determined by other than purely economic considerations. There have been times when trade policy was pre-eminently an instrument of foreign policy.'* In these words Bernhard Harms defined, in 1925, the possibilities lying open to Germany's external economic policy. When he was writing the first five years of the Treaty of Versailles had ended (on January 10), during which Germany was compelled to grant the leading countries most-favoured-nation treatment without reciprocity. The similarities with the Second World War in which we suffered a far more crushing defeat, are obvious. During the first five years after 1918 Germany's trade policy was paralysed because Section 264 of the Treaty of Versailles had deprived it of the instruments needed for prosecuting an independent policy. Harms establishes a close connection between the economic events of that period and Germany's impotence in the field of trade:

Poverty was growing, the occupied territories were oppressed. Many and vain attempts were made to solve the problem of reparations; the Ruhr was invaded, the currency collapsed, consumption dwindled, prices rose at a fantastic speed, and eventually economic and social disaster was threatening. Desperate emergency measures were taken in the sphere of foreign trade: import prohibitions, export prohibitions, higher tariffs, tariffs in foreign currency, foreign trade control with innumerable overseas trade offices, the bureaucratisation of the entire foreign trade, agreements with other States on export and import quotas, vain attempts to close the 'hole in the West', continuation of most of the rationing system, and so on and so forth.

There followed the miracle of the Rentenmark, the stabilisation at the end of 1923, the Dawes Plan, foreign loans, and eventually freedom of action and of trade policy

* Bernhard Harms, *The Future of Germany's Trade Policy*, Jena, 1925.

which, on the basis of the tariffs of August, 1925, led to the speedy erection of a system of German trade treaties beginning with the significant Franco-German trade treaty of 1927.

More than a few similarities exist between then and now. The economic destruction after 1945 was even more severe, and the currency had been even more thoroughly undermined by controls and camouflaged inflation. Since then the priority belonging to politics has become still more obvious. During the growth of our independence since the formation of the Federal Republic, our trade policy has never been more than one facet of a wider tendency, and more particularly of the Western drive towards integration. These points should be steadily kept in mind.

With the political integration the economic one went hand in hand; an unbiased assessment of the initiatives we have taken in foreign trade and in trade policy during recent years is bound to notice the way in which our measures kept step with the construction of an economic framework for the establishment of European and of world-wide integration. This process expedited our return to world markets. The Marshall Plan, the Schuman Plan, G.A.T.T., the World Bank, the International Monetary Fund, the Council of Europe, our entry into the London system of payments and trade treaties, and the Mutual Security Agency—all these are steps created by the West for its economic and political integration: and they are steps in which we also had a part. They resulted from a dynamic will towards a political harmony. Thus, after each of the two wars, it was not so much the restrictions which were imposed, as the emergence of new political conceptions which ultimately determined our return to world markets. It would be impossible otherwise to understand the speed of this return since 1948 in the face of the far more serious restraints imposed by unconditional surrender as compared with the Treaty of Versailles.

Are We a Disturbing Element in World Markets?

If the priority belonging to the political element is borne in mind, the dynamic nature of our economic and trade

policy will be better understood and we shall not succumb
to the temptation either to see in these forces a disruptive
element in the Western markets, or alternatively to celebrate
them as a 'triumph of German initiative'. Both extremes
would be equally misplaced. The entry of the Federal
Republic into world markets is the outcome of a growing
political trust, of a will towards a common political order
whose task it is among other things to grapple with the
economic and relatively technical problems of German
competition. The economic interest which our trade partners
felt in our return, both as a market and as a supplier, was a
further factor. We know that the E.C.E. at Geneva has
continually pointed to the dislocations caused to the world
economy, to the intensification of the dollar gap, and to the
clogging of European reconstruction so long as the German
economic vacuum was allowed to exist.

The Occupation Statute

The subordination of our independence, and hence of our
foreign and trade policy, to the supreme power wielded by
the French, American and British Governments is clearly
expressed in the revised Occupation Statute. The Occupying
Powers have reserved the right to exercise full control should
they judge it essential for security or for the maintenance of a
democratic order in Western Germany. This is the general
political framework with certain reservations where our
information is incomplete; it forms the base of a position
where, in international law, we do not yet enjoy full independence. Against this background a multifarious initiative
in the field of foreign trade has developed, an initiative
supported by the energies of our merchants and industrialists
set free by the establishment of a market economy, by the
Trade Unions and by our efficient and industrious workers.
The result has been to give us a close integration in world
economy.

Subject to the above reservations, we can say that, by the
beginning of 1953, the Federal Republic had begun to
matter in international life, and that the Federal Government
has become the real ruler of Western Germany, with an

authority recognised by the entire nation. Undoubtedly this is due to internal measures and to the active share taken in the integration of the West. The Occupying Powers' authority which—according to Professor Carlo Schmid's words in the Parliamentary Foreign Affairs Committee—at one time was not based on the unconditional surrender but on the tacit recognition given it by the nation after the disaster of 1945, has ceased to belong to the Occupying Powers. The E.D.C. and the relevant treaties will complete the development towards full independence.

CHAPTER IV

INTERNAL LIBERATION

Lack of an Economic Order

Our return to world markets after the Second World War shows two developments, which often manifest themselves in the same way:

(1) Recovery of freedom of action in trade and in trade policy; hence replacement of the Occupying Authorities, who originally had a monopoly in the administration of, and the treaty-making for, foreign trade.

(2) Development of our own initiative in trade policy within the framework of our new freedom of action.

A genuine foreign trade policy of our own begins with point 2, a policy of the kind enjoyed by every autonomous State. But this autonomy is governed by new rules laid down in the G.A.T.T. treaties, the O.E.C.C. and in other forms of integration. The continuing barriers to our Eastern trade indicate the point where we are still subject to restrictions.

The two phases tend to overlap in time. We have enjoyed a trade policy of our own only since the foundation of the Federal Republic in 1949; yet traces of independence were observable in the J.E.I.A. and in its predecessors. As soon as the Allied restraints were loosened, trade policy and foreign trade began to assume an independent shape. It would be worth a special study to determine to what extent an independent economic dynamism was in this way touched off, a dynamism which could be found at work even during the period of maximum restraint. Important, however, as the political element is, the economic forces at home and abroad also have a life of their own which causes them to seek contacts beyond the frontiers and across the intervening obstacles. It is manifested in daily negotiations between German and Allied authorities, in the resolutions of German

federations and Chambers of Trade, the pronouncements of
foreign bodies like the International Chamber of Commerce,
the financial Press at home and abroad, and, in short, in
the deep-seated human forces and wishes which seek for
openings and for trade along rational lines. These forces
made themselves felt as early as 1945–6—in the shape of
resolutions and in plans for foreign trade in Bavaria, in the
Hanseatic towns, and in the Ministries of the different
Länder. Their strength grew with the transition to a sound
currency and market economy, and with the simultaneous
expansion of trade abroad to which this economy led.

In considering the period before 1948 we must bear in
mind that there was no such thing as a real free market
economy to provide incentives for foreign trade. The motive
forces for foreign, as well as for domestic trade had been
paralysed, and not only by dismantling and other Allied
restrictions. The controls over the economy, and the currency
chaos, stifled foreign as well as domestic trade. To export
meant to swim against the stream, the more so since there
was no connection between the remunerative prices abroad
and the inadequate controlled prices at home. The Allies
exported raw materials by order and paid for the import of
foodstuffs: they did not really know themselves what to do
with the different Zones. And so they contented themselves
with looking after their own troops and preventing disease
and famine; there was also an idea of meeting the neighbouring countries' requirements of timber and coal from German
supplies. The really disastrous characteristic of this period
lay not in the existence of any plans for retribution or
destruction, but in the absence of any economic sense whatever.

Post-1918–Post-1945

Since industry failed to work at home, it could not be
expected that foreign trade should work. Here again a
comparison with the post-1918 period may be instructive.
The Treaty of Versailles imposed a unilateral and unconditional most-favoured-nation treatment. It impeded our
trade policy, but it did not destroy our trade: on the contrary,

by Section 264 the German market was opened unilaterally by compulsion, a procedure which showed how deeply the Allies were interested in having us as economic partners. On the other hand, on September 20, 1945, Proclamation No. 2 of the Control Council prohibited in principle all foreign trade. The details were laid down in Military Government's Laws No. 53 and No. 161. 'By Law No. 53 all transactions involving foreign currencies or contracts of supply or payment relating to foreigners, and the import and export of capital goods are prohibited', while Law No. 161 prohibits all trade and all travel across the frontiers of occupied Germany. Exemptions can be granted which 'take the form of general or individual sanctions given by the competent Occupation Authorities'.* Foreign trade in the ordinary sense did not exist in 1945–6. Any exports took place by order of the occupying authorities, who took charge of the goods and issued a requisition receipt (e.g. Form 80-G of the British Zone), which was eventually met by the German financial authorities. No alternative method existed, since foreign firms, in view of the existing Trading with the Enemy Acts, had been prohibited from trading direct with German concerns.

Whereas the Treaty of Versailles tried to give the Allies a one-sidedly favourable position in the German market, the Control Council of 1945 prohibited our foreign transactions altogether. In this way the prophecy of an illustrator in an American weekly was fulfilled, who in the depth of the war drew a map of Germany showing the country isolated in every possible way: telephone wires cut, rails torn up at the frontiers, harbours blockaded, and Allied troops along all the frontiers preventing any contact with Germany. Inside this Chinese wall the German business-men sat on their crates, looking mighty glum.

After 1918 it was possible to hope that freedom in trade policy would be restored within five years. After 1945 foreign trade was supposed to cease altogether, so far as the occupied region was concerned, a region cut off, divided, and deprived of any sort of working economic order. In 1945–6 German

* Joachim Wapenhensch, *The New Law of Foreign Trade*, Berlin, 1948.

exports meant Allied requisitions on rather centralised lines in the British and French Zones, and on relatively de-centralised lines in the American Zone. These exports were handled by the occupying authorities, and were entered in occupation accounts. The German exporter received the order, which was credited to him at the internal price. The collection of the foreign exchange equivalent concerned the occupying authorities. In principle the different Zones resembled each other, though there were differences in the practical details and in the ultimate motives. The Americans were least reluctant to allow a meaningful foreign trade to develop on a federal basis, and with the help of German authorities and firms. If, despite the early trade fairs at Munich, Stuttgart and Wiesbaden, and despite the exhibition of samples in New York, the results on the whole were meagre, this was due to the obstacles provided by the Control Council and to the absence of any business incentive in the existing economic anarchy. It is true that the French relatively soon produced a system of trade agreements with the neighbouring countries; but the bulk of the exports went to France, and the whole system centralised in the Office de Commerce Extérieur was designed rather to extract German goods than to promote a genuine form of foreign trade. In the British Zone, finally, a fear of competition could soon be recognised which contributed to shape the dismantling policy and the various investigations into technical and business details as well as the structure of foreign trade in the British Zone. On the whole this period remains somewhat obscure. Sources are scarce and un-reliable: it would be an equally attractive and thankless task to study the sources for this period in detail and with proper care. Here we must be content with the main outlines.

FIRST BEGINNINGS

German Authorities—German Plans

In the three Western Zones the development of our trade policy passed through a number of stages which originally developed almost entirely independent bodies for the conduct of foreign trade. In the French Zone OFICOMEX looked after exports from Germany, the proceeds being credited by an originally rather complicated system to the funds of the Occupying Powers. A good deal was extracted from the Zone in this way. In the British Zone, too, foreign trade at first was purely a matter for the military authorities. Exports formed part of an accounting system in which German supplies were requisitioned and set off against services by the occupying troops. The payments agreements governing exports were settled by the War Damage Assessment Commission, while payments were made into and out of the Government funds within the framework of the zonal emergency budget. In the three Länder of the American Zone, on the other hand, German bodies, the Overseas Trade Offices, were instituted at a fairly early stage. These worked jointly with the occupation authorities, and were encouraged from the beginning to get overseas trade moving again. Beginning with the overseas trade Division of the greater Hesse Ministry of Economics, and continuing with the overseas trade Division of the Council of the Länder, Dr. von Maltzan helped in creating the first beginnings of an independent overseas trade organisation. Later, Dr. von Maltzan had an opportunity to use the experience gained in the Bizone, and later still in the Federal Republic. The first beginnings of the overseas trade organisation in the American Zone are also deserving of interest because, at a later stage, the Americans played a leading part in developing J.E.I.A., so that a number of their ideas were embodied in the independent machinery set up later in the Federal Republic.

Preparations for developing a German trade apparatus were made, as early as the winter of 1945-6, in the Ministries of Economics of the three Länder in the American Zone. In this way a Division for foreign trade under Dr. von Maltzan was set up in the Ministry for Economics and Transport of greater Hesse. This included a section for trade. The Americans had in view at an early stage 'the gradual evolution from controlled State barter to a free exchange of goods'. It is true that the German share at this point was restricted to the receipt and delivery of goods without any exchange of currencies between the German and the foreign party. Exports required two distinct contracts, one domestic and one foreign. The domestic contract operated between the supplier and the Land (which was competent for foreign trade); the foreign contract operated between the Land and the foreign importer, American Military Government acting as middleman. The last-named contract involved an exchange of goods without any monetary transaction: the Foreign Trade Office was, in effect, doing business for the State; it operated as partner, both to the German supplier and to the foreign importer.

The following bodies were at that time concerned with foreign trade in the different Länder of the American Zone:

(1) The Foreign Trade Division in the Ministry of Economics.
(2) The Foreign Trade Office of the Land.
(3) The standing working committee for foreign trade in the Council of the Länder of the American Zone.
(4) The joint representatives of the Minister of Economics and of the Foreign Trade Office of the different countries with the Office of Military Government, United States, in Berlin.

The Foreign Trade Offices acted, so to speak, as a turn-table for our exports. Their function was to supply Military Government with lists of export goods in the form of offers by individual firms to purchase and process raw materials, to collect the proceeds and to employ them for financing imports. At the same time the Offices had to compile lists of imports and to purchase goods offered by Military Government. The accounts were kept at the branches of the Reichsbank in the capitals of the different Länder. The Foreign Trade Offices were organised as limited companies on the boards of which representatives of the Land Government and experienced business-men were present. The individual Foreign Trade Offices thus had no direct contact with their foreign customers. They constituted a sort of large-scale merchant-house, having a monopoly of the

Land's foreign trade. They worked in close contact with the food and other rationing offices of the Länder. The Ministry of Economics carried on 'foreign trade' with the different Länder of the American Zone and with those of other zones, and eventually with other countries, in this case with Military Government as middlemen. The accounting and clearing business with the Länder of the American Zone, to say nothing of inter-zonal business, was often extremely complicated, as in the case of foreign trade proper. Nevertheless, the Foreign Trade Offices of the American Zone did provide an opening for the gradual reinstatement of German business-men. Export orders were largely prepared by Germans, and it was only the finalisation that lay with the Americans. In 1946 Dr. von Maltzan had taken charge of the Foreign Trade Commissariat in the Stuttgart Council of Länder, and after 1946 was in charge of the Foreign Trade Division of the Administration for Economics at Minden. The main problem now was to extend the methods of German co-operation in foreign trade developed in the American Zone to the British Zone as well. The British offered fairly stiff resistance at first, which was overcome only in the spring of 1947 by Col. William H. Draper, Jr., the head of the Economic Division of O.M.G.U.S. Later the Foreign Trade Advisory Council was formed. There followed the first discussions on the new organisation of our foreign trade with the heads of the Economic Divisions of the United States and the British Military Governments (Col. Draper and Sir Cecil Weir), until eventually J.E.I.A. was formed in conformity with the Washington Agreement of December, 1946.

West German Initiative

Thoroughly though our foreign trade had been cut off after the defeat of 1945, the first attempt to build up some measure of foreign trade, on however small a scale, by Allied, and through it by German, initiative, soon became apparent. During the period immediately after the Potsdam Conference of 1945, when men still believed that a unified control by the four Powers was possible, the four Occupying Powers had chiefly in mind the appointment of a Permanent

Secretary for Economics; and in fact a group of German experts were asked to draft an opinion on our balance of trade and of payments. The present head of the Foreign Trade Division in the Federal Ministry of Economics, Dr. Hermann Reinhardt, took part in this work, which was done at Hessisch-Lichtenau. These attempts to work out an economic scheme for the whole of Germany soon became meaningless through the partition. The process of building up foreign trade thus became an affair of the different Occupying Powers as early as 1945. German initiative became active early in the American Zone, and was fostered by the Occupying Power; and Professor Ludwig Erhard, together with Dr. van Scherpenberg, at that time head of the Foreign Trade Division of the Bavarian Ministry of Economics, was enabled to take the first steps towards foreign trade based on commercial practice as early as 1945-6. At this time all the Land Governments of the American Zone were supposed to be working out a plan for controlled exports. An *ad hoc* committee composed of Dr. Ludwig Kastl (Bavaria), Herr F. Sperl (Greater Hesse) and Herr Steinkopf (Württemberg) worked out the first draft. The resulting memorandum of March, 1946 arrived at a minimum figure of RM.6 milliards, consisting mainly of high quality finished goods. This was supposed to assure rations on a basis of 2,000 calories, as well as the essential raw materials.

The introduction of the memorandum read as follows:

We herewith transmit the following guiding lines for foreign trade in conformity with the request made at the meeting of the Foreign Trade Sub-committee on February 18, 1946, when we were asked to supply proposals for the regulation and control of German foreign trade. In our view this regulation should be carried through without delay. An explanatory memorandum on the importance of foreign trade for Germany is attached.

A resumption of foreign trade is of vital importance for the feeding and employment of an over-populated Germany in its present form and economic structure. To provide the population with food, even on a modest basis, necessitates increased imports of foodstuffs in the immediate future.

Germany is bare of raw materials, and this will shortly put an end to industrial production unless the necessary raw materials are supplied. To work out and fulfil an emergency import programme is urgently necessary.

In the long run imports can be paid for only if openings are provided for the corresponding exports. The German population is aware that today its existence depends, as never before, on adequate exports. Given the state of the German economy, no large-scale exports of staple goods are possible. The primary requisite is to send abroad high value finished goods adapted to individual requirements.

German foreign trade is an important element in the European economy; without it the latter cannot develop in a sense desirable for all the nations. But our foreign trade can flourish and can fulfil its vital tasks only if it is increasingly freed from the restrictions and controls hitherto regarded as essential. This demands a large measure of understanding, goodwill and initiative from all concerned. Such a policy would conform to the Potsdam Resolutions, which expressly state that Germany must be given a chance to live, so that it can fulfil its tasks in a democratic community of nations.

The business-men of the world must resume their old connections if the disasters caused by the war are to be overcome. Civilisation cannot be saved unless world trade is allowed again to assume its old shape.

The following outline is confined at this stage to the parts of Germany under American administration. But it is also of the greatest importance for the other Zones. Germany's foreign trade can grow only if inter-zonal trade can work with the smoothness necessary for a single economic area.

Today the plan sounds conservative enough, if not actually tame; still, it did suggest that the Allies should provide the financial pump-priming for exports. It failed to gain the approval of the Allies, and another proposal was worked out. This was put forward at the end of May, 1946, and though sanctioned by the Military Governments on a Land basis was not accepted by O.M.G.U.S. in Berlin.

This plan put the Prime Ministers of the Länder in charge of foreign trade. For this purpose it was proposed to form a Control Council for Foreign Trade to work under the Council of the Länder; the greatest possible freedom was to be given to private initiative. 'The employment of import and export organisations under State control is to be deprecated.' The different Ministries of Economics were to permit firms to deal direct with the foreign countries. The establishment of foreign agencies was also envisaged as well as journeys abroad for business purposes; business correspondence with foreign countries was to be permitted. Military Government was to continue to finalise export deals, weight being given to the difference between dollar prices abroad and the maximum permitted prices inside Germany. The proposals were modest enough, but at that time were not yet practical politics. Today one is inclined to regard the proposals (which were worked out in a similar form later by private persons in the British Zone) as insufficient. They must be judged in the light of prevailing conditions, nor must we forget the heavy pressure exerted by the Americans as well as by other parties. The plan as a whole reflects the situation as it was in 1946. It ran as follows:

May 29, 1946.

PLAN FOR THE CONTROL OF FOREIGN TRADE

A. GENERAL CONSIDERATIONS

1. *Competence*

   (a) The control of foreign trade lies with the Prime Ministers of the Länder.

   (b) For this purpose a Foreign Trade Control Committee will be appointed at the Council of the Länder; it will consist of the Foreign Trade Sub-committee with an economic representative for each Land as assessor.

   (c) Foreign trade will be controlled by the Ministries of Economics of the different Länder, in conformity with outlines published by the Council of the Länder. The latter are empowered to set up a subordinate authority for the purposes of controlling foreign trade.

   (d) In principle private initiative should be utilised to a maximum degree for the whole of foreign trade. The employment of State import and export organisations is to be deprecated, as before.

2. *Participation in Foreign Trade*

(*a*) Firms will be granted permission to trade independently with foreign countries by the Land Ministry of Economics, which has to satisfy itself of the existence of the necessary personal and economic qualifications. Permission to trade will be granted only on application, which is subject to cancellation. Where applications are refused or sanctions are cancelled, the firms affected have the right to appeal. Appeals will go before a committee set up by Military Government.

(*b*) The establishment of branches, agencies, etc., requires sanction by Military Government. Applications should be sent to the Ministry of Economics.

(*c*) Applications for sanction to proceed abroad on business and for the necessary currency should be sent to the Ministry of Economics and must be sanctioned by Military Government. Applicant's passports should be marked accordingly. The conditions under (*a*) apply with the appropriate modifications.

(*d*) Lists of firms granted sanction and of cancellations should be submitted to Military Government.

3. *Correspondence*

Firms permitted to do foreign business shall submit their foreign business correspondence to the Ministry of Economics or to a body to be designated by it for a preliminary censorship. On being granted permission to carry on foreign trade, every firm must sign a declaration undertaking to confine its business correspondence to the appropriate transactions in the light of any existing regulations, and to submit such business correspondence to the Minister of Economics or to a body designated by him for purposes of a preliminary censorship.

Business contacts and business correspondence with foreign firms designated to the Council of the Länder by Military Government (blacklisted firms) are prohibited.

B. SPECIAL ARRANGEMENTS

1. *Exports*

(*a*) The Council of the Länder will compile a list of goods, the export of which is prohibited or restricted; this list to be published by the Ministries of Economics in the three Länder.

(b) Export transactions will be finalised by Military Government (O.M.G.U.S.). Prices, conditions of payment and conditions of supply must be supplied to the Minister of Economics. Separate pro forma accounts, in duplicate, should be supplied covering:

    (i) The foreign price (if practicable, in American dollars).
    (ii) The permissible domestic price due to the exporter.

(c) The Ministry of Economics must satisfy itself that:

    (i) The goods are permissible exports.
    (ii) Their export is practicable in the light of the general state of the German economy.
    (iii) That the price agreed in foreign currency is adequate. Special attention should be given to ensuring that no capital transactions are made possible by special price arrangements.
    (iv) That the domestic price quoted by the firm conforms to the legal regulations.
    (v) That the transaction does not contravene any other arrangements.

If, upon examination, no objections arise, the Ministry of Economics submits the documents to Military Government (O.M.G.U.S.) for finalisation.

(d) The exporter will supply, in triplicate, an export currency declaration to be submitted to an authority to be designated by Military Government on the proposal of the Council of the Länder.
The resulting foreign currency will be collected by Military Government (O.M.G.U.S.).
Military Government will advise the appropriate Ministry of Economics of the receipt of the foreign currency. On receipt of the advice the Ministry of Economics will meet the invoice in Reichsmark. Where payment is made in instalments an appropriate partial payment will be made to the exporter.

(e) Goods designed for export may be despatched only if a certificate of sanction accompanies the way-bills or bills of lading. The Council of the Länder will issue the regulations necessary for export transactions and dealing with certificates of despatch and of payments, with statistical returns, etc.

2. *Imports*

   (*a*) Subject to the import plan sanctioned by Military Government, imports should in principle be effected by admitted
firms; State organisations should be excluded as far as
possible.

   (*b*) Import transactions are finalised by Military Government
(O.M.G.U.S.).

   Individual transactions should previously be submitted for
sanction to the Ministry of Economics. The latter has to
satisfy itself:

      (i) That the transaction will not exceed the available
imports as sanctioned by the Control Council.

      (ii) That prices, conditions of supply, quality, etc., are in
accordance with the needs of the German economy.

   (*c*) Where goods are under State control, and the imports are
effected by private firms, the Ministry of Economics will
ensure that individual firms are given equal treatment by
the assignment of appropriate quotas.

   (*d*) If, on examination, no objections are found, the Ministry
of Economics will transmit the documents to Military
Government (O.M.G.U.S.) for finalisation; the latter
will concurrently settle all questions connected with
payment.

3. Special priority should be given to transactions by which a
high value is added through processing. Such transactions will
be governed by the regulations applying to the import and
export of goods. The Ministry of Economics will examine the
conditions arranged with the foreign customer regarding the
goods (raw materials or semi-finished), which should be imported in bond, and regarding the fee for processing and
conditions of supply and payment.

Admittedly the local representatives of Military Government in the different Länder frequently sponsored purely
local interests. Many transactions carried through in the
American Zone would have been impossible at that time in
the British Zone. Thus in the spring of 1946 exports of
concrete to neighbouring States were used to demonstrate
the importance in the export trade of a large cement works,
which was thus saved from dismantling.

Other German measures too became possible at an early stage. For instance, a memorandum addressed by Dr. von Maltzan in June, 1947, to the Bipartite Economic Control Group proposed the establishment of German foreign trade agencies in important cities abroad, at first London, New York, Brussels, Milan, Vienna, Zurich, Stockholm, Prague and Montevideo; later, agencies were to be opened in Moscow, Paris, Istanbul and the Far East. These plans were sponsored by certain officials of American Military Government, e.g. Miss Ethel Dietrich and Col. W. H. Draper, Jr. It was found, however, that the time was not yet ripe. Yet the first foundations had been laid.

Frustration All Round

It is clear, however, that in 1946 the economic conditions for large-scale trade were wanting, however good the organisation might be. A workable market economy did not exist. Imports were drawn into a vacuum, exports were frustrated, and the internal economy was subject to interference and insecurity of every kind. The virtual cessation of foreign trade is illustrated by a passage from *Trade and Commerce* (Monthly Report of the Military Governor of the American Zone, No. 6 of January 20, 1946).

According to this publication export prices were hard to determine in the absence of official quotations for Reichsmarks. The systems for supervising trade existing in the countries with which Germany would deal were being examined to adapt the buying and selling procedure or the supervisory machinery to the position existing in the different countries. Steps were being taken to proceed jointly with the British to permit technical contact between German and foreign concerns. Proposals for opening a limited and supervised postal and telegraphic service between Germany and other countries were being worked out. In December endeavours were continued to discover, interrogate and eventually accept candidates for a central German export and import administration. Representatives of the Länder Governments arrived in Berlin to take over the work previously done by Military Government in working out an export programme. Contact was efficiently established with the Governments of the German Länder and methods were formulated for handling the import of foodstuffs from the United States. Regular conferences were provided for with the working committee for imports and exports at the secretariat of the Council of Länder in Stuttgart.

Imports

The gap between imports and exports to be financed by the American Administration to realise the foodstuffs programme of 1,550 calories sanctioned in the American Zone was being worked out for the fiscal year 1946–7.

Preliminary negotiations for the import of seed clover from Czechoslovakia and of other seeds from Denmark, the Netherlands and Great Britain were concluded.

Exports

Lists of available exports were handed in by the three Länder. Certain industries requiring a minimum of essential raw materials were selected and an export programme was being prepared. Most of the factories producing ceramics, glass goods, pottery and scientific and domestic instruments were found to be adequately equipped to resume production provided they had coal. It was also assumed that export surpluses of fountain pens, pencils and other goods could be achieved if the producers were given small quantities of raw materials.

The American Zone was actually exporting electric current to Austria. Exports of salt and potash to Czechoslovakia were under discussion; the same applied to exports of refrigerators, various gases and carbon rods to Denmark. Export openings for scrap, building timber, optical instruments, pharmaceutical products and oil-boring and oil-refining machinery to the Netherlands were being studied. Arrangements were made to export hops to the United States through the U.S. Commercial Credit Co. Negotiations were in progress with the Norwegian Government to supply hydraulic installations ordered and manufactured before the German capitulation, but not yet supplied.

Plans in the British Zone

In the British Zone progress at first was much slower. It is true that, as early as the summer of 1946, the German Economic Council in Minden had written a memorandum on the best way to speed up the development of foreign trade, a document demonstrating the readiness of responsible Germans to stimulate exports which would lighten the burden resting on the Allies. Today this plan too reads like a lesson on the elements of the German economic structure and on rational economic conduct. It can hardly be assumed that these fundamentals were unknown to the Allies. The memorandum, much of which was drafted in Hamburg, stresses the need for a closer nexus between Germany and other countries, for the expansion of German exports (primarily finished goods) to finance imports of foodstuffs and raw materials, and for the reintroduction of private business-men in dealings with foreign customers. It was argued that the offer of German goods through an anonymous and monopolistic trading corporation would speedily result in failure, even if the German exporter supplied the names of his foreign customers to the corporation. The memorandum dealt with long-term export plans as well as with the possibility of an emergency export programme which would utilise existing finished goods and raw materials. Here too the proposals seem today almost to suffer from an excess of modesty. Thus it was not suggested that the German exporter should be paid at world market rates, but merely at the rates ruling internally. The foreign exchange rates would have to be established by a gradual system of trial and error at the world centres. A foreign exchange account and a Reichsmark settlement account, neither having any connection with the other, were proposed. Foreign trade offices run by the State were described as undesirable in view of their bureaucratic clumsiness unless Military Government should decide that direct relations between German and foreign business-men were not yet practicable.

There follows a particularly significant passage:

Hitherto the exports of the British Zone have consisted almost entirely of raw materials, particularly coal and timber; they have consequently remained slight. Admittedly it was natural that, in the first period of the Occupation, the coal so urgently needed by neighbouring countries should have been exported; yet a continuation of this practice would involve very serious economic injury. A densely populated industrial country cannot pay for the needed foodstuffs and raw materials by exporting its own raw materials. The imports must be processed and thus be raised to twenty or forty times the value of the imported raw materials. In this way alone it is possible to pay our suppliers. The exporting industries [the Memorandum continues] should have priority in the allocation of raw materials, since many producers naturally hesitate to process their last remaining stocks. This instinct for self-preservation can hardly be met by compulsory measures. On the other hand industrialists would no doubt be ready to use their stocks if they had a firm assurance that raw materials used in producing export goods would speedily be replaced.

It ends by declaring that large industrial capacity is waiting to turn out goods, that foreign business correspondence should be freed from control, and that German business-men should be allowed to travel abroad.

The memorandum was rejected in London, though it had been approved at a high level by Military Government and by the British members of the Commission set up by the Control Council.* This happened at a time when the British taxpayer had to contribute largely to keep the Zone going. Evidently this expense could be supported so long as it eliminated German competition.

The difficulties of neighbouring States were intensified by the fact of Germany's isolation, but nothing much could be done. As early as 1946, all the neighbouring States under Dutch leadership applied to the European Committee of U.N.O. to be allowed a say in the economic future of Germany. The Netherlands in particular were actuated by a desire to resume old trade connections. Despite these vigorous endeavours, negotiations for an exchange of goods with the Netherlands did not begin until early in 1947, when the Netherlands offered to import goods worth $60 millions from the two Zones.

5   * *Exportdienst*, vol. 1, no. 1, September 19, 1946.

OFICOMEX

In the French Zone the accounting work for exports was done by OFICOMEX. Foreign trade transactions could be effected only by the Foreign Trade Offices of the Occupying Power. The German producer sold to OFICOMEX in Reichsmarks and on the basis of German internal prices. The German importer purchased from the same office, also in Reichsmarks, and at the prices current in the Zone. Thus sawn timber was purchased at RM.116 a ton, and was sold at $19 (RM.190) to France. The proceeds could be used to buy wheat in the United States at RM.200 a ton, including freight. For exports and imports alike the rate was RM.10 to the dollar. Of the dollar proceeds, 20% was retained for any reparations payments. From August, 1945, to January, 1946, the Zonal exports amounted to $18·8 millions, leaving $15·5 millions for imports after the 20% had been deducted. A sum of $14·5 millions was actually so spent. Of the exports, $11·5 millions consisted of raw materials, and $5·4 millions of industrial equipment. Consumption goods and finished products were exported to an amount of $1·6 millions, and foodstuffs to an amount of $0·5 million. Imports of foodstuffs cost $9·6 millions, and $1·3 millions were paid for ancillary services, chiefly rail charges, which came to about 10% of total imports. These are official figures but it is not certain that they reflect the total exports.

O.M.G.U.S.

In the American Zone the authorities were not directly interested in exports of German raw materials. The different authorities set up by the Occupying Power were anxious rather to stimulate exports in general on a decentralised basis. But these attempts too were frustrated by the chaos ruling in markets and currency. And though a decentralised system was used, German exports in the American Zone too were handled by Allied authorities. The depersonalised nature of this method did not do full justice to German finished goods (both consumption and capital goods) embodying a high degree of skill. Despite all the endeavours of bureaucratic bodies, valuable goods of this sort cannot be

marketed without personal contact between the business-
men concerned. Although O.M.G.U.S. received from the
one Foreign Trade Office of Greater Hesse alone nearly a
thousand offers valued at RM.45 millions in the period to
September, 1946, business was actually done only in potash,
timber and other raw materials. Similarly disappointing
results were recorded in Bavaria, whose exports consisted
chiefly of easily marketable raw materials, e.g. hops and
sawn timber. Ultimately these exports thus did not differ
much from those of the British Zone, though in the latter
the Occupying Power was much less interested in exports than
were the Americans. American Military Government did,
in fact, try hard to get exports of finished goods moving.
As early as 1946 the head of the Export and Import Division,
Mr. R. J. Bullock, took a collection of samples of German
goods to New York. It comprised china, cameras, toys, and
leather and fancy goods, for the American Christmas trade
of 1946. A number of deals were put through at acceptable
prices; but the total suffered from the difficulties affecting
German output. At an early stage the Americans gave top
priority to exports, e.g. in the allocation of raw materials,
yet for the time being it did not prove practicable to allow
individual exporters to act on their own initiative. In this
way bureaucratic obstacles resembling those in the other
Zones came into being. Nonetheless, the requisitioning
stage had been left behind, and attempts were being made
to promote exports, though with varying degrees of energy,
and from conflicting motives.

Frustration

First steps had already been taken at this stage, but they
were frustrated by the methods in force. The producer in the
American Zone had to hand his offer to a Foreign Trade
Office of the Land. The offer was in English and in triplicate,
and took the shape of a *pro forma* invoice with exact details
of prices, which were not allowed to exceed internal net
wholesale prices. Where practicable illustrations, catalogues
and samples had to be attached. If possible, offers had to be
made not subject to the availability of raw materials; the

goods offered were supposed to be manufactured from existing stocks. If the contract was concluded, the required raw materials were supposed to be made good as a priority from stocks held by the Regional Economic Offices. The Foreign Trade Offices listed and numbered the offers, and submitted them to O.M.G.U.S. for final approval.

O.M.G.U.S. thereupon got in touch with the purchaser named in the producer's offer: there was no direct contact between the two. The deal could be concluded only if the customer was prepared to pay in free dollars, the cross rate between Reichsmark and dollar generally varying between RM.2·5 and RM.3. In the first instance offers could be made only to the countries listed by O.M.G.U.S., the most important being the United States, France, the United Kingdom, the Benelux countries, Scandinavia, Czecho-slovakia, Austria and Brazil. At this stage trade with neutral countries was prohibited, but it was sanctioned in 1946, particularly with Switzerland and Sweden, provided custo-mers agreed to pay in dollars. On conclusion of the trans-action by O.M.G.U.S. the Foreign Trade Office of the Land was informed by Military Government, quoting the export licence number and giving instructions for the immediate despatch of the goods. The Foreign Trade Office thereupon asked the producer to despatch the goods free to the German frontier or port. The relative documents in a prescribed form had to be handed in at the Foreign Trade Office to be passed on to O.M.G.U.S. At the frontier the German authorities ceased to be responsible for the goods, which were now taken over by the customer's forwarding agents. To send goods free to destination or free to foreign port was impracticable, since no foreign currencies were available to pay the freight.

Payment was made in dollars by the overseas importer direct to O.M.G.U.S. or its local agent in the Land. The foreign exchange transaction was thereupon entered in the account by the finance division of O.M.G.U.S. without any Germans coming into the transaction. The foreign exchange was used to finance the import of foodstuffs.

All in all, conditions for normal foreign trade were entirely wanting in 1945–6. Imports were mainly restricted to those of Category A, i.e. to essential foodstuffs, while raw materials, even when required for exports, could enter only within the limitation of a difficult and complicated export machinery. Raw materials for home consumption were in principle not admitted at all. Exports, on the other hand, consisted mainly of raw materials like coal, sawn timber, salt, etc. Despite every endeavour on the part of the lower American authorities and despite all that could be done through a number of export fairs, exports of finished goods were minute, as is clearly shown by later statistics. The following were the chief obstacles:

(1) Direct contacts between the German exporter and the foreign importer were prohibited. The Allied authorities uniformly were parties to the contract, the preliminary work being done by the Foreign Trade Offices. The German exporter was not allowed to communicate by letter or telephone; transactions were generally effected on foreign initiative, if German products were urgently needed.

(2) No guarantee existed that raw materials would be supplied to make good those used up. To export meant the sale of a capital asset, and the ultimate disappearance of the last available stocks.

(3) There was no connection between domestic and foreign prices. However favourable world prices might be, the German producer received only the domestic fixed price, carefully checked by the authorities, with the result that the Reichsmark equivalent of the dollar proceeds showed remarkable differences in the rate. With goods whose world price had risen particularly steeply, the dollar sometimes was worth no more than 1 Reichsmark.

(4) The foreign customer was compelled to pay in dollars. In practice no trade treaties or even clearing agreements existed, though admittedly foreign trade agreements with eleven European countries had been reached in the French Zone as early as 1946. In fact, however, these were really agreements for the supply

of goods, settling the exact value of exports to the country concerned during a given period. The actual amounts were minute since over 80% of exports from the French Zone were directed into France.

(5) None of the Zones permitted the import of so-called 'non-essentials'. An early agreement between Switzerland and the British and American Zones showed at how many points potential trade met closed doors. An agreement concluded early in 1946 in the French Zone allowed German exports worth 25 million francs during the first nine months; Swiss exports in exchange were, however, limited to 5 million francs.

Imports into Germany were confined to important foodstuffs and raw materials, and so far as Europe was concerned, these could not easily be supplied since Europe was itself short of raw materials. Thus German exports, such as they were (in the main they consisted of expensive raw materials) resulted in a high surplus in the balance of payments.

Obstacles could be found everywhere, even at the most insignificant stages. In the French Zone it was regarded as a step forward when German firms were allowed to enter into correspondence, via OFICOMEX, with their clients abroad. Correspondence had to be submitted to OFICOMEX in unsealed envelopes. At first business correspondence had to be in German or in the language of the Occupying Power—a substantial obstacle in the way of resuming trade with South America.

Exports and Calories

The first chapter of 1946 ended with the Stuttgart speech of Mr. James Byrnes, the American Secretary of State. The first step towards reintegrating Western Germany with the Western world was imminent. On December 2, 1946, the Foreign Ministers of Great Britain and the United States resolved upon economic union between the British and the American Zones; detailed regulations for economic co-operation were worked out. The Bizone became a reality with the beginning of 1947: the objective was to reach its economic independence within three years. Foreign trade was to be handed over as soon as possible to a German administrative Office of Economics. Before the end of 1946 the administrative outlines for the Foreign Trade Branch of the Bipartite Control Office were announced. At its head was Freiherr von Maltzan with Dr. Schöne as deputy. At the same time the Executive Committee for Economics at Minden was asked to work out a draft plan for the foreign trade balance of 1947. Dr. Rudolf Mueller, at that time head of the Economic Council, accordingly drew up a plan providing exports of approximately RM.1 milliard, and imports of approximately RM.2·4 milliards. Consumption of food was supposed to be equal to 1,550 calories daily, requiring imports of foodstuffs worth RM.1·37 milliards. Raw material imports were estimated at RM.1·03 milliards. A rate of 2,000 calories daily was estimated to imply foodstuff imports of RM.1·825 milliards. Efficiency would increase correspondingly, permitting raw material imports worth RM.1·3 milliards, and exports worth RM.1·9 milliards. At 2,000 calories the deficit of the balance of trade in the Bizone would be reduced by RM.0·1 milliard to RM.1·225 milliards, the mark being taken at 40 cents. The actual course of 1947 and of most of 1948 showed how large an element of illusion existed even in this plan. The plan, for instance, assumed exports of finished goods worth about 70% of total exports. In fact, the exports of 1947–8 continued mainly to consist of coal and sawn timber, while imports of raw materials and foodstuffs remained at a low level.

The History of J.E.I.A.

At the same time the management of foreign trade was reorganised by the formation of the Joint Export-Import Agency. This body had the monopoly of foreign trade, and until 1949 was legally the contracting party in foreign trade dealings. Even later, when foreign trade conditions had been relaxed, the German exporters acted for account of and in the name of J.E.I.A. The difficulties of 1945–6 thus largely remained, though the organisation of foreign trade was on this occasion for the first time given a special machinery.

Despite these faults J.E.I.A. was later enabled to provide German exporters with a number of useful contacts abroad.

The history of J.E.I.A. is one of brave promises on paper, and small performance in practice. Up to the time of the currency reform, the following fundamental facts consistently remained in force.

(1) The division of imports into Categories A and B was maintained. The former comprised foodstuffs, the latter raw materials needed for exports. German exports could be utilised only to pay for Category B imports, and the export value was supposed to be equivalent to three times the cost of the imports. Any surplus was used to pay for Category A imports (to prevent disease and unrest).

(2) Any trade agreements concluded prohibited the supply of Category A foodstuffs in exchange for German exports.

(3) In principle all German exports had to be paid for in dollars, an irrevocable credit being established on conclusion of the contract. Foreign customers naturally accepted such an obligation only for the most urgently needed goods.

(4) Each export deal had to be sanctioned separately by J.E.I.A. Multiple deals were permitted only if prices and amounts were fixed in advance for the entire period of the agreement.

(5) No link existed between internal and world prices. German exports had to be charged for at the highest obtainable world price, which was determined by J.E.I.A. Later J.E.I.A. established so-called conversion coefficients for certain classes of goods. A high dollar price consequently did not imply a correspondingly high Reichsmark price.

Until 1948 exports on any sizeable scale failed to materialise. The programme worked out by Dr. Rudolf Mueller in 1946 had to be postponed until April, 1947, because failures in the supply of coal and current caused production to be interrupted. Direct contracts between exporters of the

Bizone and foreign customers were admitted in principle as early as March, 1947; but the bureaucratic entanglement between the German and Allied official bodies (forty-eight forms were sometimes needed) was such that this arrangement remained largely on paper.

In March, 1947, when the Trading with the Enemy Act ceased to operate, the Board of Trade published a description of the way in which German exports from the Bizone were arranged at the time; from this the following long-term objectives become apparent:

(1) German trade was to return as soon as possible to normal channels; but the 'difficult economic position' of the Bizone offered a temporary obstacle.

(2) Only vital goods could be exported from Germany to Great Britain. Admittedly this fell within the general framework of British economic policy, which was in turn dictated by the currency difficulties of the time.

(3) German prices were supposed to be as high as possible in terms of sterling, it being the task of J.E.I.A. to ensure this.

(4) In view of the shortage of coal and raw materials, J.E.I.A. would be unable to sanction anything like every application.

(5) Every contract would have to be examined by the Ministry of Economics of the Land concerned.

J.E.I.A. No. 1

On April 8, 1947, there followed J.E.I.A. Directive No. 1, permitting direct contracts between the German exporter and the foreign customer.*

* In connection with J.E.I.A. Directive No. 1 on the new export procedure, the Joint Exchange Agency issued its Directive No. 1, restoring to the German banks the right to resume business with foreign banks. In the spring of 1947, twenty German banks doing foreign business were sanctioned as a first step. Similar measures were taken in the American Zone. At the same time a Joint Foreign Trade Fund was set up at Frankfurt. It dealt with the payments connected with the foreign trade—in Reichsmarks—of the two Zones. A normal nexus between payments in foreign currencies and Reichsmarks in the pre-war sense thus did not exist, nor was one restored until the currency reform. By Law No. 53 of Military Government the control of foreign exchange was reserved entirely to Military Government. The Law established a comprehensive prohibition of exports and imports of currency, and thus complemented the similar prohibition relating to capital. (Law No. 161.)

The contracting parties had liberty in framing the export contracts, but supply and payment were regulated by a prescribed form within which only limited variations were possible. C.i.f. supplies continued to be prohibited, and risks beyond the German frontier had to be borne by the customer. An irrevocable credit, moreover, had to be established. This having been done, the J.E.I.A. branches in the different Länder could sanction the deal. Where the order exceeded $50,000, or covered the processing of imported goods for foreign customers, or where delivery ran over nine months, the final decision rested with J.E.I.A. head office. The world market price continued to be the determining factor. In principle invoices were in dollars or pounds sterling, but the exporter merely received the home price in Reichsmarks plus special expenses.

Raw Materials Shortage

J.E.I.A. continually stressed the importance of individual exports; but in practice deals of this kind lagged so long as there was no organic connection between imports and exports and the exporter had no regular supplies of raw materials. As the currency decayed, the German producer's interest was restricted to domestic barter deals which at any rate assured his supplies of raw materials. It is true that this involved a growing decline in domestic stocks; but even so this sort of barter was more attractive to individual merchants than the drain of stocks across the frontiers. The latter sort of transaction continued to be undertaken only on compulsion. In the British Zone in 1946 total exports amounted to $145 millions; of these

$117 millions were accounted for by coal.
$12 millions were accounted for by timber.
$2·8 millions were accounted for by salt.
$2·1 millions were accounted for by potash.
$1·2 millions were accounted for by lead.
$1·5 millions were accounted for by semi-finished and finished goods.

Exports of finished goods thus accounted for only about

1% of the total. This sufficiently characterises J.E.I.A. practice of the period.

The general picture of exports from the British Zone in 1947 was described by *Exportdienst* (No. 17 of May 1, 1947) as 'a striking realisation of the British aim, which was to direct Zonal exports so as to minimise competition with British exports'. In other words, the objective was either to import the goods into Great Britain, or else to divert them into countries which were not strong potential customers. This applied particularly to exports of Ruhr coal, which were directed into those Continental markets which could not be supplied by British coal because of the lagging production in Britain. These conditions did not materially change during the first half of 1947, as is shown by the following figures for Bizonal exports:

Of a total export of $66·4 millions

$45·6 millions were accounted for by coal.

$8·8 millions were accounted for by timber.

$1·5 millions were accounted for by salt.

$2·2 millions were accounted for by iron and iron alloys.

$0·4 million was accounted for by potash.

Thus finished and semi-finished goods barely accounted for 10% of the total. The American Zone provided the only exception. In Hesse, for instance, more than half the total exports during the first half of 1947 were accounted for by optical goods, machinery and chemicals. The sales, however, came to no more than $9·3 millions for 1946 and the first half of 1947. On the whole the individual export deals were on a small or medium scale, and evidently only covered spares and kindred objects urgently required abroad.

The lack of export incentives, in view of the precarious supplies of raw materials, is reflected in the complaints, e.g. of Mr. Remington, the American head of J.E.I.A.'s Export Division, who was surprised to find in the spring of 1947 that in one part of Westphalia, near Minden, export goods worth about RM.60 millions were being kept in stock by manufacturers who explained that they could not be sure of obtaining fresh supplies of raw materials. To ensure such supplies a new export-import procedure was promulgated in the summer of 1947, permitting exporters to arrange for supplies of raw materials by direct negotiation with foreign producers. Such deals, however, were confined to special export programmes; it was provided, moreover, that the raw materials acquired had to be used in their entirety to manufacture export goods. This in turn involved a complicated system of checks by German and Allied authorities. Given the prevailing world shortage of raw materials, little business resulted, though large hopes were aroused. In the summer it was further decided to institute a 10% foreign exchange bonus, half of which went to the exporter and producer to pay for raw materials, business journeys abroad, etc., and half to the workers for imports of foodstuffs, etc. This bonus was devised as an export incentive for the first great export fair at Hanover (August, 1947); but it did not provide a real stimulus to business. Nevertheless, a series of modest steps towards the normalisation of foreign trade can be discerned. Large-scale exports would have been impossible, however liberal the policy adopted by J.E.I.A., since a currency capable of doing its work did not exist.

The First J.E.I.A. Agreements

Gradually J.E.I.A. did conclude agreements with foreign countries—in the first instance on a basis of reciprocity. By the middle of 1947 such agreements were in force with the Benelux area, and with France, Italy, Austria, Switzerland and Czechoslovakia. These agreements allowed the parties to supply each other with goods during a period of three and a half months, on the expiration of which the existing balance became due in dollars or sterling. Agreements covering goods were not at this stage combined with these reciprocal payments agreements because of the uncertainty hanging over the actual possibility of supplying the goods. The agreements in the first instance had no great significance; their immediate function was to ensure a rapid settlement of accounts in dollars or pounds. The governing principle was that the Bizone must export only on a dollar basis; supplies of goods in exchange were sanctioned only in exceptional cases.

Imports were fixed on a quarterly basis—in the first instance exclusively by the Allies. Soon, however, German authorities took a part in drawing up the plans. This short-term planning required similarly short-term agreements, which at first took the form of loose clearing agreements with a currency of three or six months. These loose agreements predominated; they mostly covered the method of payment between Military Government and foreign countries, special stress being laid on the prompt settlement of dollar or sterling balances. The agreements provided for the supply of lists containing goods required, but at first contained no binding obligation to supply or to sell, and in practice did not lead to any but a small turnover in goods. Closely itemised agreements for the supply and purchase of goods did not occur before 1948.

First Agreement with Belgium

The way in which the trade treaties developed is exemplified by the case of Belgium. The first agreement was concluded between Allied and Belgian delegates at Brussels in mid-February, 1947, after discussion of the question of the resumption and promotion of trade between the Belgium-Luxembourg Economic Union and the united Anglo-American Occupation Zones in Germany. The core consisted of a payments agreement valid until July, 1947, by which the Belgian Government opened a non-interest bearing account in Belgian francs at the Belgian National Bank, in the name of Military Government. Payments connected with all trade transactions were entered in this account, with the exception of payments for coal, timber and potash, which had to be paid for direct in dollars or sterling. In an annexe to the memorandum of July 20, 1947, the Belgian Foreign Minister expressly complained that the account did not cover the whole of trade with Germany, i.e. did not include coal, timber and potash, with the result that Belgium was unable to cover its most important imports by supplying goods to the Bizone. Imports and exports between the two countries, so far as they were covered by the agreements, were thus confined, where Germany was concerned, to the supply of finished goods; and these, in view of the difficulties affecting German production, failed to reach a substantial volume. At the same time J.E.I.A. virtually excluded altogether imports of so-called non-essentials from Belgium, while it caused the great bulk of foodstuffs to be imported from the United States and the dollar area generally. The agreement thus had little practical effect. Among its provisions there was one for a quarterly settlement in cash (in dollars or sterling); over and above this any balance exceeding 85 million francs had to be settled immediately. Today the preamble of memoranda of this kind, fashionable at the time, can be read only with a feeling of irony: it was agreed, so we read, that special importance attached to the expansion of the mutual exchange of goods in 1947 above the level reached in 1946.

There follow further so-called points of agreement, e.g. on the desirability of business journeys into Germany, provided that the travellers used their own means of transport and made no claim for food or accommodation. The memorandum continued that such journeys should not be included in the Land quota, since these quotas were necessary chiefly because of the transport, food and accommodation difficulties existing in Germany.

It was also agreed that postal services should be improved and accelerated in both directions, that telephonic and telegraphic connections should be resumed, etc. In practice all this was so much verbiage; this also applied to the so-called list comprising goods 'calculated to provide a lasting basis for trade'.

The actual exchange of goods resulting from this agreement was naturally insignificant. New negotiations followed in October, 1947, in Berlin. The Anglo-American delegates pointed out that the difficulties in the Bizone prevented a detailed programme from being drawn up. The Luxembourg delegation asked urgently that exports, e.g. of slate, should be resumed into Germany; and it was agreed to enter this article on the list of goods judged to be appropriate for importation. For the reasons mentioned, however, no agreement was reached on the actual quotas. Among the Anglo-American arguments on this point one is specially worth noting, viz. that 'owing to the slow rate of reconstruction in Germany' the need for building materials was small and the question therefore not urgent. The protocol of October, 1947, again begins with the preamble: 'Moved by a desire to develop so far as possible trade and commerce between . . .' The lists of goods again were not binding; all that the two parties submitted to each other were lists of products 'probably available for export' or 'regarded as desirable imports'. Important goods which Belgium could have supplied immediately in large quantities, e.g. fish (particularly herring) could not even be discussed, since foodstuffs of Category A were not embraced by the negotiations. Only with the agreement of August 6, 1948, were specified lists of goods with prescribed amounts or values introduced; these formed the framework within which the parties bound themselves to sanction exports or imports.

Virtually all the trade treaties of the time showed a similar development. For the leading German exports the Allies required payment in dollars; the supply of goods in exchange was only exceptionally permitted; and German exports were further handicapped by the rule that maximum world prices had to be obtained. The German supplier was paid at the lowest possible rate in Reichsmarks. But even in 1948 (at any rate until the currency reform) foreign trade failed to increase. Thus the German-Greek Agreement concluded early in 1948 provided for supplies from the Bizone worth $5 millions, against supplies from Greece amounting to $3·5 millions. The difference had to be paid in cash—ultimately from American dollar aid to Greece.

Yet in 1948 the Marshall Plan was beginning to cast its shadow before. The Plan contained the promise of largely increased aid for Europe, including West Germany, and aimed at promoting the recovery of Europe by large American supplies. We can thus understand that a report from the

Economic Division of O.M.G.U.S. as early as January, 1948, discussed two ways in which German exports could be handled. Either imports could be continued at the 1947 rate; these would then suffice simply to minimise the danger of disease and unrest. The cost of importing industrial raw materials would then continue to be covered by the proceeds of exports. This method, however, would retard the rate of industrial recovery. The alternative possibility was a large increase in imports of foodstuffs and raw materials designed to make full use of the available industrial capacity. This would involve increased expenditure, since the imports of the Bizone would attain approximately three times the 1947 amount. In this case it would be further necessary to create normal economic incentives for German exports; in other words, the rate of exchange and the entire policy governing trade treaties would have to be revised. At last productive ideas were abroad.

Ultimately the men in charge of J.E.I.A. at the time were in no position, given the universal economic chaos, to create a sensible foreign trade. At the beginning further complications probably also existed in the staffing of J.E.I.A., and there were some regrettable blunders in making appointments. Thus the official at J.E.I.A. concerned with imports of hides was a porcelain expert. Weeks generally passed between the giving of an instruction and its implementation; between the issuing of J.E.I.A. instructions and their arrival, in the original, at the different Foreign Trade Offices and Ministries of Economics. Even under the new chief of J.E.I.A. Mr. William Jones Logan, the banker, foreign trade had no chance of improving during this period before the currency reform. In the twenty-eight months from August, 1945, to the end of November, 1947, the two Zones imported amounts worth $1,360 millions, of which $1,035 millions, or 77%, covered foodstuffs paid for by the American and British taxpayers. In 1947 only 7% of the imports covered commercial goods, chiefly cotton, hemp, jute and artificial silk cellulose. Exports from the two Zones in 1946 amounted to $153 millions, and in 1947 to $222 millions, most of them being raw materials.

Monopoly Prices

In fixing prices J.E.I.A. followed a typical monopoly policy: the object was to obtain the best possible export price based on the maximum world market price in competing countries. The Reichsmark prices, however, were based on the fixed prices ruling at home, so that very strange exchange coefficients resulted, ranging down to one dollar per Reichsmark. In Bavaria, for instance, Diesel motors were rated at 52 cents per Reichsmark, milling machinery at 59 cents, and textile machinery at 82 cents. Coloured glass brought in up to 86 cents, and Gablonz glass and jewellery from 30 to 59 cents. J.E.I.A. thus treated German exports as possessing a scarcity value to be paid for as far as possible in spot dollars. This was the reason why, as late as 1948, General Clay refused the import of Dutch vegetables against German industrial exports, claiming that goods capable of bringing in dollars on any market must not be allowed to be used for barter. Failure also attended Dutch negotiations for supplies of fish. The same fate overtook Norwegian efforts to find an opening for fish. The supplies of fish were paid for in unconvertible sterling, while imports from Germany had to be paid for in dollars. Before the currency reform J.E.I.A. consistently refused to conclude barter agreements embracing goods of Category A (foodstuffs) and Category B (raw materials) as well as industrial products. This rule wrecked a number of negotiations, e.g. with Turkey, Denmark, etc. The new spirit of the Marshall Plan was required to overcome this absurdity.

The Dollar Clause

An illuminating debate was that between Mr. A. F. K. Schlepegrell, of the Foreign Trade Treaty Division of J.E.I.A. and Dr. von Maltzan in 1948, arranged by the German Service of the British Broadcasting Corporation. Von Maltzan pointed out that a very keen demand existed for German goods, particularly in Europe, but could not be remotely satisfied because of the dollar clause. He continued:

The reason for this discrepancy does not lie in insufficient production, but in the fact that the Bizone sells in principle only

6

against dollars, and that our customers have no dollars to spare. It necessarily follows that import licences for all those German goods which are rated as unessential are refused, e.g. for textiles, leather goods, china, toys, etc. Let us take, for example, Denmark, the Netherlands and Italy. These countries have large surpluses of foodstuffs, e.g. fish, meat, vegetables and fruit. If these goods could be sold in the Bizone, the latter, for its part, would find an opening in these countries for goods which it cannot sell so long as they have to be paid for in dollars. The exchange of goods would thus increase and the German standard of nutrition would improve without any dollars being required, i.e. without further burdens being placed on the American and British taxpayers. Free multilateral trade must be the ultimate aim, but meanwhile, as an interim solution, bilateral goods and payments agreements should be adopted.

Mr. Schlepegrell could not resist observing:

While one lives on other people's money the cheapest and most essential goods have to be bought and that above all requires dollars. It is our task first to make the two Zones finally independent and then to enable them to stand on their own feet. This requires hard work in partnership both from you and from ourselves. . . . While so occupied we must always think of the whole and not of ourselves.

In fact the dollar clause did more than anything else to prevent Germany from re-entering world markets. Not until its suspension and later abolition, accompanied by a clearing system which, at first bilateral, later took its place within the European Payments Union, did it become possible for the development to take shape which enabled Germany to enter world trade as a valued customer and supplier, to the benefit of all concerned.

The Currency Reform of 1948

The currency reform of June, 1948, at first introduced a uniform conversion rate of 30 cents. To the German exporters this seemed too high; according to studies made by the Bizonal Administration for Economics, the appropriate coefficient for many German exports was under 30 cents, so that the introduction of the new rate made it impossible for them to compete. On the other hand, there were many products with a much higher coefficient, and these could continue to compete after the currency reform. According to the German export statistics of September, 1947, the conversion coefficient for exports classified as foodstuffs and as industrial products fluctuated between 0·13 and 0·66, with an arithmetic mean of 0·33. The 30 cent rate thus agreed with this arithmetic mean, although it did prevent certain classes of goods from finding a market abroad. At the same time this rate caused the average cost of imports to decline. From the very beginning the question thus arose whether the conversion rate should be judged with the interests of imports, or with those of exports in mind.

The 30-cent Rate

In view of the general impoverishment ruling at the period, the most urgent requirement probably was to give a rapid stimulus to German production; this implied an intensification of imports—the more so since German producers hardly knew what goods were wanted, and what new tastes had developed abroad. Contact with world markets had to be developed by research and by a method of trial and error in production. The 30 cent rate was well adapted to this position, since it cheapened imports and at the same time enabled appropriate German goods to bring in relatively high proceeds in foreign currency. At the same time it exerted in a number of branches an early pressure which fostered efficiency in German industry. At that time Professor Ludwig Erhard declared that the immediate problem was to ensure sufficient supplies of raw materials for the needs of domestic production. If the conversion co-efficient was reduced, say from 30 to 25 cents per Deutsche Mark, the result would be that we would earn imports lower by DM.1·25 milliards a year; or alternatively that our imports would have to become a good deal more expensive. The actual rate, with its stimulating effect on imports and its braking effect on exports, was thus well calculated to provide the stimulus for domestic production which was the need of the moment. At a meeting of the Foreign Trade

Advisory Council in Hamburg, in mid-July, 1948, Professòr Erhard said that a rate favouring exports was at the moment less important than the imperative need for industry to adapt itself by rationalisation to the competitive environment. And at the time this need was served by the 30 cent rate.

Foreign Trade Procedure

After the currency reform foreign trade procedure had the following shape. Agreements could be negotiated direct between the German exporter and the foreign importer, but only in favour and on account of J.E.I.A. In principle, individual contracts had to be sanctioned; in practice global licences were unimportant, since the foreign customer was deterred by the necessity to enter a long-term obligation to accept delivery at fixed prices. Individual imports had been sanctioned somewhat earlier, but only about one-eighth of the available foreign exchange was used for these transactions.

Step by Step

The next step led to exactly defined trade and payments agreements, though the awkward dollar clause continued in each case to be introduced. Certain goods for which a keen demand existed were refused by J.E.I.A., e.g. tea in the agreement with India, much to the disappointment of the Indians. The first contacts with overseas countries, e.g. with Brazil and Uruguay, were reached by private initiative, e.g. by one of the partners of Münchmeier's, the bankers, who tried to arrange an account with the Brazilian State Bank, the Banco do Brasil. No official agreements could however be reached. All that happened was that the Brazilian and Uruguayan authorities agreed to grant import licences for German products corresponding to purchases effected by the Bizone. The intention was to ensure that German exporters should find an opening for their products equivalent to the amounts being imported by Western Germany. Up to this point South America had used the dollar equivalent of exports to the Bizone to purchase goods, not from Germany, but mostly from the United States.

The above shows how small a part Germany played in 1948 in the world system of trade agreements. Yet the first outlines were becoming visible; definite lists of goods were drawn up; and when the agreement was concluded with Greece in 1948, the contracting parties bound themselves for the first time to accept certain quantities and prices on a world market basis. This was also the first occasion on which unconditional most-favoured-nation treatment was agreed upon. In September, 1948, the Powers adhering to the Geneva Tariffs Agreement under G.A.T.T. at the suggestion of the United States granted most-favoured-nation treatment to all the three Western Zones. The system by which outstanding balances were settled in hard currencies at relatively brief intervals was replaced by one providing for longer periods and for the introduction of so-called swings. Our opposite numbers were granted the right to export larger quantities into Western Germany so as to save them the need of paying in dollars. Under this system the Netherlands obtained a first opportunity of effecting large-scale supplies of fish, vegetables, etc. Progress was also made, in the first instance with Belgium, regarding the registration of patents and trade-marks. A far-reaching reduction in the obstacles hampering the flow of trade on the payments side was being brought nearer through the Marshall Plan and through the first groping attempts to reach a multilateral system of payments in Europe.

Relaxing

As the market economy began to operate and to set industry in motion in Germany, the narrow structure of J.E.I.A. controls and J.E.I.A. agreements was undermined from many directions. The process was speeded up when the French Zone joined the Bizone and a trizonal organisation of J.E.I.A. was formed of which OFICOMEX was a part. Yet the dollar clause continued to dominate trade relations. No country wished to run the risk of increasing its imports; all feared to lose scarce dollars when the outstanding balances came to be settled. The distinction between A and B Category imports remained. Excessive weight continued to be attached to the barter of raw materials which were scarce in every country and which ultimately none of the partners was particularly anxious to export. Curious ideas about the structure of trade and economy in Germany continued to prevail among the Allies. Thus trade negotiations with Sweden were broken off in November, 1948, because J.E.I.A. refused to permit imports of timber on an adequate scale, being under the impression that the Bizone was itself an exporter of timber.

A Closer Network of Agreements

At the beginning of 1948 the number of working agreements was small, and their turnover insignificant. Until 1949 the most important aspect of the agreements was that they provided for the drawing up of lists of goods and of quotas by value; this was an improvement on the system in force from 1946 to 1948, when even lists and quotas were not allowed to be exchanged between the parties. The agreement with Switzerland in the autumn of 1949 was the first in which quotas and lists did not appear. Instead the parties agreed to import all classes of goods, and to provide foreign exchange in payment. This step forward was all the more noteworthy since Mr. Logan, the head of J.E.I.A. at the time, was still insisting that there was no need to import non-essentials. The agreement provided for an annual exchange of goods worth $60 to $70 millions on each side; the Federal Republic agreed to make available a monthly global quota of $4·8 millions, the use to which this was to be put being left open. The fact that a quota of this sort had to be used at all arose out of the foreign exchange position. A similar agreement with the Netherlands followed. Here too transactions were not limited by value in detail; all that was fixed was an annual volume of $120 to $130 millions. Quotas were insisted on by the Federal Republic only for vegetables and electrical goods. Importers' application for foreign exchange under the two agreements exceeded the available amount 100 to 150 times, a fact reflecting the famine prevailing in the domestic market of the Republic. The deliberate emphasis on imports was consistent with the requirements of the

German market economy, which was then in need of a first stimulus.

After the Federal Republic had regained full powers to negotiate trade agreements (in 1949) the chief objective was to develop the existing trade and payments agreements, and to increase their number. In October, 1949, Dr. von Maltzan stated at Hanover that trade and payments agreements were in existence with twenty-nine countries and that there were thirteen treaties apart from these. Where it proved impossible to work out detailed trade agreements, attempts were made to reach preliminary payments agreements, particularly with countries short of dollars, e.g. South America. Without such agreements trade with these countries would have had to be carried on on a dollar basis. At this time deals on a basis of reciprocity were introduced in order to get foreign trade moving. One further important objective was to reduce dollar settlements by allowing a free choice of currencies, a beginning being made in the agreements with Switzerland and the Netherlands.

The way in which the network of trade treaties became closer is shown by the following figures:

1948	..	20	Trade and payments agreements, some with negligible turnover.
1949	..	25	
1950	..	36	Agreements with increasing turnover.
1951	..	43	
1952	..	46	

In November, 1949, the import of numerous classes of goods was freed; these goods could now be imported without licence and to any amount. They represented 37·4% of imports in the first half of 1947. At the same time import quotas for goods from Austria, the Netherlands, Switzerland and Italy were abolished at a stroke; similarly liberal terms were soon granted to Belgium and Sweden. In the same month O.E.E.C. decided to remove by December all quantitative import restrictions amounting to 50% of the total imports of all the Marshall Plan countries. There resulted a further liberalisation for Western Germany in reciprocity to the autonomous liberalisation put in force for the countries mentioned above. In November, 1949, the first negotiations took place under German leadership, with J.E.I.A. restricted to the role of observer. These negotiations took place with France.

This first phase in our return to world markets can be summed up by saying that we were ready and able to play our part in the opening of markets which formed part of the beginning of European integration and to promote the process by our own contributions.

Gradually the German share in trade treaty negotiations became more important. We can distinguish the following stages:

(1) At first the Allies negotiated alone, without any German negotiators being present.

(2) The Allies negotiated but Germans were admitted as observers who came to listen. It took some time before this stage could be reached. When it was intended to take a German observer to Prague for negotiations with Czechoslovakia, he was refused admission to the aeroplane on the grounds that only persons in uniform were allowed to use Allied aircraft. The German observer had to remain in Berlin and to maintain the scantiest of telephonic contacts between Prague and Minden. The only early exception was Turkey, where the German observer eventually had to conduct the negotiations because the Turks insisted that they could not speak English or French and that German was the only foreign language they could speak fluently. The negotiations were thereupon conducted under the virtual chairmanship of the German observer.

(3) The Germans conduct the negotiations and the Allies observe, though they are entitled to intervene at any time.

(4) The Germans negotiate and the Allies are silent observers.

(5) By directive of November 12, 1949, the Allied High Commission transferred to the Federal Government powers to conduct negotiations for trade and payments agreements under certain conditions. These were as follows. Any invitations issued or received for discussions on matters of trade policy had to be reported immediately to the High Commission. Allied observers could take part in the negotiations and state their views. The agreements were initialled by the German delegation, but were formally signed by the High Commission, the latter reserving to itself all questions of tariffs, import quotas, rates of exchange, etc.

(6) By Directive No. 3 of June, 1950, the Allies were given a limit of twenty-one days within which to raise objections in the case of trade and payments agreements.

(7) In March, 1951, a further concession, still in force, was made. The Federal Republic now conducts all negotiations alone, without observers, but is bound by the principles of G.A.T.T. and of the International Monetary Fund. Only the supervision of treaties with certain scheduled countries, in practice the Eastern bloc, is maintained in its full scope. The Allies thus are empowered to send observers to such negotiations, and each treaty has to be separately sanctioned. For treaties with all other countries the Federal authorities have, since 1951, been under no obligation to inform the High Commission or to submit the documents after signature. All that remains is an obligation to submit a certified copy of the agreement. Directive No. 3 of 1950 remains in force today with regard to the Allied right to sanction agreements, e.g. on most-favoured-nation treatment and on the protection of trade-marks and patents. For agreements of this kind the High Commission can raise objections within twenty-one days. Similarly, in conformity with Directive No. 6 of March 19, 1951, the High Commission has still to be informed

of all prospective negotiations by the Federal Government on the reinstitution of treaties between the former German Reich and other States.

In matters of procedure the course of relaxation went through the following stages:

(1) 1946. The first steps to give German business-men a place in the economy were taken in the American Zone.

(2) 1947. The foreign trade organisations (Foreign Trade Offices) are introduced in the British Zone (in conformity with the position in the American Zone) and later in the Bizone. Import and export procedure is adjusted to find a place for German business-men by immediate contacts through J.E.I.A.

(3) 1948. The first trade agreements designed to bring about regular trade are concluded. The idea of barter confined to dollar goods and the idea of the dollar clause are gradually abandoned. The exchange of non-essentials is introduced, and with it a genuine clearing system in foreign trade is brought nearer.

(4) 1949. Deliberate priority is given to the German import market as an instrument to create opportunities for German imports. Import quotas are used as instruments of an expansionist trade policy.

(5) The Federal Republic attains an unintended creditor position resulting from the advance of German exports in almost every market. The problems which German trade policy has been trying to solve since the spring of 1953 now arise.

CHAPTER V

AMERICAN ECONOMIC AID

G.A.R.I.O.A. and E.R.P.

Germany's return to world markets—a fact which cannot
sufficiently be stressed—was the outcome of a lasting and
fruitful interaction between internal and external impulses.
This interaction resulted from a fusion of forces both inside
the country and outside. Among the external factors we
have to count not only the numerous measures which opened
the gates to world markets, but also the financial assistance
which began to reach us almost immediately after the end
of the war through means provided by the American taxpayer. It is therefore no accident that the recovery of our
production and foreign trade since June, 1948, dated almost
exactly from the institution of the Marshall Plan. The Plan
was not only a source of financial aid, but also a further
impulse serving to strengthen and consolidate the free
market economy which the American Congress made the
unmistakable object of the new economic order in Europe,
an object expressly laid down when the Marshall Plan
legislation was passed in 1948.

We had been helped before 1948; in the first post-war year
by supplies provided by the U.S. Department of the Army
and later through the so-called G.A.R.I.O.A. aid (Government and Relief in Occupied Areas). G.A.R.I.O.A. aid
followed the first $195 millions, which were provided by the
U.S. Army during 1945-6, and was intended to safeguard
the population against famine and disease. About two-thirds
of the fund served to finance the import of foodstuffs and of
artificial fertilisers, seed corn and motor fuel. G.A.R.I.O.A.
aid reached its height in 1947-8 and in 1948-9, with an
annual expenditure of approximately $580 millions; during
the total period from July, 1946, to March, 1950, approximately $1·6 milliards reached Germany from this source.
This aid undoubtedly preserved Western Germany from

famine and disease, and thus fulfilled its real purpose. But it could not contribute to economic recovery because the indispensable complement in the shape of a sensible economic order and a healthy currency was lacking. G.A.R.I.O.A. aid merely supported a population prevented from working by financial and economic chaos. Aid given under the Marshall Plan, on the other hand, i.e. the so-called European Recovery Programme aid, only began in 1948, after a reliable currency and a working economic order had been introduced. As its name implies, E.R.P. aid amounted to an economic recovery programme. It no longer confined itself to preventing famine and disease, but aimed at economic reconstruction. The aim was not to dole out food to a population held in the grip of a total inflation, but to supply capital which contributed to economic reconstruction in the form of tools, wages, machinery, etc. The structure of imports under the heading of aid accordingly changed during the life of the Marshall Plan while German reconstruction was in process; the share of raw materials grew (particularly cotton), and that of foodstuffs declined from year to year. In a country like Germany, itself a great producer of machinery, investment goods were naturally required only on a minor scale. Food-stuffs at first, and later raw materials, were the main means of production which the Marshall Plan directed into the empty stockyards of German industry, and into the empty shops serving the German population.

If pre-G.A.R.I.O.A., G.A.R.I.O.A. and E.R.P.-M.S.A. aid are added together, we find that American economic aid during the period from the end of the war until mid-1953 amounted to nearly DM.15 milliards, or approximately $3·5 milliards. This total consisted of almost equal parts (viz. $1·6 milliards) of G.A.R.I.O.A. and E.R.P.-M.S.A. aid, plus the help provided by the U.S. Army, as mentioned above. A critical observer could object that the $1·6 milliards provided under E.R.P.-M.S.A. constituted only a relatively small fraction of a few per cent in the total of West German investment since 1948. Undoubtedly the bulk of German reconstruction was financed by internal capital, but this fact does not detract from the psychological and material value of E.R.P. aid which, during the first years after 1948, enabled us to acquire urgently needed goods and thus gave the decisive first impulse to reconstruction.

Imports Financed by American Aid

Small as the part played by E.R.P. aid may seem within the total of German investments, it played a vital part in our imports during the post-war period. Pre-1948 statistics are incomplete, since the present area of the Federal Republic was not covered exactly from 1945 to 1947. According to Allied figures the imports of the Bizone from August, 1945, to the end of 1946 amounted to approximately $640 millions; exports came to approximately $160 millions. In 1947 the three Western Zones had imports worth $843 millions, and exports worth $315 millions. The following table shows, for the period after 1947, the part played within our exports by outside funds, i.e. by funds from American economic aid and from the British contribution. For the period from 1945 to 1950, the total came to $176 millions.

THE FINANCING BY FOREIGN AID OF IMPORTS
INTO THE FEDERAL REPUBLIC
(per cent of total imports)

	Total Imports	Imports from dollar area
1948	64·6	—
1949	42·7	—
1950	17·8	77·0
1951	12·2	47·6
1952	3·0	12·2

In 1948 nearly two-thirds and in 1949 over two-fifths of total imports were thus financed by foreign aid; in 1950 the foreign share underwent a first and substantial fall and in 1952 amounted to no more than 3%. With imports from the dollar area the dependence on foreign aid was very much greater, and even in 1950 more than three-quarters of the imports from dollar countries were paid for in dollars made available by the Economic Co-operation Administration.

These figures show how much German reconstruction owes to the American Administration's far-sighted policy of foreign aid, and to the understanding and altruism of the American taxpayer who had to foot the bill. But these figures also show that the Federal Republic knew how to make good use of the aid it received. Imports which in 1948 amounted to $1,554 millions, more than half being paid for by foreign aid, rose by 1952 to $3,854 millions, which were virtually financed entirely without foreign aid. Within a few years the Federal Republic has attained the object at which the Marshall Plan was aiming, and has become a self-supporting country.

The Counterpart Funds

The influence exerted by the Marshall Plan was not confined to the expanded circulation of imports we have described; it also stimulated domestic investments through the system of the so-called counterpart accounts kept in Deutsche Marks at the Bank deutscher Länder. The German importers paid into these accounts the sums owing for goods imported under the Marshall Plan. These counterpart funds were then used by the American E.C.A.-M.S.A. Administration to finance economically important investments, a system for which parallels existed in the other European countries benefiting under the Marshall Plan. Until mid-1953 counterpart funds just short of DM.7 milliards were provided for investment by this system, plus approximately DM.0·5 milliard for interest.

When German reconstruction began, the capital available for investment differed widely in the different industries. Where prices were free to develop by the play of economic forces, e.g. in the consumption goods industries, the price mechanism permitted a good deal of self-financing, and this provided a source for rapid modernisation and substantial new construction. Other industries where adequate self-financing was impossible owing to the continued existence of price controls, or where requirements went beyond the scope of self-financing, had to rely on a capital market which in practice was as yet non-existent. For such industries these special E.R.P. funds which were formed from the millions paid in under the heading of counterpart monies became an exceedingly important source of capital. The following industries were thus able to finance their investments from E.R.P. counterpart funds: electricity, coal, basic industries, the federal railways, merchant shipping, agriculture (for purposes of rationalisation) and building. The latter had a particularly favourable effect on production because it opened to the public the first prospect of a reasonable standard of living and hence of productive work in the factories. An all-round increase in the country's ability to export was an immediate consequence of these investments. An especially important part was played by the West Berlin programme, which received over a third of the E.R.P. funds. Industry in Berlin was traditionally dependent on exports, and this programme played a large part in restoring the Berlin industries to efficiency.

Equal Partnership

The chief psychological and political effect of the Marshall Plan lay in the fact that it set Germany free from the almost complete isolation of the first post-war years. We have already described this isolation in the field of foreign trade, and in fact the O.E.E.C. in Paris, which was founded in April, 1948, as an organisation of the countries taking part in the Marshall Plan, was the first international body to which the Federal Republic was admitted as a full and equal member (in October, 1949); the E.R.P. agreement with the United States (December, 1949) was the first international agreement entered into by the Federal Government. The German mission with E.C.A. which was set up to effect liaison in Washington was the Federal Republic's first foreign mission.

The return of Germany to world markets is not solely a matter of physical buying and selling. It is a continuing act of psychological, human and political integration which is expressed in our growing share in the institutions and organs of the Western economy in Europe and overseas. For every German it is therefore axiomatic, a fact forming a permanent element in his historical consciousness, that it was the United States whose foreign aid put into our hand the chief key to open the gates to world markets.

CHAPTER VI

WORK IN THE INTEGRATION OF EUROPE

THE stagnation of the German economy until 1948 and its lack of contacts with the rest of the world were of course due primarily to the absence of a sensible internal economic order and of a reliable currency. Even if it had been run by German super-patriots, J.E.I.A. could hardly have effected a greater volume of trade. Until 1948 other countries in Europe were not doing much better, despite large American subventions. The Continent generally was dominated, deliberately or otherwise, by a nationalistic isolationism, distorted by open or camouflaged inflation, by bilateralism, and by a deceptive prosperity. Many countries aimed at a maximum production without consideration for their neighbours. In consequence nationalist investment policy led to the duplication of numerous industries, a process which continued during the first years of the Marshall Plan.

Stages in the Integration of Europe

The difficult years during which Western Germany gradually re-entered the European markets become more intelligible if the problems and stages by which the foreign trade of Western Europe was gradually built up are briefly surveyed. The process consisted largely of a number of attempts to create a single market without intra-European barriers to hamper trade or payments. It was thought at first that Europe could be healed from outside without interference in the economic policy of the different countries. Yet the attempt to combine economic nationalism with internationalism is like trying to effect a harmonious union between fire and water. Much of the water came across the Atlantic in the shape of dollar-lined plans for co-operation, while the consuming fire of nationalism was burning in the various Continental States.

Bilateralist Beginnings

In the first years after the war goods and currencies were exchanged in Europe on a predominantly bilateral basis. The drawback to this system lies in the fact that trade is accommodated to the smaller side of the account, since the parties concerned dislike having to settle outstanding balances in third currencies. By the end of 1947 two hundred bilateral agreements had been concluded, prolonged or renewed in Europe alone. At first intra-European trade did not expand beyond the low level reached late in 1946, and the balances of structural creditor countries, like Switzerland and Belgium, etc., were threatening to become frozen. Surpluses could not be used in other countries. Hence it was that by the summer of 1947 the preparatory committee for the Marshall Plan (the Committee of European Co-operation) witnessed the growth of a desire for a multilateral payments system permitting the creditors on current account to employ the currencies of their debtors in third countries. Multilateralism favours the bigger side of the account, and therefore promotes the volume of trade. A beginning was made with the 'first agreement on multilateral monetary compensation', signed by France, Italy and the Benelux countries, an agreement to which the Bizone later adhered. Eight other E.R.P. countries, including Great Britain and the Scandinavia countries, joined conditionally. Month by month the Bank for International Settlements compiled a list of current debtors and creditors. When the first experimental clearing was made in December, 1947, the total debts of the eleven participating countries amounted approximately to $762·1 millions. A small amount, about 2%, could be cleared within the framework of the 'first category compensation'. But this is possible only if a closed circle of indebtedness exists between a number of countries, which can be settled by a simple clearing process. And such a condition is exceptional: while the arrangement was in force (from December, 1947 to September, 1948), only $50 millions could be settled in this way. The plan was restricted to Europe, and as yet had not the benefit of dollar injections.

Dollars for Exports to Europe

An intermediate stage consisted in the transfer of American purchases to European countries in the period from April to December, 1948. The Economic Co-operation Administration (the American authority within the Marshall Plan) was given powers to purchase for dollars from one of the E.R.P. countries goods needed by another E.R.P. country, and thus to increase the hard currency available among the E.R.P. countries as a whole. Such offshore purchases were effected to an amount of $200 millions, covering, mainly, coal, mineral oils, fats, building materials, fruit, vegetables, fertilisers, etc. Naturally there was keen competition for the right to effect such deliveries to European countries: if payment had been made in European currencies, such deals would hardly have come off. Dollars could now be earned by exporting to Europe, and thus the dollar gap in the exporting country was diminished. This solution, however, presently proved a failure because the European integration which it effected was artificial and rested on the acquisition of dollars. It was not until the summer of 1948 that the European Marshall Plan authority (the O.E.E.C.) began to work out a plan by which the individual countries concerned were to receive certain sums in dollars within the framework of the Marshall Plan, provided they transmitted equivalent amounts as surpluses to other participating countries. This dollar aid was intended to induce European creditor countries to pass on the dollars to their European debtors. This plan, too, was a failure. The debtor countries tried to obtain maximum free imports; the creditors hesitated. There is some irony in the fact that the countries which, under the offshore programme, had been falling over themselves to offer goods to their suffering neighbours in Europe, now tried to prove with equal eagerness that they had nothing to export.

On this point the *Economist* wrote cynically, in its issue of September 11, 1948:

Only a few months ago, certain countries in the E.R.P. group, hoping to be designated as markets from which off-shore purchases against dollars might be made, were loudly advertising the unsaleable surpluses they held—tobacco in Turkey, dried fruit in Greece, steel and grapes in Belgium, fruit in Italy. There were surpluses under which the economy of these countries was apparently groaning and which could readily be put at the disposal of the rest of Europe if dollars were paid for them. But today these apparent surpluses have disappeared as if by magic. Under the new scheme, if these surpluses entered into European circulation they would have to be given away. Consequently they no longer appear on the list of what is available.

The Little Marshall Plan

The agreement, however, did become a reality. All the E.R.P. countries participated except Switzerland and Portugal, who received no Marshall Plan dollars. The system of drawing rights was now introduced. Discussions were started about the prospective payments situation as between the participating countries for the period until mid-1949. The debit balances arising during the period were to be balanced by drawing rights *vis-à-vis* the creditor countries. In the agreed plan a debtor/creditor structure arose, which is still in force in many respects. France received nearly two-fifths of the total drawing rights, amounting to $805·5 millions, while Great Britain and Belgium granted nearly 70% of all the drawing rights. Britain appeared chiefly as creditor of France, while the Belgian drawing rights were distributed over ten countries. The French inflationary policy thus received a sort of sanction, while countries with a sound currency like Belgium, or those possessing a Colonial raw materials potential like Great Britain, were the chief sufferers. Western Germany granted drawing rights, of which the most important went to France, Greece, Austria and the Netherlands. Their total amount was $97·4 millions, against which drawing rights were granted to the Federal Republic amounting to $114·2 millions. On balance Western Germany thus was a debtor, though to a small amount. The drawing rights themselves were credited to the creditor countries by E.C.A. as 'conditional dollar aid'. This aid did not represent additional dollars beyond E.C.A. aid; it was a part of the dollar aid which was made conditional on the grant of drawing rights. This system was known as the Little Marshall Plan, in the sense of an intra-European aid programme ultimately based on Marshall Plan dollars. In this way Belgium had to pass on over four-fifths of the dollar aid it received, Sweden about half, and Great Britain and Turkey about a quarter, while Greece received an addition to its direct dollar aid of 55%. In France the addition amounted to 31%, in Norway to 38%, in Austria to 28% and in Western Germany to no more than 3%. Drawing rights granted to France under the Little Marshall Plan amounted to no less than $300 millions.

Western Germany's Debtor Position

This plan, too, suffered from serious miscalculations, the gravest of which was that Western Germany's latent powers of recuperation had been under-estimated. The country made no use of its drawing rights on Norway and Sweden; only half the drawing rights on Turkey were used, though they were fully availed of against Belgium, Italy and the Netherlands. The first-named countries did not export to Germany because the goods to export were not there. One notable point is that, while Britain was supposed to grant us drawing rights of $52 millions, a high export surplus actually developed, and London had to transfer about $20 millions in gold. British prices were high, and within the framework of the first wider trade agreement our own relatively cheap prices enabled us in 1949 to gain a footing in the British markets.

It is noteworthy that over 15% of all drawing rights were never availed of; nor were the payments crises overcome. France quickly exhausted its drawing rights, and thereupon found it necessary to revert to further import restrictions. The hoped-for increase in the export of non-essentials, particularly by France, failed to materialise, and involved Paris in a lively dispute with Switzerland. The domestic policy of the different countries thus proved unamenable to co-ordination from without. Countries whose economic policy was nationalistic, or pursued a camouflaged or open inflation, used the Little Marshall Plan simply as a welcome subsidy. Thus the Marshall Plan proper was abused to provide a premium on nationalism rather than to favour a healthy international market economy and international co-operation. Critics soon began to say that the Little Marshall Plan too favoured economic isolationism instead of overcoming it. The greater the scarcities arising under economic nationalism, the greater was the deficit and the better the chance of receiving a substantial subsidy from the greater or the lesser Marshall Plan. Accordingly, on October 30, 1948, an angry reader demanded, in *The New Statesman and Nation*, that the plan should be wound up: why should we pour our hard-earned gains into the pockets of unscrupulous French profiteers who did not even pay their income tax?

The system was inherently misdirected: creditor countries shrank from exporting to debtor countries because they were afraid of having to grant still greater drawing rights next year. On the other hand, there was an incentive to export into artificially expanded markets, and to neglect more difficult but in the long run more natural ones. The debtor countries, for their part, bought against drawing rights without quibbling about prices: you do not look a gift horse in the mouth. The creditor countries, moreover, tried to get rid of unsaleable stocks and of so-called non-essentials. The profound disadvantage lay in the fact that the desired multilateralism was being grafted on a deep-rooted bilateralism, which it favoured rather than diminished. None of the countries risked taking the plunge into convertibility. The artificially exaggerated productive structure of Europe, instead of being given decent burial, was painfully kept alive. All in all, the Little Marshall Plan raised the same problems as the big one. The aim was to assist difficult payments positions in order to eliminate them for the future: but in fact the crisis risked being perpetuated rather than eliminated. Turnover was admittedly increased —but in a hothouse atmosphere with gifts of dollars for fuel.

Multilateral Drawing Rights

The next agreement (1949–50) tried to effect a transition to multilateral drawing rights—a step towards a genuine multilateral system. Lively British resistance had to be overcome; London feared that if its drawing rights became transferable, some exports might be lost, and the drawing rights might go to the most efficient exporting countries like Belgium and Switzerland. The earlier agreement (1948–9) had allowed every creditor country to export regardless of the competitive quality of its goods. But if drawing rights became transferable, the less efficient exporting countries would transfer their drawing rights in dollars to the more efficient ones. It was this plan which, sponsored by the Americans, aimed at distributing intra-European exports in favour of the most efficient countries (i.e. those having a free market economy) which London resisted. Yet in the end the idea of multilateral drawing rights prevailed; it may have accelerated, if not caused the devaluation of sterling in the autumn of 1949. A country receiving drawing rights could now use part of them anywhere in the E.R.P. area; it was no longer confined to endorsing them in the country granting the drawing rights. By the agreement 25% of drawing rights were diverted into a common pool; of the total sum of $784·3 millions, a sum of only $172·4 millions was thus multilateralised. Italy was the chief beneficiary; it proved an efficient exporter and sold, e.g. to France, goods worth $23·8 millions under the multilateral drawing rights, although it had granted France only $8·3 millions in the form of bilateral rights. The balance of payments in several countries underwent a substantial change. France had a surplus, while Western Germany, the Netherlands and certain smaller Powers had large unfavourable balances. In the case of the Federal Republic this was the consequence of a deliberate policy of liberalisation, particularly with regard to certain key countries like Norway, the Netherlands, Belgium, etc.—a policy closely connected with the need to provide a first stimulus to the German economy.

The E.P.U. from mid-1950

This Agreement was replaced in September, 1950, by the European Payments Union. The E.P.U. is an important element in the composition of an integrated European market. The object was to leave bilateralism behind by combining a multilateral payments system with a simultaneous liberalisation. There is no bilateralism in the E.P.U. Each of the partners stands over against the E.P.U., which represents all the others; he is the debtor or creditor of the E.P.U. as a whole. The latter thus is a pool for the settlement of all the current payments of the member countries. Within the pool a monthly settlement takes place. Each country has a quota in the pool, within which it may incur debts or must grant credit. To facilitate a start difficult debtor countries like Austria, Greece, the Netherlands, Norway and Turkey were granted a first subvention (or 'initial position') totalling $314 millions. This sum was meant to allow the countries to settle their deficits before drawing on their quota proper. On the other hand permanent creditors like Belgium, Sweden and Great Britain had to accept the duty of granting special credits totalling $200·6 millions: they had to accept surpluses to this amount without counting them against their quotas. But the E.P.U. is not built in such a way as to allow each country to accumulate debts, or to build up a creditor position, without restriction except that provided by its quota. The E.P.U. has a braking effect which arises from the fact that countries are obliged to pay gold as their indebtedness grows. This effect is supposed to act as a corrective on the import policy and, so far as possible, on the internal economy of the country concerned. The creditor, on the other hand, has a chance to acquire dollars or gold as his creditor position grows, a privilege which, however, has to be paid for by an increase in that part of his claims on the E.P.U. which cannot be settled in gold. Each country has five *tranches*. The first fifth is free, i.e. it is credited in full. With the second *tranche* 20% has to be settled in gold, and this proportion grows by a further 20% with each successive *tranche*. When the last fifth is reached, 80% of the indebtedness has to be paid in gold; by the time that the quota is exhausted, the overall amount to be paid in gold is 40%. Conversely, a creditor must leave the first fifth of his quota in full; with each successive fifth he can draw half in gold or dollars, and by the time the quota is exhausted he can acquire 40% in gold or dollars. Compared with its predecessors, the E.P.U. represents a substantial advance. Difficult and merely partial settlements are replaced by a full and multilateral one. The drawing rights have been virtually abolished. Risky estimates of trade and payments balances, hitherto needed to calculate quotas, are now superfluous. Admittedly some elements of risk remain, even in the present settlement of quotas, which in 1949 amounted to 15% of the trade and payments of each country in its dealings with all the others. The great merit of the E.P.U. was that it freed the multilateral payments system from the continued injection of dollars, though the plan to be sure could hardly have made a happy start without the $350 millions of working capital which the United States supplied. The link established between the granting of credits and the payments in dollars among the countries taking part is a guarantee against the continuation of unlimited debts with the E.P.U. As a country's indebtedness grows, its dollar payments increase; at the same time a further increase in imports from the E.P.U. area means that the country renounces possibly cheaper purchases in the dollar area.

Germany's Experience

The developments since the beginning of E.P.U. will here be described with reference only to Western Germany's trade and payments. From the beginning the Federal Republic shared as an equal partner in the formation of E.P.U. and its predecessors; and indeed the Marshall Plan constituted an important instrument in restoring the Federal Republic to a status of equality in shaping the economic policy of Europe. We may anticipate by saying that the co-ordination of national economic policies aimed at was never fully realised. The forces of economic nationalism and of autonomous monetary policies remained at work, and in some instances were actually strengthened by the way in which the policy of liberalisation was carried through Heavily indebted countries are enabled by the liberalisation code to slow down or even to suspend their own liberalisation, i.e. to reduce their import quotas; and by so acting they continue to provide a shelter for their own monetary and economic autonomy. Creditor countries, on the other hand, remain under the obligation to continue their liberalisation in order to make it easier for debtor countries to export. Most of the creditor countries tend to have a market economy and a healthy monetary system, among them Italy, Belgium, Switzerland, the Netherlands and the Federal Republic. But such additional liberalisations cannot remove the source of the difficulties from which the obstinate debtor countries suffer, namely, an inflationary economic policy. Here limits are drawn to the E.P.U. and to the liberalisation it implies—limits which confirm that a world-wide economic integration, in the sense of an international division of labour, cannot merely be imposed from outside, but must grow from the internal economic order and from the will to achieve a free market economy.

The first year of E.P.U. was marked by the so-called German crisis which arose out of the rapid increase of imports caused by the acceleration of German production dating from the currency reform. The raw materials boom since Korea sharpened the tendency towards a debit balance. But essentially our imports surplus was caused by the swift and consistent liberalisation within the Federal Republic which operated by the spontaneous waiving of quotas for the benefit of a number of countries and through full co-operation in the liberalisation prescribed by O.E.E.C. The debit balance manifested itself in this critical form chiefly because the Federal Republic lacked international financial contacts, because old obligations and new debts (G.A.R.I.O.A., Marshall Plan, etc.) had not yet been settled, and because Western Germany's trade turnover in 1949, on the basis of which quotas had been established, did not properly reflect our economic and foreign trade potential. The original quota of $320 millions proved inadequate. We must remember that industrial production in the Federal Republic in November, 1950, was one-third higher than a year earlier. The number of persons employed rose by over half a million. Stocks of raw materials were slender, and rapidly melted as industry expanded. Admittedly exports too increased, but usually under conditions of long-term payment of the type ruling with exports of machinery, whereas raw materials must be paid for in cash. Accordingly our balance of payments showed an even bigger deficit than our balance of trade. The Bank deutscher Länder endeavoured to restrain imports by raising the bank rate, by restricting credits and by other measures. Speculative tendencies reinforced by the raw materials boom also favoured an increase in imports. The special nature of the conditions within which the development in the Federal Republic was taking place was recognised by the O.E.E.C., particularly by two experts, Peer Jacobsson and A. K. Cairncross, who were asked to advise on the position. The restraining measures employed by those in charge of our monetary and financial policy were duly acknowledge. The E.P.U. accordingly granted a special credit of $120 millions on which Western Germany could draw to cover two-thirds of its E.P.U. deficit after exhausting its quota. The remaining third had to be paid for monthly by earned dollars. Interest was payable at $2\frac{3}{4}\%$, and the loan had to be discharged in six instalments from June to November, 1951. It was secured by a special account, opened by the Bank deutscher Länder with the New York Federal Reserve Bank. At the same time the O.E.E.C. advised the member countries to liberalise their import policy as much as possible in favour of German goods. In this crisis the E.P.U. thus served as the most important credit instrument to expand the narrow financial cover for German imports. We must remember that after the First World War Germany had the benefit of manifold private connections existing between German and foreign banks, etc., and that moreover the Dawes Loan initiated a substantial influx of foreign capital. Had a genuine financial internationalism existed, our payments difficulties of the end of 1950–1 would have been barely visible, whereas in fact they were exposed to the searchlight of detailed, if well-intentioned examination among the Paris officials.

Ending Liberalisation in Western Germany

But the crisis was not overcome; it became more intense, and in February, 1951, the Federal Government suspended liberalisation as well as the issue of import licences. It was not a surprising measure; it was taken at a moment when Western Germany's economy was rapidly developing, and imports consequently were urgently wanted; yet it met with scepticism abroad where people suspected old Schachtian methods in a new dress. These suspicions were most vocal in France, but the *Economist* too declared (April 14, 1951) that since Dr. Schacht's days Germany had been wedded to the idea that Germany's debtors would not venture to ruin their vulnerable markets in Germany by taking retaliatory measures if they failed to obtain payment.

Comparisons with Schacht's policy are misplaced. Under the Third Reich currency and import controls were used as the favoured instrument of a nationalistic economic policy. An import surplus was intended to promote the control of foreign exchange and to destroy free trade; whereas the import surplus of 1950–1 was inspired by liberalistic ideas and aimed at replacing foreign exchange control through the growth of world trade.

The O.E.E.C. and the E.P.U. were forced to acknowledge the validity of the German arguments, and recommended three groups of measures:

(1) The internal restriction of credit.
(2) Import restrictions until June, 1951.
(3) Planned imports after June 1, 1951.

The improvement in the balance of payments began in the spring of 1951, and the export surplus within E.P.U. expanded rapidly after March, 1951. By the end of May the special credit had been repaid in full to the E.P.U. and thus the outstanding one-third of the dollars paid in on this occasion was recovered. Yet in the first instance the improvement was solely due to import restrictions, a measure the effectiveness of which was increased by the simultaneous fall in the prices of raw materials.

The E.P.U. also served as a substitute for international banking, a fact furnishing a specially cogent explanation of Western Germany's original indebtedness. It also served to expand the Federal Republic's sphere of trade because it took in most of the sterling area: by virtue of this conjunction even today practically two-thirds of the world's trade are transacted through the E.P.U. The advantages of the system became specially clear after the crisis early in 1951. The German quota was increased from $320 millions to $500 millions, with the result that the part played by the E.P.U. as a supplier of credit was strengthened at a time when private credit was diminishing. The German crisis further prompted the other countries to liberalise their exports to the Federal Republic. In this way our traditional leading position in the trade of Europe was restored. The adherence of the European colonial empires and of the sterling area further enabled us to recover our former typical structure of which high export surpluses with Europe and high import surpluses with overseas suppliers of raw materials are characteristics. Lastly, the E.P.U. brought nearer the partial convertibility into dollars of the European currencies to the extent that surpluses could be covered alternatively in gold or in dollars, a measure by which we began increasingly to benefit after 1952.

In the light of our general development, which did not begin properly until 1950, the German E.P.U. crisis of 1950-1 is best regarded as a phase of our recovery. Perhaps the alarm cord was pulled too early, and perhaps the competent bodies became frightened too soon. But such developments too would form part of the picture showing the recovery of a market economy—an economy to which even the Federal Republic was not fully accustomed at this stage. Abroad too people had still to form the habit of unbiased observation and judgement of German developments. For the rest, the fluctuations of our position within the E.P.U. must be regarded in the light of the violent disturbances of prices and of business generally caused by the Korean War.

The Course of Liberalisation

To reduce one set of trade barriers would be meaningless if another set were at the same time being erected. Accordingly even before the formation of the E.P.U. the O.E.E.C. resolved systematically to abolish the import quotas and thus to bring about liberalisation. By the middle of December, 1950, the participating countries were asked to remove import quotas for at least 50% of their private imports from E.P.U. countries, 1948 being taken as the base year. The first 50% were naturally the easiest to abolish, even though the rate for the three main classes of imports (foodstuffs, raw materials and finished goods) was supposed to be uniform. Liberalisation becomes more difficult as the end is approached, since the remnant outstanding becomes more and more representative in the course of this approach of the genuine protectionist element. In the autumn of 1949 Western Germany, besides carrying through an automatic and all-round liberalisation, also adopted a special liberalisation in favour of a number of European countries, which process was precisely the cause of the above-mentioned payments crisis.

In practice, the first 50% reduction was reached by the end of March, 1950, though there were large differences with the different countries. Liberalisation was carried through most vigorously in Switzerland, Belgium and the Netherlands, as well as in Great Britain, though in the last-named country State imports, which are exempt from liberalisation, are of special significance. In the first instance no doubt the quotas which were abolished had already been made superfluous by the all-round improvement of intra-European trade and payments. It is significant that the 50% rate was easily reached for foodstuffs and was far exceeded with raw materials, though it frequently remained below 50% with finished goods. A further liberalisation—to 60%—was supposed to be reached by the end of 1950, and this second stage also developed differently according to the payments position in the various countries. Great Britain raised its liberalisation from 54% in March, 1951 to 86% in December. Here, too, raw materials were more widely liberalised than foodstuffs and finished goods. All the other eight E.P.U. countries benefited by the cancellation of quotas which had originally been granted autonomously or bilaterally; in this manner a degree of uniformity was introduced into trade policy and into markets. To ensure uniformity in procedure a liberalisation code was worked out which later was kept up to date by resolutions from the Council; it came into effect on September 19, 1950, simultaneously with the E.P.U. Agreement. In its preamble the code stresses the organisation's object, viz. a world-wide liberalisation to be reached by way of a preliminary maximum liberalisation within Europe. This aim was to be attained step by step, all parties being granted admission at the same time and in the same measure to each of the member countries' markets. The stages had therefore to be fixed in a uniform manner for all. Article 2 provided for a number of stages in liberalisation, extending first to 50% of private imports and, by February, 1951, at the latest, to 75%. The code also permitted the restriction or cancellation of liberalising measures provided they were actually leading to severe economic difficulties in a member country. Measures to liberalise trade did not need to be carried through in full if this was justified by the economic and financial position of a member country. These were certainly important escape clauses sanctioning economic nationalism in a way of which many countries in fact availed themselves.

Since 1952 France and Great Britain have largely restricted their liberalisation; in structurally weak countries like Greece and Austria it has been virtually abolished, while in Italy liberalisation was almost complete. These variations reflect the unequal course taken by events and show that liberalisation inevitably took a form dictated by the economic policy of the different countries. Nevertheless the authorities in charge of E.P.U. and of the code tried hard to cause the adhering countries to follow the spirit rather than to make use of the exceptions sanctioned by the code. The

O.E.E.C. has consistently urged that any cancellations of liberalisation should be cancelled in their turn. It has created a growing sense of responsibility in trade and payments policy, and has fostered the idea that other countries' payments difficulties are the concern of a responsible import policy.

As the O.E.E.C. and its organs grew older they grew stronger as bodies expressing a moral and economic unity which must not be endangered by any difficulties encountered in leading member countries, like those of Italy in the spring of 1953. Difficulties grew visibly, particularly when the 75% stage was reached, a fact acknowledged by the O.E.E.C. which ceased to insist on the uniform liberalisation of all classes of goods, a measure calculated also to assist the agricultural interests of certain countries. An attempt was made to develop a uniform procedure by drawing up a so-called common list. In this way a genuine liberalisation was aimed at which was supposed to lead to a uniform supra-national market calculated not only to give a fresh impulse to the European economy but to have a favourable effect on production and sales in all the member countries. The essence of the common list lay in the fact that it was designed to embrace goods which had been liberalised by all the adhering countries and could therefore be imported without quantitative restriction. It embraced most textiles, textile machinery, many chemicals, timber, scientific and medical instruments and a number of agricultural products.

In practice the common list did not become a full reality, and indeed the uniform market, despite all that was done by liberalisation, has not been achieved. Nationalist obstacles were too powerful. The question thus arises whether a uniform market could be reached merely by quota reductions so long as the obstacles and differences inherent in financial and monetary policy survived. The question remains even where a country has reached a 90% or an all but 100% liberalisation. The code permits liberalisation to be cancelled at any time if sufficient difficulties exist; and the causes of these difficulties can lie in a nationalist policy beyond the scope of the O.E.E.C. But as soon as liberalisation is reduced, the danger of a reversion to bilateralism grows, and the bilateral trade and payments agreements then recover their importance. Hence even the Federal Republic is compelled to maintain trade and payments agreements with all its E.P.U. partners—agreements the importance of which lies in the fact that they allow the exchange of quotas for non-liberalised groups of goods.

The importance of liberalisation must not be exaggerated. Yet it has undoubtedly strengthened the feeling of economic solidarity directed towards the creation of a unified market; it has accordingly given a further impulse to other plans aiming at European integration.

The Federal Republic's Part in Liberalisation

The German payments position in the E.P.U. area since 1949–50 chiefly reflected the general economic development, though the price fluctuations of raw materials caused by the Korean War amplified the original debit balance and the later surplus tendencies. The rapid exhaustion of the E.P.U. quota (spring of 1951) frightened the O.E.E.C. and the Bank deutscher Länder and induced the authorities to impose a limit on aggregate imports from the E.P.U. countries, even after the transitional credit of $180 millions had been granted. There followed a steady decrease in our indebtedness, which turned into a creditor position by November and allowed the resumption of liberalisation by the end of 1951. In January, 1952, the liberalisation rate reached 60%, by April 76·6%, and by August 80·9%; and by April, 1953, it exceeded 90%. The result was the eventual exhaustion of the Federal Republic's credit quota, and a pressure exerted in favour of the further liberalisation of trade both visible and invisible. The increase in the German quota from $320 to $500 millions granted in mid-1951, by which means the original transitional credit was given a place in the Federal system, is today serving to strengthen the German creditor position within the E.P.U. By the middle of 1953 the Federal Republic's credit balance was approaching $650 millions.

8

LIBERALISATION OF GERMAN VISIBLE IMPORTS, 1952
(in millions of dollars)

Payments Area	Imports excluding State trade	Of which free of quota	%
O.E.E.C. member States	1,869·0	1,669·8	89·3
O.E.E.C. non-member States	310·7	225·2	72·4
E.P.U. area	———2,179·7	———1,895·0	86·9
Other clearing countries	446·0	307·8	69·0
Free dollar countries	593·8	—	—
Total	3,219·5	2,202·8	68·4

When the German payments position was being estimated, justice had not been done to the country's increased capacity to export, nor to the gradual saturation with imports which recurred in the course of 1951 and, even more strongly, after the raw materials slump during 1952. And in fact the temporary ending of liberalisation strengthened the tendency towards an export surplus, though this would have occurred even without the intervention of the O.E.E.C. Since 1952 the Federal Republic has resumed liberalisation in a number of ways; partly by spontaneous liberalisation with reference to E.P.U. countries beyond the rate agreed with the O.E.E.C. and partly with reference to non-E.P.U. countries. In consequence on an average nearly 90% of all imports from O.E.E.C. countries were throughout 1952 free of quotas. With non-member countries imports free of quota reached 70%, and for the whole of the E.P.U. area they reached 87%. It should also be noted that a 69% liberalisation was reached with the so-called clearing countries. Approximately two-thirds of the entire imports of 1952 were free of quotas; the latter are almost entirely confined to the free dollar countries. With this system is connected a growing liberalisation of 'invisibles', i.e. of services of all kinds.

Effects on Different Branches of the German Economy

It was our machinery and consumption goods industries that chiefly benefited from liberalisation in Europe. One striking fact is that in the Federal Republic, as elsewhere, the protectionist interests which might require the protection of quotas become more evident as the non-liberalised remnants dwindle. This applies, for instance, to industries which failed to regain lost ground either because of technical advance and modernisation abroad, or because of the obstacles provided by Allied controls during the early post-war years.

Finally, the lessons of the liberalisation which was pressed ahead in the Federal Republic as early as 1949–50 show that exports and world trade generally can be powerfully stimulated through imports. Certain countries, like the Netherlands and Switzerland, were enabled to gain large and lasting advantages from the early liberalisation of 1950; these countries were thus enabled to strengthen their markets for a number of goods in the Federal Republic.

Trade Agreements with E.P.U. Countries

Our trade with the E.P.U. countries is largely determined by liberalising principles. The various trade agreements, e.g. with France, the Benelux countries, Italy and the Scandinavian countries, are accordingly restricted to goods not covered by the wider agreements, and they are of real significance only where a country is unable sufficiently to liberalise itself in the E.P.U. area. Consequently treaties with largely liberalised countries are today of relatively small importance. They will become important only when they begin to deal with other fields than that of goods proper, i.e. when they develop towards comprehensive trade treaties in the classical sense.

Italy

An example is supplied by our relations with Italy. This is one of the countries with which we began negotiations relatively early after the war—at first within the framework of a loose agreement concluded by the Occupying Powers. By February, 1946, arrangements were made on the exchange of coal, iron and steel against agricultural products. Even at this early stage the Italians stressed their traditionally strong position as importers of coal, iron and steel and as suppliers of fruit and vegetables. There followed discussions conducted by J.E.I.A., and here again the accent was placed on potential supplies; no definite values were mentioned. The first major agreement under J.E.I.A. was reached in 1948. Next came that of April, 1949, in the conclusion of which the German administration played a fairly important part. But German-Italian trade was not put on a normal footing until after 1949. From then onwards it gradually began to regain its earlier structure. Italy was always an important buyer of a wide range of German finished goods, whereas Germany had always concentrated its imports on fruits and vegetables. In the course of the negotiations it appeared that the Italian economic structure had undergone a wide change.

GERMAN FOREIGN TRADE WITH ITALY
(in thousands of dollars)

	1936	1948	1949	1950	1951	1952
Imports	84,090	67,658*	88,241	120,548	130,631	152,998
Exports	97,015	26,931	59,977	115,733	160,631	223,176

* Reichsmarks or Deutsche Marks.

The industrialisation of Italy had gone ahead and Italians were now more strongly interested to find an opening in the German market for Italian industrial products. At the same time competition between the two countries became more intense in other markets. The industrialisation of Italy had been powerfully helped by the Marshall Plan and by earlier American aid.

Trade remained relatively slight in 1949, though its composition became more interesting for the two countries. A real advance was reached only through the agreement of July, 1950, in the framing of which the German authorities played a major part. The significant point was that this early agreement was in fact something rather more than a simple agreement and approximated to a treaty: thus for example it restored German rights of domicile, regulated the position of German property within the competence of the Italian Government, and annulled the Italian wartime legislation. Admittedly Italy did not have much to say in many of these questions; yet it was significant that a State now showed itself ready to annul wartime legislation in an open agreement and at the same time to grant German traders rights of domicile. Security with a legal backing thus became an early objective, and there is some justification for calling this agreement the 'Little Peace'. A year later the Western Powers generally ended the state of war.

As early as 1949 we made Italy an offer of autonomous and maximum liberalisation, as had been done with the Benelux and other countries. But in Italy the time was not yet ripe. The continuing devaluation of the lira had made the Italian tariffs meaningless, and accordingly the Italians thought it necessary to find a substitute in a far-reaching system of quotas.

Nineteen fifty-one was the great year for Italian foreign trade. The country had fully exploited the world boom set off by the Korean war and its exports had reached a large volume. Substantial export surpluses with E.P.U. countries resulted, and the Italians felt encouraged to proceed to a virtually complete liberalisation. The German-Italian Agreement of 1952 was entirely inspired by these liberalising tendencies and quotas played a relatively unimportant part in it. Even so, the Agreement merely added strength to the existing export drive which had been set free by the Italians' liberalising policy. The Federal Republic granted large quotas for fruit and vegetables—quotas which opened markets to Italy of approximately pre-war extent. Some annoyance became apparent in Italy only because of the even stronger development of Dutch imports, which until 1952 largely exceeded those from Italy—a reversal of the pre-war state of affairs. It must be added that the Dutch imports were helped by the Federal Republic's poor fruit and vegetables harvest in 1952.

The structure of Italian exports became more favourable: finished goods claimed a bigger share. For German industry the Italian market has become progressively more interesting for a number of goods with a high labour content, e.g. cutlery, china, etc. In 1951–2 the trade in raw materials also gained in extent. Italy supplied rice, hemp, mercury, sulphur and ores, while the Federal Republic sent coal, iron, steel, scrap, etc. From 1952 onwards the Italian economy strongly reflected the effects of liberalisation, which showed themselves in a stabilisation of prices, the greater strength of the lira, a sound fiscal situation and a higher national income. There are also less pleasing aspects: unemployment is still severe. Competition has become fiercer, and a number of undertakings have had to close. The volume of Italy's foreign trade was maintained in 1952; but since mid-1952 difficulties have appeared in the E.P.U. area resulting from French and British import restrictions and from the general textile crisis of the early summer of 1952. The Italian E.P.U. balances began to shrink dangerously—the result of falling exports rather than of growing imports. Accordingly the Federal Republic systematically increased its imports from Italy. (Agreement of April 23, 1953.) The further liberalisation undertaken since April, 1953, gave the Italians help in the industrial sector, in the tourist industry, etc. As in the Treaty with the Netherlands, the quota arrangements contained a clause permitting the quotas to be exceeded for market garden produce. Certain objections coming from the farmers were also overcome, with the result that large concessions regarding imports were made to Italy in the Agreement of 1953. This measure seemed all the more significant since German exports to Italy had been almost completely liberalised since the end of 1951— partly within the E.P.U. liberalisation and, beyond that, independently. The Italians have repeatedly stressed that, so far as they are concerned, no difference exists between these two types of liberalisation; it is liberalisation as such that is the core of their trade policy, and if recourse had to be had to quotas they would be reintroduced uniformly.

The Agreement of 1953 provides that, if liberalisation had to be abandoned, long-term production and supply contracts would not be affected. Special importance was attached to ensuring that any restrictions should be distributed as uniformly as possible over all classes of goods without any secondary protectionist objective. In this sense the Agreement of April, 1953, should be regarded as a model, since it aims at overcoming any new difficulties by utilising the balance of payments without discrimination. This has brought with it a certain bilateralism: current business is maintained on a basis of non-discrimination, a far more practical method than any recommendations issued by the O.E.E.C.

Capital Investment

The co-operation existing between the Federal Republic and Italy has been growing increasingly clear; it subsists from industry to industry, but within the framework of a general agreement providing for a maximum of free trade. This applies particularly to capital development in Southern Italy and in Sardinia. These regions have been suffering for decades from structural crises (over-population, poverty, etc.); today they have become a field for capital development in which the Federal Republic and Italy jointly participate, besides certain American and other firms. Southern Italy has a population of about 18 million; there are considerable undeveloped regions, and much of the soil is by no means poor. By constructing power stations, irrigation works and roads, by building factories and sinking pits (sulphur, coal processing in Sardinia) much could be done to develop the region. Plans, some of them looking twelve years ahead, provide for an annual investment of DM.1·2 to 1·4 milliards, of which DM.700 millions are provided through the Budget. The rest is to be financed from a number of sources, some of them foreign.

An obstacle is provided by the high Italian tariff. Although large concessions were made in the G.A.T.T. negotiations, the Italian tariff is probably the highest in Europe. Yet the so-called transitional tariff (applied independently by the Italian authorities) lays down a number of duties which are actually below the level provided for by G.A.T.T. Complaints about the height of tariffs can nevertheless frequently be heard. Moreover, since the transitional rates can be applied independently by the Italian authorities, it is always possible that they may be replaced by even higher ones.

France

Trade relations with France suffer from the unsolved problems troubling French economic and monetary policy, problems which are a constant source of worry to the E.P.U. The far-reaching cancellation of liberalisation in France since the beginning of 1952 is one manifestation of these difficulties. Yet it must be admitted that these particular restrictions did not have a specially serious effect on our exports.

GERMAN TRADE WITH THE FRENCH UNION
(in thousands of dollars)

	1936	1948	1949	1950	1951	1952	1953
Imports	49,938	69,256*	70,295	295,514	256,872	299,221	345,921
Exports	108,808	88,445	168,808	190,244	310,045	343,569	351,465

* Reichsmarks or Deutsche Marks.

Actually our exports to France have doubled since 1949; in 1953 the high level of the previous year was at any rate maintained. The tendency towards a surplus remains, despite our far-reaching liberalisation of imports from France. By this liberalisation we have enabled France considerably to expand its market, chiefly by the free grant of higher quotas. As a result the foreign trade of France has latterly tended towards a certain equilibrium.

The French Union today ranks first among the Federal Republic's foreign customers; among the countries to which the French Union exports the Federal Republic ranks second after Great Britain. Among our suppliers France follows the United States, as does the Federal Republic among the countries exporting to France.

France's foreign trade suffers from the chronic foreign exchange and payments crisis, which is reflected in the way in which, despite a number of ample subsidies, French exports continue to lag behind imports.

FRENCH FOREIGN TRADE (INCLUDING FRENCH OVERSEAS
TERRITORIES)

1938 to 1951

Year	Imports	Exports	Imports Surplus (−) or Exports Surplus (+)	Per cent of imports covered by exports	Volume of	
					Imports	Exports
1938	46·1	30·6	−15·5	66·4	100	100
1946	264·7	101·4	−163·3	38·3	115	50
1947	397·1	223·3	−173·8	56·2	105	83
1948	672·7	434·0	−238·7	64·5	101	96
1949	926·3	783·9	−142·4	84·6	104	132
1950	1,073·2	1,077·8	+4·6	100·4	105	164
1951	1,607·2	1,478·1	−128·4	92·0	123	195
1952	1,590·2	1,416·2	−174·7	89·0	125*	172*
1953	1,458·2	1,406·9	−51·3	97·0	127*	175*

* 1st to 3rd Quarter, 1953.

Since the spring of 1952 French imports have been regulated by a plan giving priority to essential raw materials.

Since 1952 it has not seemed probable that French foreign trade, particularly imports, would expand, though restrictions of French imports can be effected only by artificial measures. The French franc is over-valued and thus exercises a permanent, latent pressure favouring imports, while applying a brake to exports. In view of these difficulties the new agreement negotiated in the spring of 1953, in which the Federal Republic proposed an itemised exchange of goods, could hope at best to preserve the level reached and not to go beyond it. Thus in the case of France German trade policy is faced by the problem how to expand overseas trade and investment with the overseas territories of the French Union, a problem analogous to that encountered everywhere else in the E.P.U. area.

Benelux

The Benelux States are our most important trading partners among our immediate neighbours, and they are the ones with which we first developed trade relations, particularly since the autumn of 1949.

The Agreement with the Netherlands (July, 1948) was distinctly modest. It provided for Dutch supplies of $68 millions against German supplies worth $86 millions. Lists were exchanged stating what goods were definitely to be supplied; on the German list coal predominated. The Netherlands supplied overseas raw materials like rubber, tin, etc. It also proved possible to effect small imports of vegetables against limited exports of non-essentials on our part. The agreement led to a heavy indebtedness on the part of the Netherlands, leading in the spring of 1949 to the expansion of Dutch exports, particularly of foodstuffs.

In the autumn of 1949, on the initiative of the Federal Minister of Economics, a comprehensive liberalisation was effected within the framework of a new agreement providing for a credit margin of $15 millions. The Netherlands retained their quotas for German goods, while the German market absorbed large quantities of Dutch imports, with the result that the German adverse balance exceeded $80 millions, which by arrangement was to be paid off in three years beginning in 1950. (In fact the debt was discharged by the end of 1951.) Later agreements, e.g. that of 1951, aimed at maintaining a large volume of trade combined with some measure of equilibrium. Today our imports of goods from the Netherlands amount to approximately DM.1·2 milliards a year; exports are approximately DM.1·3 milliards. The difference is balanced by our deficit with the Dutch East Indies, and by services. The Netherlands themselves have been creditors within the E.P.U. since 1952, and have been compelled increasingly to liberalise, so that on the whole our chances of finding further openings are relatively good. On our side we have liberalised a number of imports of special significance for the Netherlands, including outerwear, wool textiles, artificial silk stockings, and electrical goods. On the other hand a strong industrialising tendency exists in the Netherlands; it is supported by American capital and applies to goods formerly imported from the Federal Republic. Since the wages and cost structure in the Netherlands is relatively low, great efforts will be needed if we are to expand our exports. All in all, Dutch-German trade has probably come near its maximum level.

A vigorous trade turnover soon developed between ourselves and the Belgo-Luxembourg Economic Union. Even before the currency reform the Allies had placed orders for railway repairs, which gave us a debit balance in our account with Belgium. In November, 1949, foreign trade between the two regions underwent a far-reaching liberalisation. It proved impossible, however, fully to implement the Agreement; the reason lay in our indebtedness and in the necessity for rapidly settling this debt.

GERMAN FOREIGN TRADE WITH BELGIUM AND THE
NETHERLANDS
(in thousands of dollars)

	1936	1948	1949	1950	1951	1952
Belgium-Luxembourg						
Imports	67,907	86,785*	142,489	119,558	181,898	274,541
Exports	86,254	93,967	112,742	163,083	242,661	298,208
Netherlands						
Imports	79,457	122,128*	110,276	298,705	245,046	280,959
Exports	160,479	72,180	98,482	277,267	349,130	323,778

* Reichsmarks or Deutsche Marks.

Today we have a substantial surplus with Belgium and Luxembourg. A further development of our trade with Belgium will depend on whether a fresh impetus can be achieved by taking in the Belgian overseas territories and exploiting their openings for capital development. This implies that further potentialities shall be provided in the Belgian Congo. At present our balance with the Congo is strongly adverse. An ambitious ten-year plan has been drawn up for developing the Congo; here possibilities exist in which we have not yet had an adequate share. When tenders are asked for, the Congo generally inclines to favour Belgium. Early in 1953, however, we were promised a larger share in public orders for the Congo.

Finally our trade with Luxembourg (a member of the Belgo-Luxembourg Economic Union) has favourably developed. Our imports consist chiefly of iron, steel and leather, against which we supply coke and consumption goods. Close economic relations with Luxembourg are advantageous, since Luxembourg has made large capital investments in Germany and is interested in further developing its financial contacts with ourselves.

Regarding the Benelux countries as a whole it can be said that, with the assistance of the E.P.U. and of special payments and trade agreements, our export trade was enabled to develop favourably. Our own farming interests continue to provide certain obstacles and the fact that these may eventually be eliminated constitutes a latent asset for our trade policy.

Scandinavia

Since business relations were resumed after the Second World War, the Federal Republic's trade with the five Scandinavian countries has vigorously expanded. Our trade with these countries followed, until 1950, the general pattern of trade with producers of foodstuffs and raw materials; it showed an adverse balance caused by the influx of foodstuffs as well as of raw materials into the German vacuum. Denmark, Sweden and Norway declined at first to open the O.E.E.C. free list to ourselves; liberalisation was adopted towards the Federal Republic only in the autumn of 1950; and consequently our exports were deprived of proper scope. It was the pressure exerted by our high adverse balance that induced the Scandinavian countries to respond to our own liberalisation (granted unilaterally in the autumn of 1949) by reducing their trade barriers. In view of the Federal Republic's payments position at the time, the adoption of liberalisation in the autumn of 1949 was a deliberate risk incurred in the hope of stimulating the exchange of economic impulses.

The partial liberalisation adopted by Sweden in 1950 initiated a second phase in which imports of consumption goods were expanded and the old contacts with German industry were resumed. In various fields where supplies had been cut off by the war, shortages could now be made good.

In other sectors the high quality and moderate prices of German products succeeded in overcoming domestic and foreign competition, with the result that our high-grade finished goods underwent a rapid increase. This development was favoured by the rise in the price of timber caused by the Korean boom; enough purchasing power was consequently available in Scandinavia to exploit the possibilities resulting from liberalisation.

THE FEDERAL REPUBLIC'S TRADE WITH THE SCANDINAVIAN COUNTRIES

(in millions of Reichsmarks or Deutsche Marks according to countries of origin and destination)

	1936	1950	1951	1952	1953	1952: 1951 Plus or Minus %	1953: 1952 Plus or Minus %
Iceland							
Imports	5·6	9·6	9·1	11·7	10·8	+28·6	—7·7
Exports	4·6	4·2	12·7	11·0	17·0	—13·4	+54·6
Balance	—1·0	—5·4	+3·6	—0·7	+6·2	—	—
Denmark							
Imports	154·3	490·7	426·2	480·9	436·7	+12·8	—9·2
Exports	182·3	353·4	535·0	630·3	758·0	+17·8	+20·2
Balance	+28·0	—137·3	+108·8	+149·4	+321·3	—	—
Norway							
Imports	87·9	217·4	245·3	278·2	247·4	+13·4	—11·0
Exports	91·3	119·1	246·5	396·0	564·5	+60·7	+42·5
Balance	+3·4	—98·3	+1·2	+117·8	+317·1	—	—
Sweden							
Imports	191·7	637·1	803·3	926·7	810·7	+15·3	—12·5
Exports	230·4	531·2	973·8	1,239·1	1,172·7	+27·2	—5·4
Balance	+38·7	—105·9	+170·5	+312·4	+362·0	—	—
Finland							
Imports	46·1	91·1	255·4	413·2	196·5	+23·0	—37·5
Exports	53·6	71·4	274·2	397·2	157·8	+38·3	—60·3
Balance	+7·5	—19·7	+18·8	+83·0	—38·7	—	—
Scandinavia							
Imports	485·6	1,445·9	1,739·3	2,011·7	1,702·1	+15·7	—15·4
Exports	562·2	1,079·3	2,042·2	2,673·6	2,670·0	+30·9	—0·13
Balance	+76·6	—366·6	+302·9	+661·9	+967·9	—	—

Today Scandinavia holds a more important position in our trade than that which it enjoyed before the war. This favourable development is all the more remarkable since, in the early post-war years, Allied controls had prevented the existence of a healthy exchange of goods. The Allies had a preconceived idea that Germany was an exporter of timber, and they declined to sanction the purchase of timber from Scandinavia. The Scandinavian countries were also prohibited from exporting foodstuffs, even in cases where we proposed to barter German against Scandinavian non-essentials. Similarly proposals made by Sweden and Denmark to barter lard, bacon, cattle, etc., against German textiles were declined (e.g. in 1947) by the Allies, from a number of motives, including considerations of competition. Endeavours made by von Maltzan to stimulate the exchange of non-essentials were thwarted by the Occupying Powers at a higher level, although the United States Element had originally sanctioned these plans. The only considerable barter transaction sanctioned by the Allies was concluded with Norway and comprised an exchange of whale oil against caustic soda. Later similar transactions were uniformly refused by the Allies even when they had been sanctioned at lower levels, much to the annoyance of the Scandinavians, who were anxious to keep their markets. Non-sanction was normally explained by the argument that raw materials and not non-essentials must be imported in exchange for exports of German textiles. No business was, however, done on this basis except for a number of contracts concluded under the miners' incentive programme of the period. The Allies did not change their attitude until 1949.

Today Scandinavia's share in Germany's foreign trade amounts to 12·7% compared with 11·6% in 1936. It should be noted that this represents a decline compared with 1952; this is due to the fact that we attacked the nearest markets first and most vigorously, partly by reason of the existing facility of communications, and partly because the opening of overseas markets reduced the percentual share of Scandinavia in our trade, though the absolute value was maintained. Moreover, the prices of certain typical Scandinavian exports have declined, and the turnover of trade with Finland fell last year for this reason by 50%. Nevertheless the fact remains that 'from the point of view of the Federal Republic the exchange of goods with the Northern countries soon exceeded the pre-war level'.*

The satisfactory development of our trade with Scandinavia is not, however, reflected in the Scandinavian foreign trade figures. The German share in the foreign trade of Scandinavia, exports and imports alike, is substantially lower than before the war—on an average by about one-third, with particularly severe declines for Denmark and Norway.

GERMANY'S SHARE IN THE FOREIGN TRADE OF SCANDINAVIAN COUNTRIES
(in per cent)

	Sweden		Norway		Denmark		Finland		Iceland		Scandinavia	
Year	Imp.	Ex.	Imp.	Ex.	Imp.	Ex.	Imp.	Ex.	Imp.	Ex.	Imp.	Ex.
1936	23·7	15·8	17·6	13·1	26·1	20·9	16·4	9·8	22·4	14·6	22·2	15·9
1950	10·6	12·4	4·1	11·2	9·7	17·6	4·6	5·5	3·6	6·4	8·2	12·6
1951	13·9	9·9	6·8	7·7	12·8	12·6	9·8	7·2	4·7	3·7	11·2	9·5
1952	17·8	11·8	11·2	8·8	15·5	12·5	12·5	9·4	4·5	5·9	14·8	11·0

Since the war production and foreign trade have increased in Scandinavia more than anywhere else in Europe. This is due partly to the fact that the industrial development of the Federal Republic and of Great Britain since the war has made of the Scandinavian countries the natural sources for providing fish, agricultural produce, timber and ores; partly it is due to the rapid mechanisation and rationalisation in every economic sector, including agriculture, which have permitted a lowering of prices concurrently with a higher rate of production. At the same time production became more and more strongly differentiated as markets began to open in every part of the world. Our decline as suppliers and customers of the Scandinavian countries thus was a result of the general course of development followed by production in Scandinavia. This led inevitably to a wider distribution of Scandinavian foreign trade over every continent.

* v. Lupin, 'German Trade with Scandinavia.' Supplement to Communications of the Federal Office of Foreign Information, No. 11 of March 4, 1953.

Today any further increases in German exports to Scandinavia are subject to certain limitations. If further openings are to be created, it will first be necessary to provide long-term openings in turn for Scandinavian agricultural surpluses. Exports of consumption goods, which have always played an important part in our trade with Scandinavia, will require further efforts from private enterprise and will be practicable only if the tastes of our potential customers are studied with greater care; quality and price alone will not suffice.

All in all, Scandinavia has proved a reasonably stable market even if we allow for the degree in which business conditions in Scandinavia depend on the trend of world prices.

The limitations to our export trade are particularly evident in our dealings with Sweden, where our 1953 surplus, including invisibles, reached approximately DM.400 millions. In consequence of a vigorous increase in production in the field of industry as well as of agriculture, Sweden has to rely today to a particularly large degree upon exports. It needs Germany, with its dense population and its rising standard of living, as an opening for its agricultural output. In Sweden the position of our economy and the development of our foreign trade are regarded as sufficiently advanced to make it reasonable that Sweden should obtain a larger share in these markets. In view of its adverse balance in visible trade and of its liberal importing policy, Sweden is consequently asking, with some energy, for a far-reaching expansion of the German market for its agricultural surpluses and its leading industrial products. The policy followed by the Federal Republic in the agricultural sector is regarded in Sweden and indeed in Scandinavia generally as a test for our readiness to play a reasonable part in international integration. Admittedly we have not yet been able fully to meet these desires. One reason for this is that Sweden is a newcomer as a supplier of grain and that earlier trade agreements prevent the Federal Republic from meeting all the Swedish desires at this moment. Another consists in the fact that Sweden is offering grain at a moment of record world crops; a moment, moreover, when the crops in the Federal Republic are approximately 400,000 tons higher than in the previous year. Nevertheless, the Federal Republic is doing its best to provide further openings for the Swedes in the agricultural sector.

In the industrial sector both countries have liberalised more than 90% of their imports. The Swedes today incline to believe that the modest nature of certain industrial quotas is unjustified in view of the stage reached by our recovery; they point to the Federal Republic's E.P.U. clearing balances and to the high amount of foreign currencies held by the Bank deutscher Länder. The answer is that the Swedes tend to treat these figures as proving that the Federal Republic's economic reconstruction has been completed; but that closer consideration will show that certain sectors of our industry are still engaged in the struggle for reconstruction at certain points which, though of minor importance in relation to the entire economy, are nevertheless important for our industry as a whole. These branches of our industry are still engaged in this struggle because, when the war ended, the damage caused by the war, the prohibitions issued by the Allies and the policy of dismantling handicapped them in the race for production or subjected them to unfair conditions. Despite the momentary advantage enjoyed by the Federal Republic's payment position, it is hoped that our Swedish friends will appreciate the difficulties which prevent us from applying a stricter standard than that employed in other competing countries which are engaged together with ourselves in the international rationalisation of redundant industries.

Similar anxieties to those affecting our relations with Sweden apply also to Denmark. In Denmark, too, people are anxious to export increasing amounts of agricultural produce, e.g. butter, pork and beef. From Denmark we import large amounts of whale oil, but neither this nor the increasing importation of iron ore suffices as a basis for a further expansion of trade. Another difficulty lies in the fact that we lack the purchasing power to import large amounts of the fish which constitute such an important item in

9

Norwegian exports. Much the same applies to our relations with Iceland, though a Treaty of trade, navigation and friendship was concluded as early as 1950. Our trade with Finland is prejudiced by the severe decline which has been ruling for the last eighteen months in the world market for timber, cellulose, etc.; these difficulties are exacerbated by the powerful rise of wages in Finland. Our trade with that country has a strong surplus tendency; a bilateral system of settlements is in force, whence it follows that outstanding balances must be settled by transfers of foreign exchange or in the form of transit business. Every endeavour is being made to maintain business, partly by a vigorous purchasing policy for a maximum list of Finnish products, and partly by stimulating transit business via Finland. It may also prove possible to increase trade in connection with the flotation of international loans.

Portugal and Spain

Our trade with Portugal and its overseas territories is a further example of the possibilities lying open to our trade policy in the E.P.U. area. We find the typical picture: a high export surplus to the motherland, and a high import surplus from the overseas territories. Here too there is an overall tendency towards equilibrium, enabling us to pay with our European surplus for the foodstuffs and raw materials imported from the Portuguese Colonies.

TRADE WITH PORTUGAL AND COLONIES
(in millions of dollars)

	1950		1951		1952	
IMPORTS						
(Country of Origin)						
Portugal	6·613		13·415		18·780	
Mozambique	2·792 ⎤		2·491 ⎤		3·704 ⎤	
Portuguese West Africa	8·279 ⎬	11·140	10·052 ⎬	13·253	7·466 ⎬	12·364
Port. India	0·069 ⎦		0·710 ⎦		1·194 ⎦	
Total	17·753		26·668		31·144	

	1950	1951	1952
EXPORTS			
(Destination)			
Portugal	10·415	18·161	25·870
Mozambique	1·402 ⎫	2·165 ⎫	4·792 ⎫
Portuguese West Africa	1·523 ⎬ 2·999	4·409 ⎬ 7·014	4·841 ⎬ 10·394
Port. India	0·074 ⎭	0·440 ⎭	0·761 ⎭
Total	13·414	25·175	36·264

A first trade and navigation agreement was signed in 1950; as usual it extended to colonial trade. It contained a most-favoured-nation clause, and it took over certain articles from the German-Portuguese trade agreement of 1926, as well as from the supplementary agreement on trade and navigation of 1935. A new payments agreement was signed in 1952, replacing that of 1950. The Portuguese Government have introduced a high degree of liberalisation. The percentage for autonomous liberalisation is 92·8 for the motherland and 81·1 for the overseas territories. Our own trade with the African overseas territories (particularly Angola) has been developing most favourably. German traders have had no difficulty in re-establishing themselves; and altogether we have been meeting with a great measure of sympathy.

A comprehensive process of industrialisation is in progress in the Portuguese colonies. It is being financed by a six-year plan adopted late in 1952 which provides for opening up the territories by improving communications—harbour installations, roads and railways. Power stations are to follow and the new industries are intended chiefly for the processing of domestic raw materials, e.g. rubber, timber, foodstuffs and seed oil. For the Federal Republic, Portugal and its colonies provide an interesting and well-balanced market, particularly for consumption goods. The old trade treaty of 1926 and the navigation treaty of 1935 are regarded by both contracting Powers as still in force.

Our trade with Spain is on a bilateral basis, since Spain is a member neither of the E.P.U. nor of G.A.T.T. The country has recently taken vigorous steps to develop its resources and therefore offers an opening for capital goods. The sale of consumption goods is extremely difficult. Recently the Federal Republic has been showing a tendency towards an export surplus which has induced the authorities to grant a substantial liberalisation, particularly for the import of citrus fruits as well as for the tourist trade. Trade with Spain offers large possibilities for industrial participation though the as yet unsolved question of German property in Spain provides a certain obstacle.

Jugoslavia

During the last few years our trade with Jugoslavia has undergone a very vigorous expansion, which goes to prove that there are countries in Europe awaiting capital development. At the same time the financial problems arising out of trade with countries of this type are present in a particularly acute form in our dealings with Jugoslavia. The country's total foreign indebtedness during the last few years has exceeded $300 millions. Part of this was financed through credits granted by the World Bank; the Federal Republic took a share in a recent second World Bank loan, partly by selling Deutsche Marks against dollars and partly by supplying funds from our 18% contribution to the World Bank. Since 1949 our trade with Jugoslavia has resulted in a large export surplus which had to be financed year by year by steadily rising credits.

GERMANY'S TRADE WITH JUGOSLAVIA
(in thousands of dollars)

	1936	1948	1949	1950	1951	1952
Imports	30,312	2,344*	8,557	22,981	38,216	61,883
Exports	31,118	1,132	15,024	37,267	43,845	76,362

* Reichsmarks or Deutsche Marks.

Jugoslavia's demands are virtually insatiable, and the Belgrade authorities are correspondingly anxious to obtain long-term German credits. The local market has, in fact, an absorptive capacity which would allow us to multiply our exports if the financial conditions existed. Difficulties again arise from the restricted market in the Federal Republic, particularly for agricultural products. A peculiarly difficult financial problem has resulted. The funds required to service and repay the German credits and claims until the end of 1955 have reached a level making it impossible to meet them even if we were to restrict our exports to Jugoslavia in the severest possible manner. A working device to permit long-term engagements in Jugoslavia must accordingly be found: the country possesses vast potentialities for economic development. Its industrialisation is based on rich mineral deposits. Favourable prospects exist for a rational system of coupling the production of raw materials and their industrial processing and for combining the development of transport and of power stations with a growing agricultural exploitation. Jugoslavia constitutes a vast potential field of development lying virtually at our door. Numerous power stations, blast furnaces, etc., have been planned. There is keen competition from other countries. All in all, Jugoslavia provides a particularly interesting object for a constructive trade and investment policy on our part.

CHAPTER VII

OUR PARTNERSHIP WITH THE STERLING AREA

FROM the German point of view the E.P.U. must be regarded as a dynamic organisation calling for expansion by a maximum extension to overseas countries to the end that our foreign trade may be promoted equally on the export and on the import side. The current problems facing the E.P.U. and the problems connected with the tendency towards the convertibility of sterling which have become apparent since the end of 1952 can be properly appreciated only if the close inter-connection between the E.P.U. and the sterling area is taken into account. Anglo-German trade will be smooth and vigorous in proportion as the two systems are more and more closely merged.*

Since 1952 our structural surplus with the majority of the O.E.E.C. countries has been becoming more clearly apparent, a surplus balanced by a structural deficit with the respective overseas territories. Germany has always exported largely to industrial countries and its opportunities for export grow with the growth of industrialisation in general. The process of industrialisation undoubtedly offers us growing opportunities overseas in proportion as the countries affected become more fully industrialised or mechanise the production of raw materials. Yet for the time being the position is governed by our surpluses with regard to the industrial countries (except the United States and Canada). Accordingly our position within the E.P.U. would probably have become untenable some time ago were it not that an opportunity existed to offer our deficits with the overseas territories in compensation by bringing into the account these overseas territories, and particularly the sterling area.

* The same problem applies, though less forcibly, to our relations with the French Union, Belgium and the Netherlands. The last-named is important because of the part played by Indonesia in the payments between the Netherlands and the Federal Republic.

Within the sterling area we have the typical high export surplus with Great Britain, and substantial export deficits with the Colonial Empire and several Dominions.

STRUCTURE OF GERMANY'S TRADE WITH THE STERLING AREA
(in millions of Deutsche Marks)

	1951		1952	
	Exports	Imports	Exports	Imports
Sterling Area	2,140	2,538	2,146	2,458
of which Great Britain	878	498	955	525
Dependent overseas territories	413	783	335	820
Independent overseas territories	788	1,237	789	1,092
Ireland	48	11	56	9
Iceland	13	9	11	12

Our trade with the sterling area as a whole shows a deficit of about DM.300 millions, resulting from our imports of wool, cotton, rubber, jute, non-ferrous metals and foodstuffs. There is also an invisible import surplus resulting from payments to British shipping and insurance companies, etc. We have already promised London invisible payments going beyond the requirements of the liberalisation code. In 1952 our invisible deficit with the sterling area amounted to about DM.80 millions, and the working of the London Debt Agreement will add to this a further DM.153 millions. Still another item may be added by the more liberal transfer of dividends, etc., arising from British investments in the Federal Republic. Our overall deficit with the sterling area is thus likely to increase. Moreover, it is in our interest to draw a maximum amount of our raw materials and foodstuffs requirements from a soft currency region like the sterling area.

We have thus deliberately promoted our trade with the sterling area by adopting a general liberalisation; with Great Britain this liberalisation has been carried out within the framework of the O.E.E.C. and has been completed by supplementary agreements on import quotas. The Anglo-German Agreement for 1953 is typical. The scope of the Agreement naturally varies with the scope of O.E.E.C.

liberalisation. In the spring of 1953 we liberalised 90% of our O.E.E.C. imports, and accordingly the remaining scope for negotiations was diminished, particularly since we conceded an overall liberalisation of wool textile imports. Conversely the British quotas have played a larger part since the liberalisation of nearly 90% granted by Great Britain in 1951 was substantially reduced in 1952. Our exports none the less took a favourable course since the British restrictions were chiefly directed against dollar goods. Our exports in 1952 increased by about 9%. The Agreement of 1953 has further increased turnover by a number of reciprocal concessions covering a wide range of German finished goods on the one hand and of British supplies covering coal, oil, iron ore, blister copper, etc., on the other.

As recently as 1949–50 the Anglo-German economic negotiations were wrecked on the dollar clause. The allied authorities in Germany, as well as the Germans, demanded such a clause, whereas the City of London tried to induce us to accept unlimited amounts of sterling. At that time the United States was still exerting a relatively strong influence on our negotiations. With Britain's adherence to the E.P.U. the problem ceased to exist; the dollar clause was dropped and London was no longer in a position to insist that we should take sterling without limit. The payments agreements now were reduced to a chiefly technical character. Since 1950 we have also been able to conclude separate treaties with the Dominions, whereas under the J.E.I.A. regime all that could be effected was a comprehensive treaty for Great Britain and all the Dominions. Here again we have gained freedom of action for our trade policy. In principle our trade with the sterling area is based on a minimum of bilateral quotas. Within the framework of the overall quotas granted us, we are in practice in a position to supply any quantities needed; our competitive ability is the determining factor.

The first bilateral treaty with one of the Dominions was that with Pakistan, concluded at the end of 1949. We introduced a far-reaching autonomous liberalisation, to which certain quotas were added. German goods on principle enjoy in the Dominions the same treatment as goods from other soft currency countries. The British Government confirmed as early as 1950 that they would not invoke reasons connected with the balance of payments in order to impose on imports from the Federal Republic into the sterling area treatment less favourable than that granted from the other O.E.E.C. countries. We, for our part, have always maintained the principle that liberalisation granted to the Dominions must be given bilaterally and autonomously, and therefore not at the same level as that granted to the O.E.E.C. countries.

Our trade with the rest of the overseas sterling area, i.e. with the Colonial Empire, also enjoys agreements favouring liberalisation. Imports are fixed independently by the Colonial Governments. In the course of the discussions on Anglo-German trade in 1953, the British Government agreed to ask the Colonies to do what they could to grant special import licences to those importers whose pre-1951 imports from the Federal Republic had been more or less negligible. Our imports from the Colonies are based on the O.E.E.C. free lists; the Colonies for their part were asked not to employ the system of open general licences in a discriminatory sense against the Federal Republic, though of course everything here depends on the way in which the principle is applied in practice. As a rule, the importers have to apply for import licences in the Colonies; thereupon the Controllers generally inquire whether the goods could be imported from Britain under the preferential tariff. Preferential quotas as well as preferential tariffs are thus employed.

All in all, British import policy is not unfavourable to our exports. The so-called free import sector comprehends precisely those goods which play a leading part among our exports.

Our trade with the Dominions too is beginning to enjoy better prospects after the passing setback caused by the sterling crisis of 1951-2. This applies to most of the Dominions, and particularly to Australia.

The British overall quotas taking the place of de-liberalised imports imply an element of competition. Yet the quotas can be handled in such a way as to conform to the actual exports offered by the parties concerned. Moreover, at the beginning of 1953, Great Britain for the first time granted the other O.E.E.C. countries additional import quotas in order to avoid hardships. The Federal Republic, too, received such a quota; it is settled quarterly and is designed to facilitate the import of de-liberalised goods in order to avoid unnecessary losses. These imports are intended to preserve our footing in certain British markets despite de-liberalisation.

Opportunities Offered Within the Sterling System

The sterling area offers us one great economic advantage, that of saving dollars. The adherence of the sterling area to the E.P.U. keeps open overseas markets for us, since we are enabled to employ the surpluses arising from our trade with Britain and the Continent to import sterling raw materials. Moreover, we can employ the balances from our exports to the other E.P.U. countries in order to pay for our imports from the overseas sterling area. A further advantage lies in the fact that we thus belong to the system of transferable sterling accounts. By this system a considerable number of non-members have a link with the sterling area. Among these there are at present:

E.P.U. countries	*Non-E.P.U. countries*
Denmark	Ethiopia
Federal Republic and West Berlin	Egypt
	Anglo-Egyptian Sudan
Greece	Chile
Italy	Finland
Dutch currency area	Poland
Norway	Spanish currency area
Sweden	Thailand
Austria	Czechoslovakia
Trieste	U.S.S.R.

The transferable sterling accounts can also be used to effect payments on current business in our dealings with these countries without sanction by the British authorities. The Federal Republic, for instance, can accept payment of its claims on countries like Italy, Norway, Austria, etc., in transferable sterling, and can use the money to pay the owners of transferable sterling accounts overseas, e.g. Thailand, Ethiopia, Egypt, etc. By the middle of 1952 credits from German transferable sterling accounts amounted to approximately £13 millions; the debits amounted to approximately £6 millions. To Britain it is an advantage that we should be members of the transferable account area because in this way numerous other members can acquire German goods against transferable sterling; this sterling can then be used by us to cover our sterling deficit.

The significance of our membership in the transferable account system, so far as Great Britain is concerned, thus lies in the fact that we provide an additional source for the import of capital goods, etc., which would otherwise have to be bought in the United States. German supplies to the owners of transferable sterling accounts thus complement British industrial exports, while the Federal Republic has a chance to reduce its high debit balance with the sterling area. This is presumably the reason why certain important Continental industrial countries have not yet joined the transferable account system: France prefers to buy in its Colonial Empire, Belgium in the Congo, and Switzerland in the dollar markets. On the other hand the industrial countries on the Continent which have no colonial empires and no hard currencies are natural members of the sterling area. The same applies to Scandinavia and to the Dutch currency area.

This also is the reason why the Federal Republic is interested in adhering to the E.P.U. and to the sterling area, and in seeing the closest possible nexus established between the two areas. So long as we can use the surpluses arising in the E.P.U. to discharge our debts in the sterling area, the surpluses arising in our European trade will not become economically or politically troublesome to the other countries. Moreover our membership of the sterling area provides us with opportunities for taking a part in the capital development of the Dominions and of the Colonial Empire; and indeed we already have heavy commitments in India, Pakistan and Australia and in parts of the African Colonies. We must never forget that before Britain joined the E.P.U. it had insisted on settlements in sterling and would not allow any balances to be settled in dollars. So long as something like a merger exists between the E.P.U. and the sterling area we are the less likely to relapse into bilateralism, a relapse which would run counter to our interests as a world trading power.

The question whether the dollar area can also be brought in remains open. Multilateralism within the E.P.U. and the sterling area does not alter the fact that these regions constitute an importers' club based on the existence of the dollar gap. It cannot be the objective to turn these areas into a self-contained payments system discriminating against the dollar. This is the reason why the more recent endeavours in London to develop sterling convertibility met with such lively interest on our part. The aim clearly is to amalgamate the different British types of settlement represented in bilateral, transferable and American sterling accounts, and to make them interchangeable. This would be equivalent to making these sterling accounts transferable into dollars. The danger that such sterling accounts would be converted into dollars in too much of a hurry would be diminished if owners of such accounts existed who were capable of competing with American industrial exports without at the same time insisting on the conversion into dollars of the sterling thus earned. These conditions exist in the Federal Republic for the reason that we have a trading deficit with the sterling area and that this deficit is likely to increase.

It is true that before the last step towards dollar convertibility can be taken, the different European countries will have to consolidate their fiscal and their credit policies. If this can be brought about all-round convertibility should become possible, a convertibility which, with reference to the dollar area, would presumably have to be total, so as to ensure that any remaining balances are settled by a more ample flow of American capital into the rest of the world.

On June 3, 1953, an Anglo-German monetary agreement entered into force which allowed the Deutsche Mark to be used throughout the sterling area as a unit of account and currency. The Deutsche Mark is thus placed on a par with other currencies like the dollar, the guilder, etc.; its status as an international means of payment should thus be enhanced.

India

Within the sterling area special opportunities are offered to trade with the countries lying on the Indian Ocean. A vigorous process of industrialisation and of the development of raw materials is in process in these regions, providing special openings for our capital goods. On the other hand the large part played by raw materials in the exports of these countries, except India, coupled with the wide fluctuation in prices ruling during the last few years, has given the balance of payments in these countries a somewhat insecure structure. This implies an element of risk for our export of consumption goods. As a rule our trade with these countries shows an adverse balance. India forms an exception; it is predominantly an industrial country and thus offers us openings for the division of labour and for an export surplus in the same way as that existing in our dealings with most of the European industrial countries. The industrial nature of the Indian economy has become even more pronounced since the formation of the Dominion of Pakistan, which as yet remains a typical producer of raw materials.

GERMAN TRADE WITH CERTAIN EASTERN DOMINIONS
(in thousands of dollars)

	1936	1948	1949	1950	1951	1952
INDIA						
Imports	—	—	18,661	24,774	28,661	29,708
Exports	—	—	11,874	17,593	50,996	54,203
PAKISTAN						
Imports	—	—	16,776	21,867	46,916	34,767
Exports	—	—	617	9,140	15,060	22,948
CEYLON						
Imports	3,213	(6,395)*	8,338	11,479	21,897	12,528
Exports	1,198	831	1,170	1,609	3,483	4,382
AUSTRALIA						
Imports	18,251	(43,450)*	29,841	63,871	84,292	47,385
Exports	14,238	2,462	10,074	27,311	59,530	39,136
NEW ZEALAND						
Imports	2,696	(22,329)*	21,820	19,439	26,969	18,824
Exports	2,220	395	944	692	5,006	4,519

* Reichsmarks or Deutsche Marks.

It naturally follows that our trade policy towards these countries should be strongly directed towards participation in the work of capital development. This was stated in express terms, e.g. in the agreement with India in the spring of 1952:

In view of the fact that India stands in need of technical assistance to build up new industries and to improve existing ones, the Government of the Federal Republic are prepared to take steps to ensure that German companies and private persons shall place their experience at the disposal of interested Indian parties. The two Governments will give help in promoting contacts in a variety of spheres. It is understood that any agreements must be concluded directly between the parties in conformity with the existing foreign currency and other regulations.

These arrangements were strengthened in the course of the negotiations in New Delhi at the end of 1952. The Federal Government declared themselves ready

on request to place their services at the disposal of the Government of India, to cause German companies, firms and individuals to give the benefit of their experience to interested Indian parties for the development of new industries, the improvement of existing industries or the development of technical research. It was further agreed that such technical aid was to embrace the technical and practical training of Indian nationals in the German Federal Republic.

Similarly arrangements were reached with Pakistan and Ceylon. They are likely to be increasingly introduced into treaties with other countries providing openings for capital development, and possibly to be given a wider scope.

Trade with India did not get under way properly until 1950, when India recognised the Federal Republic as a soft currency country, thus enabling the Republic to compete with other soft currency countries under the free list and overall quota schemes. At the same time India was granted an autonomous liberalisation for any goods which we were liberalising for the O.E.E.C. countries. Import quotas were provided for our farm products. Since then we have further liberalised our dealings with India. The trade agreement of November, 1952, moreover, provides for direct payments between the two countries. A trade treaty of the classical type has not yet proved possible, evidently because India is afraid that this would mean the formal recognition of the Federal Republic as the successor of the Reich, which might inhibit its freedom of action in dealing with the Far East (e.g. China) where the Indian Government are particularly anxious to maintain cordial relations. Instead it was decided to enter on separate negotiations on urgent special questions, e.g. the right of domicile, navigation rights, etc., though the form which the agreements were to take remained open.

An extremely powerful urge towards industrialisation is at work in India; imports are restricted to the indispensable minimum, i.e. primarily to machinery. The German negotiators, however, have succeeded in obtaining so-called token quotas which will allow German industry a certain minimum cultivation of its former markets. These quotas constitute an important concession without precedent in Indian trade policy. We on our part were unable in principle to meet the Indian wish for complete assimilation to the O.E.E.C. countries in the matter of liberalisation; we did, however, give an assurance that we would concede the widest possible autonomous liberalisation to Indian products.

India provides one instance among others of the opportunities lying open to our trade policy in the countries awaiting capital development. In virtually all of them very large projects are in process of realisation. One example is found in the vast coal and iron mining plans and the irrigation and electrical power projects in Australia, all of them coupled with far-reaching plans for industrialisation. Industrialisation on a wide scale is also being carried through in the Union of South Africa as well as in New Zealand, particularly in connection with the construction of paper mills and power stations. In Pakistan a textile industry and various metal-using industries are being built-up. Everywhere the output of farming products and raw materials is being expanded; this also applies to India, where the World Bank is interested in the Damodar Project* near Calcutta. Openings are made easier by the existence of our adverse

* Cf. Herbert Gross, *New Markets—Overseas Openings*, Düsseldorf, 1953.

balances with these countries; on the other hand, capital development work is hampered by the permanently precarious nature of the balance of payments. From this the question follows whether our technical assistance, our machinery exports, etc., should be linked with the export of capital. This question becomes the more interesting since strong temptations exist to extend our interest from the production of raw materials to local factories, particularly in India—factories which would produce goods previously imported from Germany.

It might look as though, by erecting this sort of factory, we were sawing off the branch supporting our own exports. Possibly; but ultimately we are compelled to follow the existing course of development and to replace our former exports of consumption goods by exporting our technical knowledge and our technical goods. By doing so we help to raise the standard of living and the consuming power of these countries, and thus to create markets capable this time of absorbing our exports of valuable finished articles. Such a development raises questions on the protection of our local businesses, and of German capital, and of securing the transfer of salaries for German engineers and managers. All this intensifies the need for reaching wide general treaties in the classical sense, though modernised, to cover trade, navigation and friendship. In the long run it may be found that a certain reciprocal development occurs between the basic general treaties and the trade and payments agreements of the day. If this happens it will be the part of the latter to foster the exchange of goods and to stimulate our exports, and at the same time to reap the fruits of a growing partnership in the capital development of the countries.

Arrival of the first German Trade Delegation under
Dr. von Maltzan at Rio de Janeiro

Professor Erhard in conversation with the American Secretary
of Commerce, Mr. Charles Sawyer, Washington, July, 1951

CHAPTER VIII

THE FUTURE OF EUROPEAN INTEGRATION

HITHERTO our foreign trade with the E.P.U. area has been dominated by a fruitful exchange of dynamic impulses and rising turnover. Our trade also showed a tendency towards a surplus based upon our high balances with Europe, though a small limiting factor could be introduced by bringing in the overseas sterling area. Our surpluses within the E.P.U. area reflect our overall surplus position, which is increased by the tendency towards a surplus with the clearing countries and is not totally eliminated by our debit balance with the dollar area. One could make light of this situation, particularly in view of our obligations under the London Debt Agreement and of a possible further liberalisation of the items making up our invisible balance of payments within the O.E.E.C. Yet this situation might increase our dollar gap in visible trade. We are today faced by the paradoxical co-existence of a dollar gap and a Deutsche Mark gap, and, though the E.P.U. helps to close part of the dollar gap, another part of the gap is merely shifted to a different place and the gap as a whole is not eliminated—a position familiar to all the E.P.U. countries.

We are thus faced with the question whether our policy towards the O.E.E.C. requires readjustment, or whether we have reached the limits of our trade agreements policy in Europe such as we have hitherto pursued. This question concerns ourselves particularly because, within the E.P.U., we are the leading, and structurally, perhaps lasting creditor country. We shall endanger our exports if we fail to reduce our credit balances on expansionist lines calculated also to ease the problems with other countries; for if these countries were compelled to deliberalise, our own exports would be the first to suffer. The nature of the problem is made clear, for instance, in our dealings with Italy; we would have to increase our imports or else to take a larger part in the capital development of Southern Italy. The different danger points in the relationship between ourselves and the E.P.U. show how important it is to establish a link between an increase of imports and capital exports through a system of treaties supporting the payments system established by the E.P.U. The structure of the German-Italian Agreement of 1953 shows the beginnings of such a development. Our negotiations with Belgium aiming at a wider share in trade with the Congo point in the same direction and our discussions with the Netherlands gained fresh potentialities through the fact that they were linked to discussions with Indonesia, whose payments continue to be made within the guilder area. The British endeavours finally show how greatly the German surplus tendency could serve, through a development of the British system of sterling accounts and through the greater freedom of action which this system implies, to permit German export surpluses to be set off against increased imports from the sterling area.

All these endeavours reflect so many tendencies towards an expansion of the field belonging to the E.P.U. and the sterling area. The search is for multilateral solutions embracing the largest possible areas and avoiding a relapse into bilateralism. The structure of the German balance of trade and of payments shows that our interests conform to these tendencies. If convertibility could be established between the E.P.U. and the dollar areas, our E.P.U. surplus (in 1952 approximately DM.2 milliards) and our dollar area deficit (approximately DM.1·8 milliards) would be virtually eliminated, leaving a small balance in our favour. These figures show clearly and forcibly how deeply we are interested in the principle of convertibility. Admittedly any solution we might obtain along these lines would not solve the European problem as a whole if it involved an increase in the other countries' dollar deficit. But this does not invalidate in principle our interpretation of the facts. Moreover in practice things would happen differently. If dollar convertibility could be achieved, rates of interest would presumably find their own level so as to disperse American capital over Europe and over the sterling area; the Federal Republic, too, might benefit in the shape of dollar credits. Yet convertibility and a liberal trade policy could merely prepare the way to a solution of the difficulties connected with the balance of payments; they could not achieve it. It is inherent in the transition towards convertibility that an undue strain need no longer be placed on trade or clearing policy or on bilateral methods, and that an interconnection can be established between markets for other commodities than goods.

The Dynamics of Integration

Such considerations lend strength to the sort of ideas which see in the integration of Europe a means not towards European isolationism, but towards attaching the Continent to world markets as a whole. We must remember that the Marshall Plan legislation of the spring of 1948 aimed expressly at the economic and financial restoration of Europe based on a healthy fiscal policy and on healthy currencies as well as an expansion of trade not only among the countries immediately concerned, but also with other countries. Special stress was laid on the reduction of trade barriers; and finally there was a close connection with G.A.T.T. and with the rules of the Havana Charter, the spirit of which is conserved in the Marshall Plan. Article 6 of the Paris Convention adopted by the European Marshall Plan countries (April 16, 1948) states that the contracting parties reciprocally and in dealing with like-minded countries will aim at the reduction of tariffs and of other obstacles to the expansion of trade so as to create a healthy and balanced multilateral trade system harmonising with the principles of the Havana Charter.

It is thus clear that the measures for the integration of Europe do not aim at a closed economy but are simply a preliminary stage leading to the integration of Europe in a system of multilateral world trade. Hitherto the E.P.U. system has functioned only because American aid at the rate of about $4 milliards a year flowed into Western Europe, or because equivalent payments in gold flowed from

Europe into the United States.* Liberalisation and multi-lateral payments took place under the overall shelter which the E.P.U. area enjoyed in the form of dollar aid ('aid not trade'); the resultant attachment to the dollar area was not one which was capable of working in a businesslike way.

Dollar aid paralysed the will to dollar saving; moreover it favoured the retention of economic and monetary isolationism, thus raising the questions, to what extent Europe's growing external trade is based on aid from Washington, and to what extent on a genuinely progressive division of labour. The system continues to grant premiums to countries standing in need of aid and taking the appropriate measures. The exceedingly close connection between liberalisation and the O.E.E.C. on the one hand and dollar aid on the other gives an artificial element to every endeavour and does not remove the danger of a relapse into bilateralism and nationalism.

This artificial element is reflected in the repeated instances of countries shrinking from convertibility, which is ultimately equivalent to a shrinking from adopting a free market policy in international as well as in domestic trade.

Limited Unions

What has been said explains our interest in the convertibility of the European currencies as opposed to attempts at reaching partial solutions through the internationalisation of individual sectors of industry. Admittedly the Federal Republic played a strong part in the preparation and institution of the Coal and Steel Community and in negotiations about similar bodies, e.g. the Agricultural Union, the Health Pool, etc. But the merit of this support would become questionable if it involved losing sight of the ultimate objective. We readily played our part in the Schuman Plan precisely because we expected that the Plan would lead to something more than an *ad hoc* union among the nations concerned. It is regarded rather as the symbol of a genuine and comprehensive integration.

* E. S. Kerber, 'United States Foreign Aid in 1952', Survey of Current Business, March, 1953, Washington.

The Federal Republic are helping to make the Schuman Plan a reality because the existence of a comprehensive European market in the sphere of the basic industries will help to safeguard the industries of the States concerned against a depression. The Government are convinced that in this way a road will be opened towards a general prosperity benefiting every inhabitant of Europe.

In these words (contained in the Government's report on the year 1951) the Federal Chancellor has described the positive support given to this partial integration of Europe. But his words also permit the question whether such partial groupings will invariably help the creation of a common market before this market has been created in some other way. And this raises the further question whether such partial groupings can assist the development of a genuine comprehensive market which in fact can come into existence only by virtue of convertible currencies.

At first the Marshall Plan stimulated a sort of investment nationalism: it encouraged a number of E.R.P. countries to develop their industrial capacity without regard to the existence of similar capacities elsewhere in Europe—a development by no means intended by the authors of the Plan. Little attempt was made to achieve an overall arrangement of productive capacity. The main effort was therefore concentrated at an early date upon the reduction of trade barriers. Liberalisation and the Payments Union establish a horizontal union of markets on the principle of the reciprocal reduction of barriers, though their efficacy is restricted to the extent that artificial exchange rates and economic autarky are retained. Thus even this horizontal liberalisation suffers from the lack of clear co-ordination among the basic elements in the common market.

The danger that symptoms rather than the roots of the trouble may be attacked is increased if the aim is restricted towards forming partial groups of States, while the co-ordination of other markets into a common one remains untouched. Objections to the system of partial integration have been laid down in detail in papers written by the expert advisers to the Federal Ministry of Economics and in contributions by Professor Dr. Helmut Meinhold and Professor Dr. Fritz Meyer.* The special interests which may have led different countries to support the Coal and Steel Community may be worth special study.

For France and the other Western European coal importing countries it would obviously be no sacrifice but an extremely desirable object to obtain a free non-discriminatory and non-monopolistic access to West German coal. Again with steel the countries which had expanded their productive capacity through large investments in the first years after the war were primarily anxious to obtain an outlet, and this sufficiently explains their wish to see a general market established.†

The system of international integration by sectors of industry also involves the danger that while a uniform market is created for the sector concerned, a balanced system becomes more difficult in other markets. A kind of economic 'old maid' is played in which the necessary adjustments are shifted from one sector to the next. Accordingly in their opinion of December 14, 1952, on the Schuman Plan, the experts pointed out that it would be meaningless to effect the integration of one sector of the European economy if the resulting effect upon the balance of payments would be to bring about quota restrictions or currency manipulations impeding the division of labour in other sectors.

Any integration by sectors, even for as important a part of the economy as coal or steel, must be accompanied either by the simultaneous integration of a maximum number of other sectors, or by a general and equably progressive liberalisation in all the other countries. A series of integrations effected one after the other in different sectors, if it led to the desired objective at all, would at best do so by a long and circuitous detour.

There follows a sentence trying to attribute a measure of significance to partial groupings:

* Papers on questions relating to the establishment of a European and Agricultural Community, Foreign Office, Bonn, 1953.
† F. W. Meyer, loc. cit., pp. 227 ff.

The true economic significance of the Coal and Steel Community lies in the fact that its inner dynamics can enforce a progress beyond the integration of one sector to the complete integration of the entire European economy.

What then would be the 'true economic significance' of a European economic integration? Surely it would be to create a single common market allowing the greatest possible freedom of movement to labour and capital and, by concentrating production on the most favourable locations, opening to individual concerns the benefits of a larger and consequently a more uniform rate of mass production. At the same time such a market would provide further opportunities for a concerted policy in dealing with the problems of employment and of the trade cycle; it would permit a rationalisation of the costs of production. The various economic processes could thus be reduced more easily to the common denominator of a currency. Such a currency, based upon the potential of a great uniform market, might then achieve convertibility with the dollar and with other currencies. Accordingly the objective in pursuing an effective European market is to transfer to this market the free movement of goods, people and capital which today is confined to the smaller national markets.

In order to establish such a market the basic economic factors in the different countries will first have to be co-ordinated. These factors at this stage comprise financial and monetary policy, credit policy and trade barriers. It will further be necessary to co-ordinate budgetary policy, primarily by limiting expenditure and by achieving a lasting balance between expenditure and revenue.

From what has been said it follows that any partial integration which fails to co-ordinate these basic factors is likely, while integrating one sector of the community, to bring about disintegration in other sectors and to threaten markets with a measure of atomisation. Moreover, so long as currencies remain inconvertible, it is impossible to form a correct view on true costs and on their differences as between the different sectors. Valid data for an intelligent reorientation of locations and lines of production would thus be wanting.

Trade Problems of the Limited Groups

Where integration is carried through by sectors trade policy is hampered by the fact that it becomes impossible to negotiate on all the products of the partial market. The countries concerned regard an opening of the individual markets as an obvious consequence of the partial grouping. The countries which in this process have to give more than they receive in the way of openings thus suffer a weakening in their negotiating power. An agrarian union, for instance, might deprive our own Government of the ability to offer an increased opening to other countries' agricultural produce in exchange for an opening of their markets to German industrial products. Moreover, if such a union were to be formed, our own agricultural markets could be subjected to pressure, and at the same time our own agriculture would not enjoy the advantages arising from lower prices for agricultural machinery which the existence of a partial grouping ought to provide. Integration by sectors thus either creates artificial structures with artificial prices and with a strong tendency towards new super-national authorities, or else tends to prevent the integration of other markets. This is the reason why other proposals for partial integrations (one example is provided by the proposed creation of a European Health Pool) are likely to lead to a dead end rather than to a genuine common market. The French health plan, for instance, aims at the formation of a new super-national authority which is supposed to control a common market for drugs, for medical-surgical material and for the pharmaceutical industry. Such proposals contain the danger that economic policy may be divided according to professional sectors and that a new *dirigisme* may arise which might be employed all the more vigorously since the general instruments of economic policy (e.g. monetary and credit policy) would not be available to the various subsidiary sectors which a partial integration implies.

Agrarian Union

The same objections apply to the plans produced hitherto for the creation of a partial grouping embracing the agricultural markets of Europe. On this point the technical experts in their paper of February 22, 1953, said:

Integration in individual sectors hampers inter-communication among the different streams of goods, preventing instead of promoting co-operation between the different economies. An isolated integration of the agricultural markets without appropriate measures in the industrial sphere would lead to severe distortions in the exchange of agricultural for industrial goods. If super-national bodies are created in the different sectors instead of one supreme body responsible for the entirety of European economic policy, the danger arises that action will be concentrated on the interests of the different sectors. This could mean that a multiplicity of unco-ordinated and partial plans might be drafted. In international negotiations the formation of an isolated union would offer smaller opportunities for give and take than would a wider integration. . . . No sort of integration can become a lasting success unless currencies too have been or are made convertible.

Attempts of this sort moreover involve the danger of a regional autarky, particularly in countries which have been introduced more or less by historical accident into certain groups set up for economic co-operation. The European and other Marshall Plan countries form a somewhat mixed gathering; among them are Turkey, Greece and Trieste; countries like Finland and Spain remain outside. The way in which the different countries draw on American aid has also differed widely. If this fortuitous collection of regions were to be formed into a single market, a limited bloc might be formed; yet many of the member countries have worldwide interests. The countries of the Coal and Steel Community can admittedly meet each other's needs to a great extent; yet this regional limitation of the basic industries has no bearing whatever on the interests—in the sphere both of trade and of world economy—of the other industries in the participating countries.

The same problems apply to the statutes of the European Community of 1953. Article 82 aims at the creation of a common market among the member countries, a market based on the free circulation of goods and capital and on the free movement of nationals. To fulfil these tasks the Coal and Steel Community is charged with co-ordinating the currency, credit and financial policies of the member States. We here have an attempt to transform a partial grouping into a comprehensive political and economic union whose economic fortune will, however, depend on whether the common market does not cut itself off from other countries to a greater extent than that previously enforced by its least protectionist member.

All in all, it appears that the methods of integration hitherto employed have reached the limits of utility and stand in need of transformation. Either a uniform market will have to be created by currency reform, by the introduction of uniformity in dealing with problems of finance and of the trade cycle and by the introduction of a general plan for lowering tariffs (cf. the Pflimlin Plan); or else a move will have to be made towards a political union amounting to a European Community—in other words, a political unit will have to be created, which would imply a comprehensive market not limited to sectors of the economy. If this is admitted, then vertical integrations restricted to single sectors possess a real significance only if they are regarded as starting points or as measures for introducing into the general scheme branches of the economy which, at the national level, are under the influence of powerful State control or of monopolies and which in no other way can be subordinated to the higher order. The latest statements by M. Jean Monnet suggest that the Coal and Steel Community is seeking to transform itself into an instrument for achieving a general economic and political integration.

The more the course of European integration tightens the nexus between Europe and the world economy, and the more it stresses and promotes the latter, the more strongly will it agree with the course of our own trade policy. Today this policy has reached the point where it is more powerfully interested in overseas business and in a general participation in the tasks of capital development.

CHAPTER IX

OPENINGS IN LATIN AMERICA

IN our trade with Latin America two forces are at work, each troubled by contradictions. The one lies in the traditionally close cultural and human contacts between Germany and the Latin-American world. The other works towards a relaxation of our economic connection with Europe in general and compels us to look for fresh bases on which to build a larger world trade. Indeed, our trade with the so-called clearing countries is characterised by the fact that the most important among these—at least in the Middle East and in Latin America*—generally felt a cultural and political sympathy towards Germany though at the same time our normal trade with them involved difficult if also interesting problems. Visible trade in the sense of exchanging goods for goods appears to be growing more and more difficult, since most of the countries concerned are in a process of a capital development which is changing the structure of their foreign trade and increases their demands on our technical, economic and financial help.

The many proofs of our traditional friendship with Central and South America are distinctly encouraging. It was ties of this sort which undoubtedly provided the first steps towards rebuilding our totally destroyed trade with Latin America. Herr von Maltzan expressed this well in an address (October 12, 1949) to the Latin-American Society in Hamburg:

We feel that we possess certain reserves in South and Central America—reserves which dictatorship, war and years of severance could not destroy. These are reserves of an immaterial nature which we have succeeded in preserving in the South-American

* The South American countries, with the exception of Venezuela, Peru and Bolivia, are so-called clearing countries; all the countries in Central America, including Mexico, are dollar countries.

market. . . . During the last decades German investments have not been confined merely to material things; in our dealings with South and Central America we have had the human element at heart; we have built schools, and with our own means have developed educational institutions. If today hundreds of thousands of people in South and Central America remember gratefully the educational work done by German schools; if these memories recall to them the German people, and cause them to feel respect towards the former activities of German nationals; if, in consequence of all this they regard German affairs with a far-reaching sympathy, then in our eyes these facts constitute powerful reserves which we are entitled to take into account as a lasting fund on which to draw in our future economic and political dealings.

It was in this spirit that the first important treaty with Uruguay (in 1949) was hailed on both sides of the Atlantic. The Uruguayan delegation had negotiated the treaty in Frankfort, and was received personally in rapid succession by the Federal President, the Chancellor and the Minister of Economics. Both in Germany and in South America the public displayed a lively interest. The representatives of other South American countries congratulated the Uruguayan delegation on having restored connections with Germany. Further treaties followed in large numbers. Delegations arrived from Columbia, Peru, Costa Rica, Ecuador, Paraguay, Argentina, Mexico, etc., to conclude treaties. The sums involved were frequently substantial. Next the first German delegations went to South America; Herr von Maltzan led one to Brazil, Herr Karl H. Panhorst led one to Venezuela, and Herr Ludwig Imhoff led one to Chile. In this way 1950 became an important year of reconstruction in our overseas trade. It is true that the treaties concluded at this time showed certain lacunae, but they did at any rate provide a framework, the dollar clause losing in importance and swings being introduced. They provided a foundation for new negotiations which led to a growing number of treaties with countries of South and Central America. The year 1952 was particularly fruitful.

Our trade with South America requires a highly skilful policy; special regard must be paid to numerous structural changes and to new tendencies in economic policy. In this way our problems in dealing with Latin America become attached to our general European preoccupations; they cannot be overlooked despite the special nature of the German position and despite the special advantages it enjoys. Accordingly it may be easier to appreciate our South American problems if they are regarded in the light of the general economic relations subsisting between Latin America and Europe. A recent United Nations study has provided valuable material for this purpose.*

EUROPE AND LATIN AMERICA

Findings of a United Nations Report

Europe's trade with Latin America suffered notable diminutions through the First and the Second World Wars; the beneficiaries were the United States and the domestic tendency towards industrial autarky. In consequence we have to note a lasting decline in the European share in the foreign trade of Latin America, partly compensated by a vast expansion of trade with the United States. Latin American imports from the United States in 1951 were nearly four times as high as in 1938; imports from Europe rose by no more than 55%. At the same time exports to Europe were about 25% less than before the war, while exports to the United States were 75% higher. When the war ended Latin America had gained financially as the result of large exports to the United States and to Great Britain; but the wealth so acquired helped to stimulate a dangerous inflation. It financed nationalism and industrialisation—an expansion of the domestic market which, though largely artificial, was still far from negligible. Domestic consumption gained at the expense of exports. Despite the existence of large sterling and dollar balances, the state of the balance of payments soon led to difficulties which were reflected in a chronic dollar gap. Admittedly the Caribbean countries, which were

* *A Study of Trade between Latin America and Europe.* Produced jointly by the Economic Commission for Latin America, the Economic Commission for Europe, and the Food and Agriculture Organisation. Published by the U.N. Department for Economic Affairs, Geneva, January, 1953.

particularly important suppliers of raw materials to the United States, did not suffer so much. The financial difficulties increased with the distance from the United States, and were intensified by a far-reaching interruption of trade with Europe.

South America too is suffering from a structural interruption of its channels of trade. As Europe paid for the interruption of its Eastern trade with the development of a chronic dollar gap, so South America had to pay for the interruption of its trade with Europe with the development of a similar shortfall. Though exports to the United States were increased, a demand for capital goods arose, and its vigour was such that the increased dollar earnings could not remotely meet it.

This experience suggests that Latin America can hardly rely on being able to pay, out of its direct receipts, for the quantity of dollar goods and services it would like to buy, even in times when primary prices are at extremely high levels and when United States capital is flowing freely. In more normal periods, Latin America must either restrict its total imports to a substantially lower level, or import more from Europe or endeavour to continue to obtain dollar settlements from European countries. The last-named 'solution' makes a further reduction of trade with Europe inevitable.*

In practice foreign trade in the two continents on each side of the Atlantic has taken a divergent development. The United States increased their imports from Latin America; France, Great Britain and Belgium drew more from their own Colonies and from the sterling area, while their imports from Latin America underwent a severe proportional decline. Now the United States are not buyers of a number of South American agricultural products, e.g. grain and cotton, etc., with the result that marketing problems have arisen which at first compelled South America to rely less upon exports, but which today suggest the resumption of trade with Europe in general and with the Federal Republic in particular.

* *A Study of Trade between Latin America and Europe*, United Nations, Department of Economic Affairs, Geneva, January, 1953, p. 12.

Certain countries, like Argentina, Brazil and Chile, are today pursuing industrialisation behind the protection of an autonomous monetary policy, of foreign exchange control and of arbitrary and differential rates of exchange, which retard the production of raw materials and stimulate domestic consumption, leading to chronic payments crises and hampering trade even with friendly foreign countries. The above-named United Nations Report, despite the influence of South American experts in its drafting, utters unmistakable warnings against an exaggerated industrialisation. The danger of an unco-ordinated duplication of industrial capacities in the different countries and of an all-round rise in the South American level of costs is pointed out in unequivocal terms. A high level of costs in turn hampers exports, compels Europe to buy from the cheaper dollar area, and thus further opens the dollar gap. If trade with South America is to increase, South America therefore will itself have to pay greater attention to farming and to the production of raw materials; industrialisation will have to be directed into fields where the production of raw materials will be stimulated and cheapened instead of being hampered.

Market Changes

The structure of imports into Latin America is today widely different from what it was before the war; consumption goods have lost ground and capital goods have gained. Industrialisation has largely concentrated on consumption goods; more recently capital projects, some of them ambitious, have begun to play a part. In foreign trade the need for the import of raw materials has increased; on the other hand South American delegations are anxious to supply so-called consumption goods, e.g. textiles for Germany. An analysis of the United Nations Report on imports into Argentina, Chile, Brazil and Mexico (which account for 60% of the entire imports into Latin America) shows a substantial shift from consumption goods to capital goods. In 1951 machinery and vehicles (excluding private cars) accounted for nearly a third of the total imports as compared with approximately a quarter in 1938, and one sixth in 1928. The only countries continuing to rely strongly on raw materials are those with convertible currencies, i.e. those which can draw on the dollar area; and these have consequently succeeded in substantially expanding their imports of consumption goods. This applies particularly to Cuba and to other Central American countries, as well as to Colombia and to some extent to Ecuador; these countries consequently contain special openings for exports of German consumption goods.

Meanwhile competition for a share in the capital development of South America has become extremely keen; the different European countries are vying with each other in offering State subsidies, export guarantees, etc. The Federal Republic is particularly interested in this type of enterprise by reason of the large part played by capital goods among the total of goods it produces; but this type of business frequently requires new methods, including technical advice, the provision of finance, etc. Moreover, a general trade policy providing wider scope for this sort of business has to be evolved. The authorities are aware of these facts, and are giving them full weight in the negotiation of trade treaties and in their detailed framing.

If contacts are to be further developed, the South American countries will have to increase their output of raw materials at world prices. Omissions in this sense are severely criticised by the U.N. Report, which points out that a number of raw materials producers have omitted to expand their leading exports and are therefore experiencing severe difficulties in paying for their imports of capital goods and for material needed in their industrial development. They are at the same time risking that import restrictions may be confined to a number of less important goods, and that their resources will be dispersed over too wide and too variegated a field.

GERMAN FOREIGN TRADE WITH THE LATIN-AMERICAN STATES
(in thousands of dollars)

Country	1936	1948	1949	1950	1951	1952
ARGENTINA						
Imports	47,797	71,947*	43,842	65,472	99,893	64,491
Exports	39,396	1,174	1,783	24,865	82,775	79,067

* Reichmarks or Deutsche Marks.

(Photo: Engels)

The Turkish Ambassador, Mr. Ayasly, calling on the Federal Minister of Economics, in connection with the German-Turkish economic talks, 1952

(Photo: D.P.A.)

The Argentinian Foreign Minister, Sr. Remorino, signing the German-Argentinian Trade Treaty, summer, 1950

The German delegation at the Torquay Conference, September, 1951

Country	1936	1948	1949	1950	1951	1952
BRAZIL						
Imports	52,978	45,495*	23,674	20,678	74,951	74,349
Exports	53,806	1,673	9,792	35,106	112,506	154,344
CHILE						
Imports	23,710	3,560*	4,895	13,692	19,441	29,842
Exports	19,930	127	1,885	7,014	22,089	21,164
URUGUAY						
Imports	8,471	6,869*	18,486	13,645	9,500	27,639
Exports	6,720	429	1,795	14,123	24,503	13,628
VENEZUELA						
Imports	5,703	15,275*	7,484	8,383	14,967	20,780
Exports	9,734	1,320	6,339	16,833	24,371	25,566
MEXICO						
Imports	22,749	7,985*	8,436	6,490	24,100	31,470
Exports	20,601	735	2,083	9,167	20,218	19,885

* Reichsmarks or Deutsche Marks.

The Report further points out that stronger incentives for the production of raw materials must be provided by an appropriate economic policy. The competition from other providers of raw materials, chiefly Australia, New Zealand, etc. (for meat), and from the United States (for cotton, grain, etc.) must not be under-estimated. However favourable the terms of trade might be (for South America this applies particularly to coffee, maize, linseed, meat and wool) the producers would have to become more cost-conscious. In practice this would mean that some of the South American countries would have to come off their high horse in matters of prices and exports. A high horse might otherwise prove a Trojan horse, introducing dangerous shocks into the economic structure of South America.

German Treaties with Central and South America

During the first phase of the J.E.I.A. treaties the German negotiators were largely eliminated and all that was possible was a cautious examination of possibilities. The dollar clause and the obligation laid on both parties to confine themselves as far as possible to goods having a dollar value restricted turnover in 1947 and 1948 to a minimum. Non-essentials were hardly exchanged at all. Payments agreements with lists of the goods covered, and with fixed quotas, were all that was practicable. In this way treaties were concluded with Chile, Ecuador, Brazil, Colombia, Argentina and finally with Uruguay. The first treaty in which we could play a formative part was that (signed late in 1949 in Frankfurt) with Uruguay, though it was representatives of the Allied High Commission who acted as contracting party. The Treaty was ratified by the Montevideo Parliament and came into force on July 5, 1950. Its predecessor (concluded in October, 1948) bound Uruguay to use 85% of all German dollar payments for purchases from Germany. In the new Agreement of 1949–50 the contracting parties guaranteed each other a large-scale grant of import and export licences. The Federal Republic granted large quotas for wool, frozen meat, hides and skins, oilseeds, etc. Exports to Uruguay were to include machinery, electrical goods, iron and steel, chemicals, etc., and a wide range of consumption goods set out in a special list. A non-interest-bearing dollar account was opened in the name of the Bank deutscher Länder with the Banco della Republica Oriental del Uruguay. This was the first instance of a clearing account; the Treaty of October, 1948, had still provided for the payment for imports from Germany in American dollars. At the same time a swing of $10 millions, later reduced to $5 millions, was arranged. Each side was to provide the other with goods worth $70 millions. A total turnover of $140 millions, however, was never reached; these large figures were selected in the hope that they might have a stimulating effect on other South American countries.

The Agreement initialled at Montevideo in April, 1953, was more realistic; it provided for a turnover of $25 to $30 millions on each side, and the swing was raised from $5 to $7 millions. Deliberately, quota lists were not drawn up. The Agreement of 1950 reflected an international scarcity economy; promises to supply were more important than promises to buy. Today the shape of trade is largely left to private initiative, and the terms of the Treaty are so drawn as to give it free play. In the autumn of 1952 the Federal

Republic liberalised autonomously the leading Uruguayan products.

Unconditional most-favoured-nation treatment was expressly introduced into the Trade Agreement of 1952 (Article 2). The novel element in this Agreement lies in the deliberate renunciation of any discriminatory import policy. This renunciation takes its place side by side with the trade treaty—covering most-favoured-nation conditions in tariffs, etc.—which was concluded at the same time.

As liberalisation grows wider, the quota system tends to vanish and tariffs become more important. Once again it was Uruguay, a pioneering area for German-South American economic relations, where most-favoured-nation treatment was used to provide safeguards for the buyers' market which was becoming increasingly more important. Moreover, a so-called Mixed Commission is charged with the task of ensuring that trade can be reasonably balanced. The Commission's duty is to shift Uruguayan trade (the country is short of dollars) to the European trading partners so far as possible. Business is transacted without the employment of free dollars.

In Uruguay, too, ambitious development schemes are being planned; their realisation depends on the grant of a credit by the World Bank. The Agreement of 1953 provides for German participation in this form of enterprise: its Article 4 provides for the promotion of the sort of business where final settlements by the nature of the transaction are liable to take place after the expiration of the Treaty. In this way we have ensured the maximum promotion of German capital development contracts, though admittedly this may involve a strain on the swing. It follows that our imports from Uruguay will have to be stimulated to the highest possible degree, precisely in order to provide an adequate basis for long-term undertakings like the construction of power stations, bridges, etc. In the course of the negotiations for the new treaty of 1953, a tendency became apparent (one probably typical for the whole of South America) to take a less serious view of the political risks involved in a commercial nexus with Europe—a view based on the belief that a *détente* between East and West was becoming possible. All in all, it is becoming apparent that the South American countries are growing progressively readier to accept wider commitments in export business.

The first trade treaty with Brazil was concluded in Rio in August, 1950, and provided for a turnover of $115 millions on each side. The Treaty bore the marks of the scarcities prevailing at the time and accordingly contained an emergency clause empowering the contracting parties to export in each quarter less than 25% of the agreed quotas if their domestic requirements made this demonstrably essential. A swing was also provided amounting originally to $11·5 millions, and later to $13·5 millions. Our exports rose most vigorously in 1952. They amounted to well over twice our imports from Brazil, which remained virtually unchanged in 1951 and 1952, at approximately DM.315 millions. Our imports lagged chiefly because of the high prices of Brazilian products, which made it practically impossible to import anything but coffee. Almost all Brazilian goods were too expensive; as late as the spring of 1953 the price of cotton was something like 60% above the world level. Moreover, a mercantile risk was implied in the purchase of staple goods, e.g. cotton from stocks held by the State, since it was impossible to obtain the guarantees of quality which are normal in the cotton trade. Like many other South American States, Brazil shows a picture of exaggerated industrialisation, bureaucratisation and inflation, and of welfare economics. The consequences are a reduced productivity, a flight from the land, shortage of goods, high costs of production, and inadequate supplies of goods for export. The output of agricultural goods and of raw materials stagnates, while industrialisation undergoes a hot-house growth behind high protective barriers. We thus have all the customary post-war maladies which a constructive European (and German) trade policy would be excellently qualified to alleviate. At the beginning of 1953 the Brazilian debit balance on current account amounted to approximately $100 millions. Efforts made to reduce it were not immediately successful, partly because German firms lacked the capital resources needed for long-term investment, and partly because such small opportunities existed to import goods in exchange at reasonable prices. Attempts made by the Brazilians to stimulate their flagging exports by the introduction of a free foreign exchange market failed at first to produce worthwhile results, the more so since coffee, cotton and cocoa did not benefit by this measure. Products like hides and skins did so benefit, but the Brazilian exporters simply raised their cruzeiro prices by an amount equivalent to the expected foreign exchange discount. So long as the Brazilian inflation continues a flight into goods will subsist, reflecting itself in a tendency towards high imports and low exports. Further difficulties arise from structural obstacles, e.g. the distance between the main sources of production and their markets, the poor communications and inadequate harbour installations, and the high middlemen's margins. None the less the debit balance was reduced to $78 millions by the end of October, 1953.

On our side a lively interest is felt in increasing imports. For this there are three possibilities. First, more coffee could be imported. This may prove feasible since our coffee duty has been substantially reduced—an important administrative measure. Secondly, Brazilian export prices must be reduced to world levels. And, thirdly, our imports of Brazilian ores should be increased. Brazilian exports of iron ores are growing steadily, though the total is less than $1\frac{1}{2}$ million tons, of which a large proportion goes to the United States. The Brazilian ores are as rich as the Swedish ones, and can be won by opencast mining. The necessary transport facilities have still to be provided.

Brazil is heavily indebted to other countries, including the United States, besides the Federal Republic. Its foreign debts on current account were estimated at $700 to $1,000 millions at the beginning of 1953, of which $420 millions were owing to the United States. The latter debt had to be lightened by an advance of $300 millions made by the Export-Import Bank, so as to provide earlier payment for the American creditors. A reduction of the German credit balance was at first attempted through licensing procedure,

Brazil at any given time licensing German imports to an amount not exceeding 80% of its exports to the Federal Republic. Brazilian payments were credited to the German exporters on a special account. These balances could be sold on the open market to German importers of Brazilian goods, a measure intended to make such imports cheaper. At the same time 20% of imports had to be paid for at the official dollar rate laid down in the Agreement, so as gradually to reduce our balance. This arrangement has not proved immediately effective, since the balance continues to grow as German claims fall due. The maximum point of $96 millions was reached in the spring of 1953. This procedure did not provide any worth-while stimulus for Brazilian exports, since the discount on dollars under the Agreement proved inadequate. The only effect was to increase our imports of coffee from Brazil at the expense of Central America and Colombia.

Everything turns on the question of bridging the Brazilian Deutsche Mark gap. The reduction in the coffee duty which has since been effected can hardly be adequate, and there are limits to the amount of cotton which can be imported. Anxious as we are to import and needful though it is for Brazil to reduce the costs and increase the volume of its output of raw materials, there nevertheless remains the problem of our own financial participation in the opening up of the country. Brazil is endeavouring to consolidate its debts, one method contemplated being to raise a loan analogous to that granted by the Export-Import Bank, and another being to have recourse to the International Monetary Fund. The authorities are also endeavouring to finance German capital goods through loans with a minimum currency of four to six years; finally, they are trying to promote long-term German capital investment in the Brazilian economy. The ultimate question is whether Brazil wants to pursue a policy aiming at world-wide trade or at autarky. True, Brazil can point to its vast and as yet barely opened territories; but this is a draft on the future and the details must be entered in a clear mercantile hand: and this implies sound ideas on the importance of cultivating world markets. The close attachment of Brazil to American capital cannot eliminate every risk: the United States are faced with much the same problems in dealing with Brazil as those facing German business-men. The partial crediting at the free rate of sums resulting from exports has not reached the desired scope. The Brazilian Government consequently has drastically revised the foreign exchange regulations; at the same time some new appointments have been made in leading positions at the Banco do Brasil. The new measures amount to the introduction of multiple rates coupled with a devaluation of the cruzeiro. Brazilian exports are subsidised. What happens is that foreign exchange resulting from exports of coffee is transferred to the authorities; the exporter thereupon receives a bonus of 5 cruzeiros per dollar. For products other than coffee the bonus amounts to 10 cruzeiros. The intention is to cut down imports, partly by introducing a far-reaching reduction in the turnover of money, from which a deflationary effect is expected, and partly by artificially raising the price of the foreign exchange needed to effect imports. Before an importer receives an import licence he has to acquire a foreign exchange certificate. These certificates are sold by auction and prescribe various premiums in accordance with the goods to be imported. For this purpose the authorities have classified imports into five groups; the majority of consumption goods fall into the fifth group, where the premium is highest. For each of these groups the Banco do Brasil provides a certain sum, drawn from incoming foreign exchange, which is made available at the auction, at the same time prescribing the minimum rate to be bid for each group. This minimum rises from 10 cruzeiros per dollar for the first group to 50 cruzeiros for the fifth group. Of the total foreign exchange obtained the Banco do Brasil takes 30%, which is intended to be used to settle outstanding trade debts and to meet other Government requirements.

The authorities stress the provisional character of these measures, and the time has not yet come for a final judgement. What is clear is that our imports from Brazil have been increasing during the last months. Thus cotton could again be imported from Brazil, after a lengthy interruption, in substantial quantities. In September, 1953, negotiations were concluded at Rio providing for the restoration to the former German proprietors of most of the confiscated trade-marks. It was also decided to set up a mixed German-Brazilian Commission whose task it will be to give an expert opinion on German investment projects. The improved facilities for importing from Brazil made it easier to revise the lists of goods contained in the Agreement, and to raise the volume on each side from $115 to $142 millions. Of the proceeds of German exports approximately 30% are to be assigned to the above-mentioned investments.

Similar problems arise in trade with Argentina. The Agreement of 1950 provided for a turnover of approximately $124 millions on each side. A dollar clearing account was opened with a swing of $31 millions which was later raised to $50 millions. Imports from Argentina rose from $65 millions in 1950 to nearly $100 millions in 1951, though the drought and the generally falling tendency of exports brought it back to $64·5 millions in 1952. German exports, for their part, showed a vigorous increase—from $25 millions in 1950 to $82·5 millions in 1951, with a slight decline to $79 millions in 1952. In 1950–1 the agreed swing was heavily drawn upon by ourselves, but since 1952 a growing German tendency towards a surplus has become apparent. Trade between the two countries is severely restricted by the multiplicity of peso rates, much as with Chile. Many Argentine products cannot be acquired at all directly, but only after transit through other countries, a method which has grown in importance in recent years. As with Uruguay, the turnover originally aimed at was unrealistic. The swing of $50 millions seems unnecessarily high though we did avail ourselves of it to some extent; in the new Agreement of 1953 we, on our part, granted Argentina a similar credit. In 1950–1 we were ready at any time to export largely to Argentina, and that country's export surplus at that time was not due to any failure to supply on our part. Today, on the other hand, the existence of a high German export swing could be the result of the fact that Argentina cannot export to ourselves at a sufficient rate. A genuine long-term financing of Argentina through the Bank deutscher Länder might then become appropriate. A drawback lies in the fact that this issuing Bank is not supposed to concern itself with long-term capital exports. The new Agreement negotiated by Dr. Seeliger (valid from April, 1953 to July, 1954) is designed to bridge the gap until a trade treaty of the classical type is concluded, and meanwhile to put an end to the previous interim arrangement.

Within the new five-year-plan Argentina is attempting to return to the development of raw materials production. Yet the provisions of the Welfare State and the effects of industrialisation, protected as they are by a system of high tariffs and differential peso rates, cannot easily be reversed. It will require exceedingly vigorous assistance from other countries if the emphasis of economic development is to be shifted from industry to agriculture. The Federal Republic has already helped through long-term contracts for the supply of tractors, trolley-buses, machinery, etc. Transport equipment, power stations, bridges, railway material, and rolling mill products are all urgently needed in the Argentine. To a certain extent the country's small export surplus, which even the most recent harvests did not raise to a sufficient level, are an impediment; moreover vigorous inflationary tendencies are in existence. The social legislation continues at work and hampers the development of foreign enterprises in the country. The factories carry a burden of redundant labour, the outcome of a one-sided protection restraining the right of dismissal. What is needed is a drastic reorientation of internal and external economic policy; without this overseas trade will continue to suffer from undue restrictions and the risks attaching to loans and investment will be excessive. Necessary as the import of capital into South America is, it is equally essential to introduce an economic policy allowing European exporters to increase their imports from South America and consequently to increase their payments. A policy of this kind would enable both parties to reduce their dollar gap.

Similar problems exist in Chile. Here too a promising agreement on trade and payments (in 1950) opened the proceedings. At the same time a long-term trade treaty on classical lines was concluded. The latter, however, had to be denounced in 1953 because the differential management of peso rates began to throttle our trade. The existing regulations imply the possibility that the so-called German clearing dollar may fall to a discount against the effective dollar rate, which would mean that our imports of copper from Chile would become substantially dearer. The fact that Chile did not fix a rate for the clearing dollar also led to a speculative reduction of imports from the Federal Republic. Behind all these difficulties stands the nationalistic economic policy being pursued in Chile, which hampers the production of raw materials and artificially stimulates industrial output. Moreover there exists a growing inflation fed by budgetary deficits. Chile prefers to confine its licences to raw materials, spares, fuel and certain chemicals. The neglect of agricultural production makes it necessary for substantial amounts of foreign exchange to be made available for the import of foodstuffs. If our trade with Chile is to flourish the country will have to adopt a policy in matters of economics, trade and foreign exchange calculated to give freer play to the geographical advantages enjoyed by the local raw materials. Yet the prospects are tempting and have led to keen competition among a number of countries, which vie with each other in offering long-term credits and favourable terms of payment. French industrialists, for instance (with State backing), have offered up to seven years' credit. The country is also anxious to obtain capital from the United States. Both the Government and the public are pro-German in their sympathies, a fact which offers us favourable bases for the development of our economic relations. In 1953 these were approaching a new arrangement; similar adjustments are planned for a number of countries on the Western seaboard of South America.

Development Plans

The openings in South America are of such a kind as to direct our attention towards major projects. A number of countries are anxious to enjoy German participation, among them, for instance, Bolivia which, by nationalising the tin mines (Patino, Hochschild and Aramayo) more or less forfeited the favour of the United States and is now trying to re-establish contacts with international investment capital, contacts which might include the Federal Republic. In the case of Bolivia this includes the construction of a tin smelter, the foundation of an industrial bank, the construction of power stations and of a match factory, as well as a number of other projects, some of them having very great potentialities. But here again we continually find that it is essential to protect financial engagements by opening up supplies from Germany, which is tantamount to developing the exporting capacity of Bolivia and of other countries.

Colombia

Our trade with Colombia tends towards a debit balance and does not therefore suffer so much from foreign exchange difficulties as our trade with Brazil or Argentina. Trade agreements have been in existence since 1949. The last agreement was concluded in 1951 and provides for imports of $45 millions a year on either side. Among our imports the most important are coffee, bananas, rice, platinum, tropical hardwoods and tobacco. A swing of $11 millions is provided for. Of the credits arising from our exports, 80% can at any time be covered by imports from Colombia. In the spring of 1953 our debit balance amounted to approximately $13 millions which, however, did not have to be settled in hard currencies. We had the chance either of reducing our imports, or of looking for larger orders under the Colombian development programme (bridges, etc.).

The biggest openings in Colombia today are for machinery. The Government are anxious to confine imports to capital goods. Nevertheless a large market exists for consumption goods. The Colombian market is thus structurally better balanced than the Argentinian one. Competition is keen for a share in the development programme. The contract for the blast furnaces at Paz de Rio, 110 miles north-east of Bogotá, went to France, which was enabled by State subsidies to offer very long-term credit. A chance remains that the

Federal Republic may build a rolling mill at Paz de Rio. In the construction of the blast furnaces American firms like Koppers of Pittsburgh and Arthur G. McKee of Cleveland are acting in an advisory capacity. The works have been estimated to cost $41 millions, though the final costs are likely to prove much higher. The output aimed at is 700 tons of pig-iron a day. The production of cast-iron and of steel is intended to be 193,000 tons a year.

By helping to build up Colombia's industries the Federal Republic might thus be enabled to compensate any losses in exports of steel proper. Once again we can observe the stimulating effect of an industrialisation based on an all-round expansion; for industrialisation creates prosperity and thus opens new forms of overseas trade. The economic relationship between the Federal Republic and Colombia is marked by the fact that the Federal Republic provides the leading European market for Colombian products. Among Colombia's customers the United States has the first place, and the Federal Republic the second. The other countries of Europe follow at a long interval.

Dollar Markets in Latin America

As we look farther north, we approach nearer to the dollar area; and we find that the economies of these more northerly Republics are based on a more complete international division of labour. In those countries where currency and economic policy favour overseas trade, remarkable possibilities exist. This is true particularly of Peru; similar potentialities exist in Ecuador, with which a new agreement was concluded in the summer of 1953. With Venezuela we have not yet concluded a treaty; but since there is no control of foreign exchange considerable openings exist, particularly for electrical goods and machinery. A ten-years' trade treaty, including a most-favoured-nation clause, is in existence with Cuba. The Treaty of Trade and Navigation signed at Bonn on May 11, 1953, gives most-favoured-nation treatment to both parties. They further promise to grant every facility in the establishment of overseas branches, and to renounce discriminatory taxation. The Federal Republic had to agree to the purchase of substantial amounts of Cuban sugar, which has to be paid for in dollars: 150,000 tons for 1953 and 175,000 tons for each of the next two years. The Federal Republic had also to agree to import tobacco, cigars, copper ore and various other raw materials totalling $2 millions. The Treaty of Trade and Navigation has a currency of ten years and the Trade Agreement one of three years. Cuba, for its part, made a number of tariff concessions, listed in an annex.

An interesting aspect of the Cuban Treaty is the fact that it provides for the Federal Republic to import certain quantities of goods on account of the State, while the Cuban Government agree to reduce tariffs in exchange. The Federal Republic is thus given an opportunity of exploiting these reductions—which lessen the privileged position of the United States—by using private initiative to maximise German exports. Cuba is a free dollar country and thus enables us to earn a hard currency, though international competition is keen. The Cuban Treaty is a key treaty for the whole of the Caribbean area. It reminds us of the fact that the dollar drive should be applied, not only to the difficult markets of the United States and Canada, but also to the Latin-American regions in the Caribbean and in Central America, where large openings still await us. The Treaty gives the Federal Republic unconditional most-favoured-nation treatment, which implies tariff reductions by which German consumption goods should benefit.

Venezuela

Among the Caribbean dollar countries Venezuela offers promising possibilities of trade as a market for German machinery and consumption goods, and as a supplier of important raw materials and luxury foodstuffs. Among our imports from Venezuela, oil and oil derivatives hold the first place, amounting to DM.84 millions in 1952. The country also produces excellent coffee, which can be used with other sorts to produce a blend specially appealing to German tastes.

Manifold developments are in process in Venezuela, and

efforts have recently been made to expand its economic structure, which today is based somewhat excessively on oil—approximately 1·8 million barrels a day. In agriculture ambitious plans for the reform of land tenure and land settlement exist, largely under the auspices of the Instituto Nacional de Agricultura. The Federal Republic has already played a striking part in the settlement policy, particularly through the model settlement of German farmers in Turen, where about a hundred German families were settled, liberal credit being granted by the Venezuelan Government. The undertaking was so successful that the amortisation originally planned to run over thirty years was largely completed within two years. In industrial development, too, promising opportunities exist. For instance, the Venezuelan Government are trying to create an iron-producing industry under the auspices of the Corporacion Venezolana de Fomento. Comprehensive plans assuming a blast furnace capacity of 180,000 tons in the first year have been drawn up, and consultations have been started with German enterprises. This industry will be based on rich deposits of iron ore which can be got in opencast working, though communications have yet to be established.

There are no currency restrictions in Venezuela, so that hitherto it has not been necessary to conclude a special trade and payments agreement. The country provides a genuine competitive market, in which orders go to the most efficient. Attempts are, however, being made to conclude a treaty providing the basis for future economic relations, the form aimed at being the classical type, though doing justice to modern requirements. It would be particularly useful to obtain unconditional most-favoured-nation treatment, which we do not as yet enjoy in Venezuela. This lack handicaps a number of consumption goods, such as cosmetics, wireless sets and foodstuffs (tinned). It is to be hoped that such a treaty may be concluded in the not too distant future. It would provide a particularly effective bond with one of the most important development areas in Northern South America, the 'land of the future on the Orinoco'.

All in all, the parts of the Caribbean area belonging to the dollar region contain openings for an intensified commercial initiative. Our policy could here content itself with concluding most-favoured-nation treaties and long-term treaties of trade, navigation and friendship; the economic nationalism which forms such an obstacle in South America does not here exist. The relatively small number of agreements concluded with the Caribbean States does not therefore reflect a lack of interest on the part of the Ministry of Economics, but merely does justice to the fact that the way already lies open for commercial competition. Cuba and Mexico stand in the forefront; moreover the latter countries' communications and industries are being vigorously developed and there are large openings for German exporters. Keen competition exists with the United States; but the United States are also stimulating neighbours, whose presence should provide an incentive to our exporters in the same way as it does in Canada.

CHAPTER X

DOLLAR MARKETS—LARGE BUT DIFFICULT

UNTIL the middle of 1953 no trade treaty existed to regulate our trade with the dollar area. The fact that the dollar was convertible made trade and payments agreements superfluous; and Washington recognises the hard nature of the dollar by refraining from insisting on special payments agreements to overcome the obstacles to American exports which lie in the dollar shortage from which its customers suffer. The great barrier on the American market consists in tariffs and in an administrative protectionism. This is true despite our G.A.T.T. treaty concluded with the United States in 1950, a treaty providing for few and inadequate tariff reductions. Apart from these our exports depend on our competitive ability in the difficult dollar markets, and on the degree to which German exporters overcome these difficulties. The dollar area is a competitive market *par excellence*. Our policy naturally confines itself to concluding long-term treaties analogous to the trade, navigation and consular treaty of 1923, and to safeguarding ourselves against discrimination by arranging for most-favoured-nation treatment. Apart from this, any treaties concluded should deal with double taxation, rights of domicile, and the facilitation of entry to German representatives and visitors, thus providing conditions giving our traders a maximum freedom of action. Since the Chancellor's journey to the United States at the beginning of 1953, these tasks have been vigorously attacked; a number of agreements have been reached which afford an interim solution calculated to lead to the ultimate resuscitation of important parts of the 1923 treaty, plus the assurance of most-favoured-nation treatment. The interim treaty was signed by the two Governments on June 3, 1953, and it can be assumed that it will shortly be ratified. At the present moment German business-men can obtain visas under the trade treaty, they can acquire real estate, take a share in American firms or themselves found firms. The legal framework to permit a healthy exchange of goods and capital is thus once again in existence. The conclusion of this treaty was a signal for the conclusion of similar comprehensive trade treaties on classical lines with other countries.

GERMAN TRADE WITH THE UNITED STATES AND CANADA
(in thousands of dollars)

	1936	1948	1949	1950	1951	1952	First half 1953
U.S.A.							
Imports	94,729	1,573,729*	754,741	430,893	647,338	595,957	209,700
Exports	69,355	25,980	43,940	103,071	236,537	249,068	143,200
CANADA							
Imports	7,563	47,983*	20,453	10,101	51,402	124,695	41,400
Exports	14,141	1,033	5,439	9,734	24,784	22,357	13,700

*Reichsmarks or Deutsche Marks.

Negotiations are also going on to settle problems of double taxation, since this threat is a particularly serious obstacle to financial intercourse. Further, at the end of 1952, 3,000 trade-marks were restored which had been confiscated by the American authorities but had not been acquired in good faith by private persons. Further concessions are likely in this matter.

Tariff Problems

American tariff policy continues to confront us with numerous difficulties despite our membership of G.A.T.T. and despite the tariff agreement with the United States concluded at Torquay. The Act to simplify tariff procedure, which came into force on September 7, 1953, has not met all our expectations. Official American sources indicate that this simplification of tariff procedure constitutes only a first step and that Congress is likely to consider further improvements. These questions, like the entire problem of American protective tariffs, are part of the general problem of American protectionism which affects all countries. Admittedly American supporters of free trade, including leading industrialists engaged on mass production and including also organisations like the Detroit Chamber of Commerce, hold the view that even the adoption of complete free trade would raise American imports by only a relatively small amount. Persons holding this view point out that Great Britain, for instance, despite the preference which it enjoys in Canada, is steadily losing ground to American imports. Yet these objections are not really sound. For one thing, every additional dollar earned is so much gained, and even a slight increase in our exports can be of substantial importance to individual concerns. Moreover, the American tariff tends to fluctuate rapidly; it is continually under threat from the Tariff Commission, from escape clauses, from the Buy American Act, etc.; and these uncertainties involve risks making it questionable whether the high outlay connected with the cultivation of the American market is really worth while. To ensure for a long time ahead the field of operations constituted by the American market is one of our most urgent tasks, the importance of which is well understood in Bonn. The lively activity of our trade policy in dealing with clearing and E.P.U. countries cannot disguise the fact that these activities are merely necessitated by the greater instability of soft currency markets which are more largely exposed to the risks inherent in import quotas, foreign exchange control and to other forms of economic nationalism. The unceasing anxiety to secure our foreign trade with the clearing countries, even for a brief period, shows how far we still are from having reached the conditions of classical trade treaties with these countries, whose problems are still largely masked by the disturbances resulting from their currency policy. These troubles do not exist when we are dealing with the dollar area. Here all that has to be done is to consolidate the dollar markets by long-term treaties and, of course, by an active policy aiming at tariff reductions. How far these objectives are reached must admittedly depend largely on the attitude taken up by the United States towards questions of world trade.

Accordingly our exports to the United States or to Canada (to which country, as to the United States, we are not linked by any trade treaty except by the G.A.T.T. provisions) will stand and fall by our competitive ability. But, if we are successfully to cultivate the American market our endeavours must be supported by an efficient information and market research service. This is why the network of economic sections attached to our Consular offices in the United States is no less important than the various offices of the Society for the Promotion of German-American Trade, which body is working in close liaison with the German-American Trade Association in Frankfurt.

We cannot here enter upon the manifold problems facing German exports into the dollar area.* It is a market full of difficulties which can be alleviated for our exporters only through the machinery described above. The fact that the American market is for many goods the largest and richest in the world is not in itself strictly relevant for European exporters, since this market is based on a foundation of American mass production and mass salesmanship. Outsiders will find the easiest entry for special goods and for such exports as components fitting into American mass production. Closer analysis of this market shows that most of its purchasing power goes to American mass-produced goods with which foreigners will find it hard to compete. The interesting aspect of the American market consequently lies in specialised goods for which openings exist which by European standards permit mass exports, however small these openings may appear when measured against the total American turnover. Our task will therefore be carefully to study the market, to plan our campaign and then to export German components, specialised instruments, etc. Evidently these goods will have to be supplied at advantageous prices, must possess a technically superior quality and will have to be available whenever wanted. Much money will be needed to study these possibilities; hence the great importance of the bodies previously mentioned. The assistance of private

* The best survey is given in Dr. Matthias Schmitt's excellent '*Das deutsche Dollarproblem.*' Schriften der Gesellschaft zur Förderung des Deutsch-Amerikanischen Handels mbH., Frankfurt, 1953.

bodies for market research is particularly important in the United States; so also is the fuller investigation of the special psychological, sociological and technical conditions of this market. It will hardly be possible to avoid mistakes, though they should be reduced to a minimum through collaboration with the above-mentioned organisations and with private market research institutions.

Easier openings may be found to exist in the neighbouring areas, e.g. Canada and the Caribbean countries already mentioned, like Mexico and Cuba. Development is vigorous in Canada in the different sectors of agriculture, mining, forestry and manufacturing industry, and in this process European immigration and the formation of affiliates of European concerns are favoured. Today a fair number of German concerns have formed branch offices and branch factories in Canada and Newfoundland. These are essential instruments for the export of German technical knowledge and capital; they are essential also in the development of overseas business, and it would be meaningless to lament any resulting loss in exports, if only because the new openings also provide new business connections. In any case German official and private bodies agree in advising that the idea of the dollar market must not be confined to the United States, and that those other dollar markets must also be explored where the stage of development is more favourable to German capital exports than it is in the United States.

One such dollar market is that of Liberia, where a Hamburg concern has acquired large plantation concessions designed eventually to produce exports to Germany, which will then be paid for by the export to Liberia of German consumption goods and machinery. Liberia is a free dollar market, and competition among European exporters is keen. It should be possible to conclude a long-term treaty of trade, navigation and friendship akin to that recently concluded in Monrovia by Spain. The chief raw materials available are rubber and ores, among the latter notably rich iron ores. Finally, Newfoundland is an important under-developed part of the Canadian dollar area, of which Labrador also is a member. Development in

Newfoundland is being promoted by large subsidies from the Canadian Government; it embraces a number of ambitious industrial projects. In a large number of these important German industrial concerns are already engaged.

The Dollar Gap

Since the end of the war our relations with the dollar area have been governed by preoccupation with the dollar gap. The danger exists that this may lead to a faulty development of our export trade. The dollar gap in our visible trade, which in 1952 still amounted to approximately $500 millions, is largely the financial reflection of structural changes in our position in the general system of world trade—changes which also apply to Western Europe in general. The shape of the gap is determined by the absence of any trade with Eastern Europe, and by the interruption of European trade overseas (particularly with Latin America) caused by the war. Through the war and through the risks affecting post-war development in Europe, our overseas trading partners have not been encouraged to develop their European trade. They thus fell under the attraction of the dollar area and, like ourselves, suffered the inconvenience of the dollar gap. The interruption of the previously existing trade between Western Europe and (a) the countries behind the Iron Curtain and (b) Latin America caused a vacuum, which could be filled only by enormous loans and subsidies from the United States. Vitally important as were these various forms of dollar aid, they nevertheless had dangerous after-effects because they also retarded the re-establishment of trade between the European countries and their other trading partners. Hence arose what is today called the structural dollar gap, which in turn has led to ideas like dollar saving and dollar drives. While dollar saving aims at reducing imports from the dollar area, the dollar drive aims at establishing a balance by increasing exports to the United States, Canada, etc. There is a certain measure of conflict between the two objectives; in a sense the less dollar saving, the more dollar drive, and, conversely, the more dollar drive, the less dollar saving. At present the total dollar gap is still so large that both principles can be employed without conflicting with each other. Both require considerable commercial expenditure, but of the two dollar saving promises to carry back world trade more effectively into the existing channels of trade. Behind dollar saving stands the modern idea of capital development overseas, an idea which in fact has already touched the dollar area, particularly in its peripheral regions, but is most effective in Latin America, in the sterling area, the E.P.U. area and the clearing area. These circumstances are worth pointing out because the dollar drive is in danger of being estimated in accordance with unduly high standards, viz. those of the dollar gap. Such a valuation could lead to a hypertrophy of the dollar drive, leading in turn to losses in other and easier markets.

A structural dollar gap has always existed in Europe. Before the war it amounted to $2,000 millions; today it varies between $4,000 and $5,000 millions. An exact direct balance will never be obtainable except at the cost of destroying a sound overall division of labour. Ultimately the objective must be to attain a reasonable success in dollar saving and in the dollar drive, and so to eliminate the gap without entirely removing the dollar deficit. To bring this about would be the task of the final stage in the restoration of order in currency problems, a process leading to the convertibility of all Western currencies and hence to a balance through the aid of international capital movements. In this sense our relations with the dollar area are not confined to achieving a balance of goods and services. They are also concerned with the movements of capital, and with an international currency and capital policy calculated to allow credit and capital to move at the call of the natural rates of interest. We must also remember that our overall payments with the dollar area were, in fact, balanced in 1953, viz. by the dollar payments of the American occupying forces, etc. The dollar gap must not be made an excuse for further *dirigisme;* rather it calls for a free-market policy which could cause the dollar gap to vanish even though the dollar deficit actually increased.

CHAPTER XI

OPENINGS IN THE MIDDLE AND FAR EAST

A POLITICAL and economic revolution is in progress in the Middle and Far East. The growing independence of those countries offers us wide commercial opportunities, but also corresponding risks. Our commercial policy in this region is therefore confronted by new tasks calling for new methods. Conditions differ from those applying in Europe inasmuch as the exchange of goods by itself is not everything. The picture is dominated by an economic expansion which implies the absorption of capital, which in turn means an import surplus. It thus becomes our task to act not only as importers, but also as suppliers of capital. Large investments will have to be made before the high level of turnover is reached which will eventually give us a large share in those countries' imports of consumption goods. The risks involved in trade with the Near East result from this region's limited resources and its ambitious investment plans. One difficulty lies in the fact that we were not really able to establish diplomatic and consular missions until 1952. Before this our business with the Near and the Middle East had to rely in practice on private initiative without really significant support from the Government. As the centre of gravity shifts from the pure exchange of goods to investment, the engineer becomes more important side by side with the traditional merchant. This involves far-reaching innovations, requiring not only the dispatch of technical specialists, but also a new psychological relationship. We shall have to act as consultants, to give tactful aid to public authorities, and to support domestic concerns. All this makes trade with the Near and Middle East one of the most fascinating tasks for our trade policy and for a new partnership which during the coming years will have to link trade policy and industry.

GERMAN TRADE WITH THE NEAR AND MIDDLE EAST
(in thousands of dollars)

	1936	1948	1949	1950	1951	1952
TURKEY						
Imports	47,791	26,623*	24,690	51,993	83,639	93,473
Exports	32,032	2,015	13,003	56,331	105,018	136,384
EGYPT						
Imports	14,968	17,437*	16,874	23,541	24,515	30,413
Exports	17,327	1,644	2,558	19,143	29,712	38,422
ARABIA						
Imports	—	—	—	16,079	36,563	34,716
Exports	—	—	—	2,513	3,049	4,464
IRAK						
Imports	—	4,369*	3,293	18,170	32,935	40,346
Exports	—	1,552	1,443	335	2,261	4,720
IRAN						
Imports	9,279	5,864*	6,569	9,319	25,402	16,403
Exports	12,269	1,671	6,386	9,272	19,945	20,969
LEBANON						
Imports	—	—	—	—	—	122
Exports	—	—	—	—	—	11,453
SYRIA						
Imports	—	—	—	—	—	3,607
Exports	—	—	—	—	—	9,420

* Reichsmarks or Deutsche Marks.

Few of these countries are in a position to export on a large scale to the Federal Republic—partly because they lack the goods to export, and partly because the Federal Republic on its side finds it difficult to increase its imports, since its inevitable reliance on dollar countries restricts its freedom of action. Our balance of trade is adverse only with those countries which are large suppliers of oil, i.e. in practice Iraq and Saudi Arabia. Our balance of trade with countries like the Lebanon, Iran, Egypt, Turkey, etc., shows a substantial surplus. A further difficulty lies in the fact that the quality of the goods we import, particularly foodstuffs, is often inferior. Expansion should be possible with a restricted range of goods, for instance cotton, though we cannot neglect the fact that in price and quality American cotton is preferable. Turkish wheat also is growing in importance.

Practical experience shows that clearing methods are not necessarily the right way to develop trade with these countries. If this method is to be used, trade must be balanced, whereas in the present case what matters is investment and, generally, business designed to stimulate further transactions; and here swings and kindred arrangements are less appropriate. Accordingly the treaties concluded with the Arab countries soon abandoned fixed clearing arrangements. With the Lebanon we settle in free currency, i.e. in sterling or dollars. A clearing agreement arranged with Syria failed to be ratified by the Syrians because it did not meet their requirements for free transactions. Treaties, in fact, have been concluded with only a small number of countries, e.g. with Egypt, where a genuine trade and clearing agreement has been concluded. With the Lebanon a most-favoured-nation agreement is in existence. A detailed trade and payments agreement is in force with Turkey; the pre-war trade treaty with this country has in the main been resuscitated. We have no treaty with Jordan or Saudi Arabia, but an arrangement was reached with the Yemen early in 1953. Dealings with Ethiopia and with the Anglo-Egyptian Sudan are carried through by means of a transferable sterling account. An economic agreement exists with Afghanistan, providing for transactions on a reciprocal basis, most of the business being done by the Afghan Government. The Government imports by open tender in the Federal Republic, while exports follow lines laid down by arrangement between the Afghan Trade Delegation and the Federal Government.

For the Federal Republic the most important among the Near and Middle Eastern countries is Egypt. This is largely due to the great Assuan project. Egypt offers us raw materials and provides an opening for consumption goods and for participating in the country's ambitious plans for industrialisation and irrigation. Among raw materials Egypt can offer manganese, zinc, lead ore, phosphates, etc.; the most important is cotton, the high quality of which should assist our textile exports. The Egyptian bazaars, on the export side, offer a market still capable of development for our consumption goods. Openings for capital development in Egypt comprise the Assuan Dam, the erection of fertiliser factories, power stations, and irrigation and railway works, the motorisation of agriculture, the construction of bridges and silos, etc. All the Arab States have ambitious plans for industrialisation and expansion, which we could further stimulate.

Egypt in this connection is a sort of test case. If we manage to make a success of capital development there, similar openings will arise in other Arab States, which are watching the Egyptian experiment with interest. Egypt is thus the key to our Eastern trade in general. The openings, however, are the object of keen competition. The Federal Republic is somewhat handicapped, e.g. by the lack of an efficient bank. Important as is the work done by the German-Egyptian Chamber of Trade and by our diplomatic mission, we shall have to send some of our ablest industrialists to Egypt if we are to compete successfully with other industrial countries.

The Assuan project alone will cost DM.1·2 to 2 milliards, of which something like 60% could be covered by German exports, the rest coming from Egyptian sources. The new barrage would retain the entire flow of the Nile, and would thus go far beyond the existing dam. It would open fertile regions to a growing population, and would provide a wider basis for the supply of food. The present imports of rice and grain would become largely superfluous.

Wide as are the opportunities it offers, the Assuan project would have to be considered in commercially realistic terms. So far as the Federal Republic is concerned, large preliminary sums would have to be spent even if the World Bank were to give assistance. The Assuan Project will embrace a power station, a long-distance cable system, a nitrogen plant and blast furnaces, though it has not yet been decided where the last-named are to be located. The blast furnaces are a long-standing ambition; they will presumably be located near the mouth of the Nile and will not be so much of a State project. The financial questions will be particularly difficult because the foreign contractors are expected to supply something like 25% of the investment.

The Assuan Project forms the centre of new capital developments, as does the Damodar Project in India and the Alpine Project in Australia. The dimensions alone are impressive. The dam will have a length of 3·2 miles and the reservoir will have a capacity of approximately 226 milliard cubic yards. It will thus be five times as big as the biggest American barrage, and about a thousand times as big as the Eder Valley barrage.

Other projects are being planned in other Near Eastern countries, e.g. that for a 250-mile two-road railway in Saudi Arabia. In Turkey barrages are to be erected and harbour installations improved. The growing pressure of exports in Turkey overtaxes the existing transport facilities, one factor being the country's growing tendency to export instead of to import wheat. A process of structural change is going on in Turkey, exemplified in road building, industrialisation, urbanisation, and raw materials expansion.

It remains to include our exports to Israel (DM.3·5 milliards), for some time a politically contentious undertaking. The resulting picture of the openings for German trade in the whole of Asia Minor and the Middle East as far as Pakistan is such as to place the highest demands on the constructive imagination of our traders and of those in charge of policy.

Much diplomatic skill and convincing proofs of goodwill were necessary before the representatives of the Arab League could be persuaded of the necessity for concluding the agreement with Israel, and could be convinced that we fully understood their own problems. In this connection the German engagement in Egypt has become a political test for demonstrating our will to strengthen economic and cultural relations with the Moslem world.

Our connections with Iran might have become closer but for the Allied opposition to German purchases of oil. Here influences are at work which are beyond our control and which are entirely understood in Iran. For the moment the oil crisis has weakened Iran, and really ambitious development plans cannot be carried through apart from the construction of certain sugar and textile works, etc.

The Far East

Favourable developments are in process in the Far East and have since 1951 elicited a vigorous trade policy on our part. Profitable contacts exist with Indonesia, which belongs to the guilder zone and has a connection with the E.P.U. as a non-participating country. The Federal Republic has granted far-reaching autonomous liberalisation to imports from Indonesia. The first trade agreement of 1951 provided a turnover on each side of 243 million guilders; our main imports were rubber, copra, palm kernels, palm oil, tobacco, coffee, kapok, etc. Our trade with Indonesia has always had a structurally adverse balance. A new schedule of goods was attached to the trade agreement of April 22, 1953. It provides for imports of 320 million guilders, with rubber, copra, tin, etc., again at the head of the list. Our main exports will be iron and steel, steel sheets and other metal goods, machinery, chemicals, electrical goods, transport equipment, optical apparatus, etc. In order to do justice to the difficult exchange position of Indonesia (probably due largely to the fall in rubber prices), an item has been entered among our exports covering a 'general quota for the promotion of German exports to Indonesia' and amounting to 45 million guilders. To this amount the Indonesian Government are not compelled to license the import of German goods if the exchange position makes the granting of licences undesirable. A reduction of our exports to Indonesia is in any case compensated indirectly by our surplus with the Netherlands. The latter country continues to carry on a heavy transit trade of German goods to Indonesia. The goods are indeed sent direct to Jakarta, but a substantial part of the payments is made via the Netherlands. For 1952, for instance, the visible trade statistics show that our direct trade with Indonesia was adverse to the amount of DM.90 millions which, however, was probably reduced to DM.40 or 50 millions if the Dutch transit trade is taken into account. Most of the payments are today made between the Bank deutscher Länder and the Indonesian State Bank, any balances ultimately outstanding being settled by the Dutch Central Bank. The Agreement of 1953 provides for a Mixed

Commission to ensure that a serious unbalance in this trade is avoided.

Indonesia, too, has ambitious development plans; the Ministry of Transport alone means to spend 320 million guilders. The grant of German credit would therefore be welcomed by the Indonesians. The plans of the Indonesian Government (whose writ does not yet run throughout the country) differ from those worked out in certain other relatively backward countries by being confined within reasonable limits.

Japan

Our trade with Japan at present shows a surplus. This results largely from transit dealings under the clearing agreement. Structurally our visible trade with Japan suffers from certain handicaps. The Federal Republic imports goods and raw materials on short-term credits, but we export costly industrial products which are supplied and paid for on a long-term basis. This originally involved a strong adverse tendency which compelled us to cut down certain imports in order to bring the balances within the limit of the swing. The first treaty was concluded in 1949 between the Occupying Powers of both countries. In 1951 we negotiated on our own. Trade with Japan suffers from the disappearance of the Manchurian Hinterland, which formerly supplied us with many raw materials. The structure of our balance of trade and of payments with Japan resembles that with Great Britain. We had an export surplus with Japan proper and employed the balance on purchases from the subsidiary raw material regions, i.e. Manchuria in the one case and the rest of the sterling area in the other. Whether our trade with Japan can be further intensified will probably depend on whether a raw materials reserve such as that previously provided by Manchuria can be introduced into the clearing system. If it should be possible, for instance, to introduce one of the producers of raw materials in South East Asia or in the Pacific area into such a clearing system, we would be able to increase our exports to that country and to pay for them out of our surplus with Japan; at the same time our exports would help to balance the payments of this country (of Indonesia, for instance) with Japan. No trade treaties exist with the other great suppliers of raw materials in the Far East; this also applies to the Philippines. As the Philippines are gradually detached from the American system, growing opportunities will be offering in those islands. It should therefore prove possible to conclude a fairly comprehensive treaty between the two countries.

Thailand is today for practical purposes a dollar country, with which we have a substantial export surplus. No trade treaties exist between the two countries. Thailand belongs to the Transferable Account Area and accordingly our exports primarily earn us transferable sterling. The Thai Government are considering large orders for power stations, railways, harbour installations, etc. There also exists a large market for German consumption goods, including beer. Bangkok is virtually the sole free currency market in South-East Asia.

All in all, East Asia is becoming an increasingly interesting market requiring a new psychological and political approach. We need capable business-men, who must also be good psychologists, to open up this market. They will have to understand the mentality of oriental nations who are steadily growing in political independence and will have to deal with the local merchants, industrialists and officials in the right way.

No trade treaty has been concluded with the Chinese People's Republic, but a number of clearing transactions have been arranged from time to time. We also export direct to a number of Chinese places. These exports, however, fall within the framework of the embargo lists.

CHAPTER XII

LOSSES AND POTENTIALITIES
IN EASTERN EUROPE

THE decay of East-West trade has raised problems affecting the whole of Europe and causing particular injury to Western Germany. The exchange of goods with the countries east of the Iron Curtain has declined severely for all countries, but the German share has fallen beyond the average, though it must be noted that the Eastward trade of the Russian Zone has correspondingly expanded and that the regions east of the Oder-Neisse Line have fallen entirely within the Russian system. The diminution in Europe's Eastern trade was accompanied by a corresponding increase in the dollar gap and, more recently, by an intensification of competition among the industrial countries of Western Europe for trade in the Western world. The longer trade between East and West continues to be interrupted, the more dangerous will be the effects of the development of two distinct systems fostered by the planned economy within the Russian sphere. The development of ambitious industrial programmes based on the heavy industry complexes in East and South-East Europe is creating duplications within the Russian area analogous to those produced in Western Europe as a consequence of the Marshall Plan and of economic nationalism. This process is accompanied by a diminution in the output of raw materials and agricultural produce, a process which is intensified by the fact that the tension between East and West prohibits an exchange of goods between these two regions which would be calculated to retard this diminution. Investigations made into the structural changes of trade between East and West are available; particularly valuable ones have been produced by the European Economic Commission in Geneva.* It appears that Western Europe's

* Economic Bulletin for Europe, 2nd Quarter, Geneva, November, 1952: Developments of Trade between Eastern and Western Europe from 1950 to mid-1952.

share in the imports of the Eastern European countries, including Russia, fell from 61% in 1938 to 15% in 1951; at the same time the share of Western Europe in these countries' exports fell from 72% to 19%. While trade within the Eastern bloc increased, the dollar gap grew on the Western side while overseas exports increased, though at a slower rate. Accordingly the share of Eastern Europe in the imports of Western Europe fell from 8·1% in 1938 to 2·7% in the first half of 1952, while the share in exports fell from 7·3% to 2·3%. Within this general decline that of Western Germany was particularly severe. In 1938 the share of Eastern Europe was approximately 13% of Germany's exports and imports; in the first half year of 1952 it had fallen to 1·3% of exports and 1·2% of imports. Germany belongs to the group of countries whose Eastern trade has suffered particularly heavily, while Switzerland, Austria, Italy and Great Britain were more successful in maintaining themselves, to say nothing of countries like Sweden, Denmark and Finland, in whose foreign trade the East actually now plays an increasing part.

Our trade with the East continues to stand under Allied supervision. Our relations with it are based on agreements which, from 1947 to 1949, were concluding by the Occupying Powers. No agreements exist as yet with Albania, Roumania or Russia. A payments agreement was arranged with Hungary in the autumn of 1947 which at present continues automatically from year to year, subject to three months' notice. The same is true of Poland; the first agreement was concluded in the summer of 1949.

A similar trade and payments agreement has been in force with Czechoslovakia since December, 1948, and with Bulgaria since October, 1947. Until 1951 the Allies were entitled to send observers to attend the negotiations and to be kept informed of their progress. Since 1952 no Allied observers have attended, but the Allies are still entitled to be advised of the intention to negotiate and to receive information at certain stages before an agreement is concluded. At present any treaties have to be submitted to the High Commission after they have been initialled, and the latter

Dr. van Scherpenberg with Mr. Nehru of the Indian Foreign Office during the German-Indian Trade Treaty negotiations at New Delhi, October, 1952

German-Pakistan Trade Treaty negotiations, Karachi, September, 1950

Dr. Reinhardt, and Mr. Triantaphyllis in conversation during the German-Greek Trade Treaty negotiations, 1953

Mr. Ushiba and Dr. Strack, heads of the delegations, signing the German-Japanese Trade Treaty, 1953

can raise objections within a period of twenty-one days. Agreements tend to be largely based on the treaties concluded earlier by the Occupying Powers. Nevertheless, it has proved possible to modify them in conformity with existing conditions, particularly by arranging the provisions for swings according to the state of payments. Since the autumn of 1951 much of the supervision of trade has lain with the Federal Trade Department, which considers in detail all the proposals.

SHARE OF EASTERN EUROPE IN THE FOREIGN TRADE OF CERTAIN WEST EUROPEAN COUNTRIES

(percentage)

		IMPORTS			EXPORTS		
		1938	1951	First half 1952	1938	1951	First half 1952
I.	Increased Turnover						
	Finland	7·7	15·1	15·8	1·7	11·3	18·0
	Iceland	1·8	7·1	5·6	1·2	8·1	8·5
	Portugal	—	—	—	2·0	1·8	2·9
	Sweden	—	—	—	6·3	6·4	6·6
	Denmark	—	—	—	2·4	2·8	2·8
II.	Reduced Turnover						
	Austria	30·8	9·8	9·9	25·8	12·3	11·9
	Sweden	7·6	6·2	5·2	—	—	—
	Italy	10·1	3·4	3·4	6·0	3·9	3·7
	Turkey	11·8	5·0	2·9	12·2	7·8	6·0
	Switzerland	11·0	2·8	2·8	9·3	5·1	3·5
	U.K.	5·8	2·4	2·7	4·5	0·6	0·6
	Denmark	4·5	4·8	2·4	—	—	—
	Norway	5·8	2·3	2·1	3·1	3·5	2·6
	The Netherlands	7·0	1·5	1·3	5·8	1·4	1·3
	Western Germany	12·9	1·5	1·3	13·1	1·8	1·2
	France	4·0	1·1	1·2	4·9	0·9	0·9
	Belgium-Luxembourg	7·1	1·4	1·0	5·5	1·9	2·3
	Eire	2·2	1·1	0·5	—	—	—
	Greece	17·6	0·1	0·1	8·9	0·4	0·2
	Portugal	2·0	0·5	0·1	—	—	—
	Spain	4·5*	0·1	—	1·1*	—	—

* 1953.

13

The importance of trade between East and West has frequently been stressed in the Federal Parliament and the Federal Cabinet. It has been pointed out that Eastern trade is important and requires fostering within the general framework of international obligations. The licences required for export to the countries of the Eastern bloc are granted only after examination by the Central Export Control. To coordinate the different tasks related to Eastern trade a West-East Division has been formed in the Federal Ministry of Economics with Dr. Kroll at its head. Today part of the work of this Division is handled by the Trade Policy Department of the Foreign Office.

The Federal Republic's trade with the East has been severely hampered by the Embargo Lists which in many instances affect it more adversely than many other European countries. By virtue of long-term contracts concluded before the Embargo Lists were drawn up, certain countries, e.g. Great Britain, even now possess a greater freedom of action. In many instances Great Britain can appeal to over-riding contracts, many of them with a five-year currency, e.g. with Poland and Russia. Moreover, our negotiations with the countries of the Eastern bloc suffer from the difficulties encountered in determining the volume of trade which can eventually be realised without merely remaining on paper. Among our difficulties is the effect of the Embargo Lists on exports of machinery, instruments, etc.; on the other hand our own importers are sometimes unable or unwilling to buy, the result partly of our heavy imports from the dollar area and partly of the obstacles caused by our agricultural policy.

GERMAN TRADE WITH COUNTRIES OF THE EASTERN BLOC

(in thousands of dollars)

	1936	1948	1949	1950	1951	1952
POLAND						
Imports	23,339	11,873*	33,416	16,139	13,639	13,879
Exports	21,355	136	8,240	15,954	19,938	15,430
CZECHOSLOVAKIA						
Imports	45,115	27,796*	24,833	25,041	17,006	18,175
Exports	56,049	5,422	13,633	18,228	20,882	8,064

* Reichsmarks or Deutsche Marks.

	1936	1948	1949	1950	1951	1952
ROUMANIA						
Imports	37,228	322*	1,099	2,263	363	3,040
Exports	41,758	15	910	5,258	4,799	9,757
BULGARIA						
Imports	23,211	365*	2,875	1,323	2,405	3,406
Exports	19,205	114	734	3,933	696	1,478
RUSSIA						
Imports	60,162	4,169*	799	178	441	3,957
Exports	73,495	—	—	1	28	151

* Reichsmarks or Deutsche Marks.

Meanwhile the economic structure of the East is relaxing its contacts with the West. Hence a smaller export surplus of agricultural products, coupled with a certain reduction in the Eastern bloc's requirements of industrial finished goods. The economic policy hitherto pursued by the East has in any case made it unlikely that trade will be restored to the pre-war volume, and some of the hopes cherished about Eastern openings may turn out to be illusory. The Economic Commission for Europe, for its part, is not looking forward to any extensive imports of grain, timber or coal from Eastern Europe, though it does regard an annual saving of $300 millions as possible. Recently the Eastern bloc has been offering wheat, maize, cattle, etc.; we for our part have not shown ourselves anxious to buy; moreover, our freedom of action is restricted by the International Wheat Agreement.

Despite these and other obstacles it should be possible to expand trade with the East. It is an instrument for saving dollars, and should not be neglected despite the risks inherent in long-term contracts. Although the existing embargoes impose certain limitations, competition is keen, particularly from France and Great Britain. So far as the long-term prospects of Eastern trade are concerned, the West is far from holding all the trumps.

The autarkic tendencies of the East will grow stronger with the lapse of time. Protectionist tendencies are already discernible in glass, ceramics and textiles. The authorities in Bonn are well aware that everything must be done to stimulate trade with the East, and to create the organisations necessary if East-West trade is to be built up as efficiently as possible. In this sense we must welcome the foundation of the Eastern Committee of German Industrialists, at the head of which are a number of leading representatives of trade and industry under the chairmanship of Dr. Hans Reuter. Private initiative is a useful complement to State action, particularly in dealing with countries like Russia, Roumania, Albania, etc., with which no trade agreements are in existence. In these cases private discussions with Eastern delegates, e.g., from Roumania, are important. Under this head also fall contacts established at Geneva through the United Nations, particularly through the East-West discussions of the Economic Commission for Europe, e.g. in the spring of 1953, and on earlier occasions.

In mid-1953 our Eastern problem was marked by export surpluses which in some instances were large. This is one more instance of the surplus tendency in our trade which is ultimately the result of our low imports and of our agricultural protectionism. Yet it should certainly be possible to increase our trade by shifting purchases from the dollar area to the East, and by intensifying our transit trade, particularly from overseas clearing countries.

Eastern Europe is one of those regions whose virtual elimination from our trade has helped to distort the structure of our foreign trade. Yet despite the tendencies towards autarky existing in the East, those regions provide a reserve which could be used to stimulate business and which, properly exploited, could do much to stabilise our balance of payments and the volume of our exports.

CHAPTER XIII

RETURN TO A LIBERAL TARIFF
POLICY

DURING the first post-war years tariff policy in general moved into the background. Foreign exchange control and import quotas were regarded in this period of economic nationalism and of autonomous monetary policy as the proper instruments of economic policy in the foreign sphere. Powerful as are the vested interests which can benefit it, a tariff has no such disruptive effect on world trade as have foreign exchange control and import quotas. To be effective a tariff presupposes the existence of some sort of nexus between the different market economies in the different States—economies based upon a common currency system. And a tariff is proved inadequate only when a country adopts the monetary autonomy which goes with economic nationalism. Admittedly tariff policy was used after the First World War to provide a protection for unrealistic price levels: this was the comprehensive tariff system (Heinrich Rittershausen). Such a function—that of protecting the price level as a whole—was undoubtedly that of the American tariff legislation of 1922 and 1930; the object was to raise rates all round and thus to weaken the internal symptoms of deflation. And even the super-protectionist American tariff did not destroy the economic unity of the world and permitted the existence of a large volume of trade; the foreign suppliers could after all make an allowance for even the highest tariff walls and, if necessary, leap over them. Import quotas and foreign exchange control, on the other hand, create more or less insuperable barriers and destroy world trade. The fact that many countries attached no particular importance to tariffs after the war provided they could use the other two instruments shows how great has been the change since the period after the First World War.

We are gradually returning to more normal conditions; liberalisation is extending and for their payments in Europe many countries are returning to multilateralism. Accordingly tariffs are regaining some of their importance as an instrument of trade policy, and as early as 1949 signs were not wanting that the world was tending to return to tariff and trade treaties of the classical type. The Federal Republic therefore found itself obliged to prepare a fiscal apparatus enabling it to negotiate effectively. The first necessity therefore was to enact the new tariff legislation.

The Federal Republic's New Tariff

Shortly after its formation the Federal Republic began to work out a tariff of this nature. In view of the prospect that the Federal Republic would take part on equal terms in the third round of the Torquay tariff negotiations (autumn of 1950) the work was specially accelerated. After the collapse of 1945 the Allies had claimed the right to legislate in matters of tariffs. The military Governments of the British and the French Zones in the first instance suspended tariffs. It was only in the American Zone that tariffs were imposed, though at different rates in the different Länder. At this early stage therefore chaos prevailed which was eventually cleared up in 1947 for the Bizone and later for the French Zone by the restoration of the tariffs provided by the treaties in existence before the war. This measure was applied to all countries irrespective of whether they had most-favoured-nation agreements or not. At the Tariff Conference at Annecy in 1949 the Occupying Powers made these measures binding *vis-à-vis* the other adhering States by the so-called Statement of Annecy; in other words, a one-sided servitude was imposed on Germany. It was not until some time later that autonomous tariff alleviations (e.g. in the French Zone) recalling the 'hole in the West' existing after the First World War were eliminated.

Certain similarities with the Treaty of Versailles are obvious. But there is a difference from the most-favoured-nation treatment in force at that time; then the German market really was largely open to other countries, whereas the servitude of unconditional most-favoured-nation treatment, as introduced in 1949, largely remained on paper because imports were in any case regulated by the supreme control exercised over them by the Allies. Moreover, before the currency reform tariffs had ceased effectively to regulate imports. As imports were gradually freed the significance of tariffs as instruments of trade policy began to grow.

It now became apparent that the Bülow tariff of 1902, which was still in force, had become out of date in its vocabulary, its rates, and its entire structure. In the chemical sector alone, technical progress demanded new rates; moreover the specific duties laid down in the Bülow tariff had lost most of their protective effect by reason of the all-round increase in the price of imports. As an instrument of trade policy the tariff had lost its usefulness since the fall in its protective effect caused by the rise in prices had deprived the German negotiators of any adequate margin for concessions. Accordingly, on October 10, 1949, i.e. only a few weeks after its constitution, the Federal Government resolved to form a mixed Tariff Reform Committee to be composed of representatives of the appropriate Departments of the Länder, of business organisations and of Trade Unions. This body was asked to prepare without delay the outlines for a draft of a new German tariff. It was decided to use as a basis for this tariff the revised European tariff outline of 1949, which is based on *ad valorem* duties. (This outline had been previously adopted by the study group for the European Customs Union sitting in Brussels.) Our anxiety to effect a rapid tariff reform was increased by the fact that by it the one-sided servitude imposed in the Annecy Statement found its natural end. The Bülow tariff, which was designed to replace the free trade tariff in force under Caprivi, took nearly ten years to be worked out; the new tariff reform was completed in barely two years. The Tariff Reform Committee was virtually in permanent session and succeeded in completing its labours in the remarkably brief period from the end of October, 1949 to the beginning of April, 1950.*

* Dr. von Maltzan, 'The New Tariff in the Light of Trade Policy', in the *Handelsblatt*, No. 115 of October 3, 1951. See also the Federal Government's memorandum, 'Considerations relevant to the Draft of Tariff Legislation'.

The Committee was compelled to work fast since it had been arranged that a draft tariff accepted by the Allied High Commission and adopted by the Federal Government as the basis for negotiations had to be submitted to the countries taking part in the Torquay Conference not later than May, 1950. No later date was possible since the countries taking part had to be informed of the new tariff rates in order to communicate their own wishes on this subject to the Federal Government before the Conference began. The Allied High Commission differed from the proposals at certain points because the rates were regarded as too high. On this point the Federal Government's Memorandum observed: 'The Allied High Commission's wishes must be met at a later time as far as necessary.'

The European Draft Tariff worked out by the study group for the European Customs Union, which is the basis of the tariff, had originally been intended to provide the foundation for a common tariff to be adopted by a future European Customs Union. The States represented at Brussels had expressed the wish that this European Draft Tariff should be used by the different countries in framing their own new tariffs. In setting up its new tariff the Federal Government took care to comply with this wish. The tariff is based on the so-called production principle, i.e. each of the different sections embraces as far as possible the entire range of raw materials, semi-finished products and finished products needed for the different branches of the economy. The classification adopted in the European scheme was retained with an eye to the possibility of a general European collaboration.

The new tariff is an *ad valorem* tariff; indeed a general tendency towards *ad valorem* tariffs is in existence in Western Europe. In the new German tariff, rates are fixed by weight only for fiscal duties and for raw sugar, wine and must. For cinema films the duty is calculated by the yard. The essential aspect of *ad valorem* duties is that their protective effect varies automatically with variations in price; they fall when prices fall, which of course is not the case where duties go by weight. The latter type loses its protective effect in times of general boom and thus favours the expanding phase in the world trade cycle. It is one of the advantages of *ad valorem* duties that they constitute a lower burden on cheaper goods and thus enable buyers with low purchasing power to maintain a cheaper standard of living. The question which of the two types of duty is ultimately superior has still to be settled.

The foreign trade interests of the German economy made it natural for the Federal Republic to aim at a tariff with low rates of duty, though admittedly it did not prove possible fully to realise this ambition. In the spirit of the liberalising measures of O.E.E.C. and of the free trade ambitions of the G.A.T.T. system, the new tariff was used not so much as an occasion for creating a system giving our negotiators a strong fighting position, as in order to provide our negotiators with a favourable position within the framework of the Torquay Conference. We can thus claim that the spirit of the Havana Charter and of G.A.T.T., in which the principles of the Charter had found their realisation, have exercised a far-reaching influence on the Tariff Committee's labours. The latter body was able to benefit by the experience of other European countries where *ad valorem* duties had been in force for some time. In the event an average rate of duty was reached which is lower than that applying in France, Italy and Great Britain, though it is generally above the more liberal level of the Benelux countries and of the Scandinavian States.

Each rate of duty was discussed in detail with representatives of the sectors concerned. The principle employed was that the German economy should be given approximately the same competitive position at home and abroad as that existing for the corresponding foreign sectors. Excessive rates were avoided since these would have unduly raised prices at home and would thus have proved an obstacle to our exports. Moreover it was intended deliberately to increase foreign competition in the domestic market in order to compel the German economy to work more efficiently. (The same principle underlies the idea of liberalisation.) The view that a certain amount of foreign competition should be used as an instrument for enforcing rationalisation in German industry and to stimulate efficiency after more than ten years of insulation, was implied in Professor Erhard's original indifference, immediately after the currency reform to the convertion rate of 30 cents. A number of industrialists maintained that they required an initial period of protection to enable them to make good the technical and managerial advantage gained by foreign countries since 1934, and justice was done to this view in a number of individual tariffs, e.g. in those applying to the electrical and chemical industries. In principle raw materials, semi-finished goods and goods manufactured in insufficient quantities inside the country, are admitted free or at moderate rates. With other raw materials and semi-finished goods which are manufactured on a substantial scale at home, the duties were adjusted so as to provide some degree of compensation for inevitable differences in the conditions of manufacture. With few exceptions the suggested maximum rate of duty was 35%, even in those cases where the rate hitherto in force happened to have exceeded this figure. In certain special cases it was suggested that the Federal Government should raise or lower the duties if this was necessitated by special economic considerations. Later the Bundestag extended this principle to all duties, though in each case the Bundestag had to give its specific sanction, and the Bundesrat (the Upper Chamber) had first to be heard.

The Government's readiness to play its part in a worldwide division of labour becomes clear in the above-mentioned Memorandum, where the objects of our foreign trade policy are defined. These are: 'To restore normal structural conditions for groups of goods, both imports and exports, as far as possible, while substantially raising exports above the present level.' The Memorandum continues: 'It is an essential part of our foreign trade policy to effect liberalisation of foreign trade relations within a system of European co-operation, a system which has made substantial progress by the Government's own measures and which favours the objectives of unifying the different national economies in

Europe into a single system.' The authors of the Memorandum do not take the view that Germany's economic weakening since the war should be made an excuse for perpetuating this state of affairs through protectionism and other State-imposed measures; it should be made the starting point for a planned increase of exports since such an increase would be the only way to overcome this weakness. This in turn implied moderate tariffs, since exports, even when based on efficient production, presupposed a readiness and ability for large-scale imports. Hence a rejection of protectionism and the recognition of the principle that 'in the long run Western Germany can become viable only within an economically unified Europe and through the working of an essentially free-trade system'.

It might be suggested that these principles implied the complete renunciation of protective tariffs and justified a thoroughgoing free-trade tariff. The truth is that the one-sided adoption of free trade would paralyse our trade policy and might deprive us of an important instrument to promote free-trade measures among the countries with which we deal. It follows that we must maintain a complex tariff, admittedly placing a minimum burden on our costs of production but still allowing a margin for reductions which could be offered in the course of tariff negotiations.

Our Part in Brussels

At an early stage we began to play our part in the work done by the Study Group for a European Customs Union, which was formed in Brussels in September, 1947, under the Marshall Plan. From March, 1948 onwards the Western Zones were represented in the study group by observers; German exporters assisted the Allied representatives in an advisory capacity. Since the end of 1949 the Federal Republic has worked in the Study Group as a full member. The Federal Republic was the first country to adopt in practice the model tariff worked out at Brussels, though it was found in the course of these studies that, owing to the retarding action taken by Great Britain and certain other countries, much time would have to pass before a European

Customs Union was formed. The Study Group's preparatory work for the customs union was suspended in autumn of 1948; labours in this field have since passed into the hands of the O.E.E.C., the Council of Europe in Strasbourg and G.A.T.T. At present the Conseil de Coopération Douanière, an offshoot of the study group, is doing the main work, concentrating chiefly on the legal and technical aspects of customs procedure. Three leading agreements have been worked out by the Study Group:

(1) The agreement on standard tariffs. It is worth noting that the idea of a uniform international tariff goes back ultimately to German initiative. As early as 1927 Dr. Trendelenburg, the German delegate at the Geneva World Economic Conference, made a proposal in this sense, which led to the Geneva international standard tariff of 1937. The Brussels Study Group based its work on this proposal.

(2) An agreement on values for customs purposes. This agreement contains a uniform definition of value for these purposes. It therefore facilitates comparisons between the actual burden implied by a given rate of duties in different countries; accordingly it favours the formation of customs unions and economic unions.

(3) The agreement on the formation of a council for collaboration in customs questions, the main object being to study the technical aspects of the different customs systems.

Entrance into G.A.T.T.

The new tariff came into force on October 1, 1951, simultaneously with the concessions granted by the Federal Republic at Torquay. At that Conference the German negotiators were somewhat hampered by the fact that the German tariff legislation had at that time not been enacted. They were able, nevertheless, to negotiate a number of substantial reductions, while other duties were fixed for the time being. Moreover, by joining G.A.T.T. the Federal

Republic obtained unrestricted most-favoured-nation treatment, which meant that it benefited by some 50,000 concessions made by the other G.A.T.T. countries. These
concessions had been negotiated in the three successive
conferences at Geneva, Annecy and Torquay.

The General Agreement on Tariffs and Trade, concluded
on October 30, 1947, at present embraces thirty-three States
which, by virtue of this agreement, declare their approval of
certain rules governing trade policy. They also bind themselves to observe certain rules of the game which are under
permanent supervision at the G.A.T.T. conferences at
Geneva with the help of the local Secretariat of the Interim
Commission for the International Trade Organisation.
G.A.T.T. itself is a distillate of the principles of trade policy
laid down in the Havana Charter which was signed in 1948
after a number of preparatory conferences, though later it
failed to be ratified by the American Congress. Formally the
Charter is dead, but its spirit is alive.*

The significance of G.A.T.T. is contained in the openings
it provides for multilateral negotiations among all the
member States leading to an all-round reduction of tariffs
by which all the countries concerned would benefit as of
right. These concessions could not be annulled unilaterally,
i.e. without the possibility that countervailing measures
might be taken. Besides reducing tariffs G.A.T.T. deals with
various other trade barriers, e.g. questions of transit, of
taxation, of the designation of countries of origin, etc., the
uniform object being to settle world trade on an equal and
multilateral basis. Moreover any country can take the initiative at any time and can suggest fresh tariff negotiations
which the countries to which the proposal is addressed cannot
decline. G.A.T.T. is not an international organisation with
deliberative and executive bodies; it is a conference at which
the member States adopt resolutions in accordance with the
customary forms of international law, employing the
majority rule in principle. It is a dynamic institution, aiming
at the reduction of tariffs and providing a relatively lasting

* Cf. Ludwig Imhoff, 'G.A.T.T.' 1952. Cf. also Herbert Gross, 'World Trade
Tomorrow', Studies on the World Trade Charter, 1950.

basis for the concessions reached. At the conferences at
Geneva, Annecy and Torquay hundreds of negotiations were
carried through, culminating in treaties each running for
three years, after which they can be denounced at six months'
intervals. G.A.T.T. also exercises pressure for the reduction
of import quotas which, according to its principles, can be
retained or reintroduced only to safeguard the balance of
payments and even then only exceptionally and after
sanction by G.A.T.T. in consultation with the International
Monetary Fund. A close connection exists between G.A.T.T.
and the Fund since virtually all the members of G.A.T.T.
are also members of the Fund.

Our entry into G.A.T.T. marks another significant step
towards the restoration of world markets and towards international co-operation in the West. It completes the work
done by other steps we have taken in the same direction,
e.g. by joining the O.E.E.C., and E.P.U., the Brussels
Study Group, etc. It was taken after the signature of the
Torquay protocol and, so far as the Federal Republic was
concerned, entered into effect by the enactment of the
new tariff together with the German concessions made at
Torquay.

The significance of our adherence to G.A.T.T. is not
confined to the immediate tariff reductions and to the fact
that we benefit by the agreements previously reached between
the earlier members of G.A.T.T., although these concessions
are by no means negligible. The figures are these. The
German tariff contains 3,664 items; within this tariff 587
items were reduced, and 592 were fixed. The Federal
Republic, on the other hand, benefited by 1,533 reductions
and 1,037 fixings conceded by the other twenty-one countries.
Moreover, the Federal Republic benefited by other reductions and fixings exceeding 7,000 in number. We were unable
to get all our requirements met; this was partly due to the
fact that the Federal Republic joined G.A.T.T. relatively
late after a number of countries with low tariffs, e.g. the
Benelux States and Scandinavia, had made all the concessions they were prepared to make. They could or would not
make further concessions to the Federal Republic without

endangering their own protective industries. The events in Korea also exerted a certain retarding influence.

After the Torquay Conference our treaty with Switzerland enabled us to reduce a large number of items which had not been dealt with at Torquay. In some respects the tariff submitted at Torquay did after all leave a margin for negotiation, though some of the countries represented there were unwilling to make any further concessions. Switzerland on the other hand is not a member of G.A.T.T.; but its tariff is noted for its low level and the Swiss were able in a sense to continue the negotiations by offering the attraction of a strong and relatively unprotected market. To ensure participation in this market against the possibility of a future tariff increase, the Federal Republic reduced its own rates substantially and thus caused its tariff to approximate to some of the lower G.A.T.T. levels. The reductions conceded to Switzerland were extended to the other G.A.T.T. countries by virtue of the unconditional most-favoured-nation treatment enjoyed by these countries.

The Search for Further Tariff Reductions

The Torquay Conference ended with the impression that most of the countries had shot their bolt and that new ways would have to be found to develop the impulse given at Torquay. Since 1952 four main plans for a general reduction of tariffs in Europe have been under discussion.

The Benelux Plan at Torquay

At the fourth G.A.T.T. meeting, in Geneva, the low-tariff countries complained that the method of negotiation provided under G.A.T.T. gave them no opportunity for obtaining adequate or equal concessions from the high-tariff countries. The contrast between the high- and the low-tariff countries thus became accentuated; and the differences extended to the Torquay Conference. The Benelux delegates accordingly submitted a memorandum suggesting multilateral negotiations among the O.E.E.C. States represented at Torquay. It was suggested that Canada and the United States should join with the object of levelling down

as far as possible the customs rates of the countries in question
to the level of the lowest rate in force among them. The first
proposal led to the formation of a working committee. This
body was asked to study the differences among the European
tariffs, and to consider the question of levelling down European tariffs and of the compensation to be granted by non-
European States. At the sixth meeting in Geneva in the
autumn of 1951 the Benelux States submitted a fresh memorandum proposing that a basic rate, which was to serve as
general guide, was to be determined for each item in the
Brussels vocabulary. Within a certain time limit the countries
concerned were asked to reduce their rates to this basic rate,
or else to reduce the difference between the basic rate and
their own rate by a percentage to be determined at a later
time. The plan was not further discussed at the sixth meeting.
The Benelux States agreed that their own plan, which was
designed to cover Europe, should be set aside in favour of the
following plan, which was intended to have a world-wide
application.

The Pflimlin Plan

The Pflimlin Plan was conceived by M. Pflimlin, the
French Minister of Commerce, and bears the date of
September 19, 1951. The Plan was submitted to the seventh
meeting (autumn of 1952) in a new and revised form; it was
passed on to the working party dealing with the general
reduction of tariffs, for further consideration. At present the
Plan holds the centre of the G.A.T.T. negotiations. It provides for the reduction of tariffs in the member countries by
10% a year to a total of 30% in three calendar years. In
calculating the reductions the weighted average tariff burden
applying to selected groups within the overall tariff is to be
employed. Tariffs are sub-divided into ten groups within
which the successive stages by which the reduction is to
proceed will be uniformly applied. The basic tariff level is
defined as the weighted average of the tariff burden; this in
turn is represented by a fraction, the numerator of which is
represented by the total customs yield while the denominator
comprises the value of all goods, whether falling within the

tariff or not. Most of the G.A.T.T. countries hold the view that so-called classical fiscal tariffs should not be reduced under the Pflimlin Plan. Other duties, also of a fiscal nature, are to be dealt with by special regulations. Specially high duties, exceeding a certain maximum limit, are to be reduced to this maximum.

The Pflimlin Plan naturally raises a number of questions, e.g. whether the reduction in duties is to apply to duties lowered by negotiations with the non-G.A.T.T. countries. The method of calculating the level of duties as a fraction between customs yield and import value for the different groups is not likely to do full justice to really prohibitive rates of duty. In fact, the moderate rates which bring in the biggest yield play a particularly important part in establishing a customs level; the terms by which it is calculated are thus likely to provide a lower protection than that corresponding to the actual protection brought about by the tariffs as a whole. On the other hand, it it entirely reasonable to expect that the Pflimlin Plan will touch off a series of tariff reductions with the probability that many of them will be reciprocal. Though the different States enjoyed full freedom in making their decisions, a compulsion would nevertheless be at work in them to concentrate on the reduction of those particular duties which permitted a fairly substantial volume of imports and which therefore evidently did not have a strong protective effect. On the other hand, the reduction of the really high rates which seriously restricted imports would not bring much nearer the object of the Pflimlin Plan, viz. a 30% reduction of the total tariff burden. It is true that this drawback is compensated in a measure by the rule that the highest duties must be reduced to the maximum level. On the whole the effect the Pflimlin Plan can have will depend on the number of countries, particularly outside Europe, which adhere to it. By making it a part of G.A.T.T. the tariff reductions will be extended beyond Europe; it aims at an all-round lowering in every continent. Such a lowering entirely agrees with the world-wide trading interests of the Federal Republic.

14

The Plan illustrates the principle that politics is the art of the possible. This is expressed in the idea of a maximum tariff as well as in the proposal that a free limit—i.e. a limit so low that no further downward adjustment is required—shall be negotiated in favour of countries having a particularly low average tariff. All these questions, however, will have to be further discussed by the appropriate G.A.T.T. committee. The representatives of the Federal Government have given their backing to the Plan in principle and have taken a part in working out its further details.

Work on the Pflimlin Plan is being pushed ahead by G.A.T.T. with a fair degree of energy. It has the approval of the Benelux States, of France, Denmark, the Federal Republic, and evidently also of the United States, although it is obviously not yet certain to what extent the United States may ultimately be willing to adhere to the Plan. Certain adjustments will probably have to be made; the low-tariff countries in particular will probably be relieved of part of their obligation further to reduce their tariffs. Tariffs applied to groups of imports where the average duty is below a limit by a certain percentage—at one time 50% was suggested—are in appropriate cases to remain untouched. In all instances where a duty is lowered the reduction is to apply for five years. Many technical questions are still open and much preliminary statistical work will have to be done. It is therefore unlikely that the Plan will be adopted before 1955.

The Ohlin Plan

At the suggestion of the Swedish economist Ohlin, a plan was developed before the Consultative Assembly of the Council of Europe to form a so-called low-tariff club which was designed ultimately to bring about a European Customs Union or, alternatively, a free-trade zone. The Plan was adopted by an overwhelming majority in December, 1951 at a time when the efforts being made by O.E.E.C. and G.A.T.T. to liberate world trade were being pushed ahead with particular vigour. The Ohlin Plan would bind countries adhering to it to adopt a maximum duty of 35% and, over and above this, to adopt a maximum of 5% for raw materials, of 15% for semi-finished goods and of 25% for finished goods and foodstuffs. During the first year these reductions would be restricted to 70% of a country's total imports, the reductions being applied equally to each of the three classes of goods. In the second year this percentage would be raised to 80, and in the third to 90. After the third year the maximum duty of 35% would therefore apply merely to a residual 10% of all imports. The Council of Europe recommended that the convention should contain a clause providing that, within a reasonable time, a conference should be called among the member States providing for the complete abolition of tariffs as between these countries. The low-tariff club would thus be transformed into a genuine customs union. A second clause would prohibit the use of quotas.

Difficulties standing in the way of the Plan arise out of the most-favoured-nation clause and out of the British Commonwealth's preferential system. The members of the Council of Europe, who would presumably be the first members of the club, are bound, those of them who are also members of G.A.T.T., to grant unconditional most-favoured-nation treatment. Accordingly the advantages of club membership would also accrue to G.A.T.T. members who were not members of the club. Moreover, difficulties arise out of unconditional most-favoured-nation treatment when trade treaties are concluded with States which, like Switzerland, are not members of G.A.T.T. If the plan is to be a success unconditional most-favoured-nation treatment would therefore have to be restricted, or else appropriate advantages would have to be agreed upon to compensate for the wider extension of the club privileges. Questions like these wrecked the endeavours made at Ouchy and Oslo twenty-five years ago to form a customs union. In itself G.A.T.T. contains provisions for such exceptions to the extent that the club can be regarded as the precursor of a genuine customs union. A second obstacle might arise out of the British preferential system. Lord Layton, however, declared, at the Strasbourg Conference, that a compromise might well be reached on this question.

This plan too is being supported by the Federal Government, as has been made clear by the active part it has played in the discussions. Meanwhile the Pflimlin Plan has taken a more concrete shape, and it might be objected to the plan put forward by the Council of Europe that the proposal for the residual 10% of total imports would still leave considerable scope for prohibitive duties, since the duties on the remaining 10% of goods need not be reduced below a level of 35%. These aspects of the plan which aim at free trade are being vigorously supported by the Federal Government.

Finally, the recommendations made by the Council of Europe contained a proposal for the creation of a sort of second preference system. This idea was put forward jointly by the members of the Council of Europe and by representatives of the British Commonwealth. The proposals are contained in a report made by Dr. Semler, a member of the Bundestag, in the name of the Council's Economic Commission. According to this plan a preferential system is to be erected between the European members and the Commonwealth on a basis of reciprocity. The Plan aims at combining the idea of the low-tariff club and that of a preferential system by devising a sort of second preference which would naturally leave the countries of the Commonwealth a special margin derived from the Treaty of Ottawa. The chief objections were raised by Hr. Ohlin, the Swedish delegate, who feared that countries with pronouncedly low tariffs might be tempted to begin by raising their duties in order to obtain a point of vantage for granting preferences. A sort of high-tariff club might be the ultimate result.

These considerations led to the idea of a European preferential system, which would admittedly have to be recognised by G.A.T.T. in the same way in which G.A.T.T. recognised the Commonwealth, the French Union, etc. The point is that nobody is prepared to waive the principle that such a system would have to form an essential part of G.A.T.T., the main reason for this being that all are resolved that the United States shall continue to play its part in matters of tariff policy. Accordingly the report of the Secretary General of the Council of Europe aims at retaining the rules of G.A.T.T. in principle, provided it proves possible to arrange for certain modifications in unconditional most-favoured-nation treatment. A European solution could then be found in the creation of a multilateral preferential system which any country could join provided it was prepared to make the concessions arranged for in the low-tariff club project. Under President Roosevelt and President Truman the American Administration would certainly have resisted strongly proposals of this sort which (under the European version) aim at a far-reaching tariff merger between Europe and the British Commonwealth. The present growth of protectionist interests in the United States and the general state of doubt about future trade policy in the United States provide, however, a new environment for the ideas developed in the Council of Europe. To what extent the plan had previously been agreed with London is not entirely clear. To a certain extent it seems to hang in the air.

At present the plans worked out by G.A.T.T. and by the Council of Europe for tariff reductions are running parallel with one another; between them they are calculated to effect manifold breaches in the customs barriers. The G.A.T.T. Plan contains potentialities for extending it to embrace world trade.

The above-mentioned plans do not exhaust the list of tariff reduction proposals. Early in 1953 the Netherlands Government put forward a plan for the formation of a customs community and for the gradual reduction of tariffs within the framework of the Coal and Steel Community. This was the so-called Beyen Plan. The special interest which the Federal Government has shown in the Pflimlin Plan serves to stress the Government's desire that any tariff reduction achieved shall be as comprehensive as possible and shall in any case apply to the leading industrial countries, including the United States and Canada. The wider and more general the basis for such plans, the more will they coincide with our own ultimate interests, since our exports require openings in all the markets of the world. This comprehensive aspect, which is particularly strong in the Pflimlin Plan, might also become popular with the Council of Europe to the extent to which this body too is interested in ideas of world integration.

CHAPTER XIV

CHANGES IN IMPORT AND EXPORT PROCEDURE

Removal of Import Supervision—Promotion of Exports

DURING the early stages imports were reserved to the Allies. It was they who financed imports, particularly those of Category A, which were meant to prevent famine, a general break-down, epidemics, etc. Apart from these imports, which were tied to the provision of a minimum of calories, there were those of Category B, which comprised raw materials for processing into finished goods for export; any surpluses arising were used to help in financing imports of foodstuffs under Category A. During the early post-war years the dollar clause was applied to German foreign trade and consequently the only goods entering into our foreign trade had a dollar value. Accordingly Germany—a paradox in view of its poverty—was a hard-currency country *par excellence*.

J.E.I.A. No. 4 and No. 10

The first attempts to apply rational principles to our imports were made in 1947, when J.E.I.A. was founded. In the first instance imports were centralised. J.E.I.A. Directive No. 4 of August 18, 1947 was the first measure to facilitate the import of goods needed in the production of goods for export. These imports comprised goods of Category B, i.e. raw materials and semi-finished goods actually used in the manufacture of a detailed list of goods destined for export, as well as items used for maintenance and repairs under the same heading. In these cases sanctions were given by the J.E.I.A. branches. All other imports under Category B continued to be centralised, sanction being given either direct by J.E.I.A. or by German firms who had received sanction direct from J.E.I.A. headquarters.

Imports of raw materials to be processed for exports involved (under Directive No. 4) somewhat clumsy bureaucratic supervision. The Land Ministries of Economics had to satisfy themselves for each application that the raw materials could not be procured inside the country and that the conditions for processing them in the form of labour, coal, electric power, etc., were available in sufficient quantities. Moreover the proceeds in foreign exchange had to bear a certain relation to the original foreign exchange expenditure; the rule was that sanction would be refused where the ratio was less than three to one. But this scrutiny was only the beginning. When the Länder had done their work the J.E.I.A. branches satisfied themselves regarding the price in foreign currency of the imports applied for and of the physical practicability of importing the goods. Applicants were asked to submit letters and other relevant documents. A similar procedure was in force for prospective exports. Payment, which was effected by means of credits, were also subject to complicated rules. Annex G. to Directive No. 4 reserved a wide range of raw material imports to J.E.I.A. head office; the branches had nothing to say in the matter. These raw materials comprised cellulose, foodstuffs, artificial fertilisers, mineral oil, jute, rubber, copper, aluminium, tin, etc. The following raw materials were deemed to be available inside Germany in adequate quantities, and therefore did not rank for import licences: iron, steel, zinc, lead, sand, salt, gypsum, etc.

Nevertheless the whole procedure under Directive No. 4 was an improvement on previous conditions. This is also true of Directive No. 10 (November, 1947), a decentralising measure which put the J.E.I.A. branches in charge of Category B imports. The express purpose of Directive No. 10 was to restore German imports to normal conditions. A distinction was made between imports not allotted to any definite programme and those for internal requirements, i.e. those not wanted for processing and eventual export. J.E.I.A. currently kept the Minden Economic Administration informed of goods which could be imported under the new system. In dealings with foreign countries J.E.I.A.

continued to act as contracting party. In practice these measures had little meaning, since a working economy was wanting in any case.

J.E.I.A. No. 29

A rational import policy came into being only with J.E.I.A. Directive No. 29 of February 28, 1949. This Directive created an improved decentralised system for import licensing with the object of facilitating and accelerating the import of goods needed for export production and for important internal requirements. Directives No. 4 and No. 10 were cancelled. Importing Länder, manufacturers, etc., were now enabled to import direct. An Import Advisory Committee was formed to supervise imports, consisting of the director of the Allied Foreign Trade Department as Chairman and of representatives of J.E.I.A., of the Bipartite Control Office, of the Administration for Economics, of the Administration for Food, Agriculture and Forests and of the Bank deutscher Länder. The Import Advisory Committee was empowered to restrict imports of any type of goods and to issue any regulations deemed necessary. In considering the new regulations it is not their restrictive effect but the relaxation they foreshadow that deserves attention. The general trend, even while J.E.I.A. was in charge, was directed towards a growing decentralisation and to the restoration of business initiative, particularly after the currency reform when a growing freedom was being restored to the economy. Thus Section 8 of Directive No. 29 provides that an importer desirous of importing goods listed in the import plan could deal direct with the foreign supplier in conformity with the normal practice of importing merchants. He was, however, required to apply in quintuplicate for an import licence, acting through a bank undertaking foreign transactions. These banks dealt with the allocations of foreign currency and notified the importer whether his application had been sanctioned or rejected. The Import Advisory Committee determined the permissible total of imports and of available foreign exchange. Imports themselves had not yet been liberalised, but the procedure was on businesslike, decentralised lines and the Allies merely confined themselves to control at the top.

Directive No. 29 remained in force after the self-dissolution of J.E.I.A. in 1949. From September, 1949 only three German representatives remained as permanent members of the Advisory Committee; the Allies remained merely as observers and withdrew altogether in the autumn of 1950. From this point the Committee was thus a purely German body, the members being representatives of the Federal Ministry of Economics, which supplies the Chairman, the Federal Ministry of Agriculture, and the Bank deutscher Länder. At a later point representatives of the Marshall Plan Ministry, the Federal Finance Ministry and the Foreign Office were added. J.E.I.A. No. 29 had been initiated in a time of restrictions and world-wide scarcities. It was a piece of decentralising machinery designed to deal with carefully planned imports. Meanwhile the German economy began its rapid course of development, fostered by a deliberate policy of liberalisation, and it suddenly appeared that the J.E.I.A. system could no longer meet the new conditions. Nobody could obtain a clear view of the foreign exchange obligations which had suddenly proliferated through the post-Korean import boom. Many import applications were speculative and the entire foreign exchange position became thoroughly obscure. This ignorance of the true position led to a general nervousness, particularly during the import boom of 1950–1. Emergency measures were hastily taken: after discussions with O.E.E.C. imports were restricted, liberalisation was suspended, etc. Later it appeared that the restrictions had been overdone, simply in ignorance of the foreign exchange position. Accordingly a new import procedure was introduced in 1951. It was laid down in Foreign Trade Circular Order No. 56/51.

More Relaxations

The technical aspects of the new procedure need not be considered in detail. The important point is that the process of importing was divided into three stages: the conclusion of the buying contract, the entry of the goods into Federal territory, and payment. Under the new system licences are required for the buying contract—the so-called buying permits. The grant of the buying permits was designed to give the authorities a clear view of the country's foreign exchange commitments. The system is handled as liberally as possible, e.g. by allowing contracts to run for a long period and by adapting sanction to mercantile requirements. The procedure was agreed in permanent consultation with leading industrial organisations; at present it is centred (a) round the buying permit, which enables prospective foreign exchange requirements to be appreciated, and (b) round the imports and payments licences which reflect forthcoming demands on our paying capacity arising from imports.

Meanwhile some important steps were taken to ease imports. Thus, in the spring of 1953, the import of printed matter and of maps (from the E.P.U. area) was virtually decontrolled. Overall sanctions were given for commodity futures transactions. Import procedure was largely treated as simply reflecting the foreign exchange position which at present has of course become much easier outside the dollar area. Import controls are not used as an instrument of trade policy; the object is simply to allow the agreements under trade treaties to be implemented on businesslike, effective and flexible lines by framing tenders, etc., according to the principle of maximum competition. Where quotas remain, tenders are made as wide as possible in the knowledge that tendering technique can do much to promote foreign trade, e.g. by preventing the existence of a tendering monopoly. Three methods are used—through Federal offices, through the banks, and through the so-called L.V. procedure; the last-named is used for perishable goods where import has to be carried through as quickly as possible. Within the limits of the possible import procedure has steadily been perfected; the general tendency has been to check transactions after the event rather than to license them before. This method will presumably be developed in the future.

Above this sanctioning machinery there stands the Inter-departmental Importing Committee, which also has never had any ambition to indulge in commercial politics. Its sole objective has always been to allow imports to conform to practical requirements.

A high volume of imports and a maximum freedom in offerings foster competition and a lowering of costs. Consequently the tendency is so far as possible in favour of overall tenders. With many countries where we have an export surplus, so-called open tenders have been introduced, which in practice represent a sort of autonomous liberalisation. Other administrative regulations, especially those relating to import applications, have consistently been eased, e.g. by restricting the scope of certificates required from Chambers of Industry and of Commerce when import applications are made.

In future our foreign trade will largely depend on our importing capacity except in so far as we take on ourselves the burden of capital exports. Hence it is important that the process of liberalisation shall be extended to simplify import procedure and that sanctions are handled in such a way as to allow them to follow closely the movement of world markets. The aim of our import control is thus to make itself superfluous and to vanish without a trace on the day when complete convertibility is introduced.

The report of the Interdepartmental Committee for 1952 shows that 80% of our total imports benefited by this liberalised system. Important work was done by the Committee in promoting transit imports via the clearing countries. The intention was to pay for imports from the dollar area in clearing currencies. In this way we were able to play a useful part in a transit deal undertaken by the Bank of England which enabled us to buy dollar goods worth $87 millions against E.P.U. currencies. Open tenders were also carefully promoted. According to this method importers can at any time obtain automatically foreign exchange for certain goods from certain countries without quantitative restriction and without previous sanction by any official body. At the beginning of 1953, 425 open tenders were running for imports from a number of European and overseas countries. In 1952 buying permits amounting to DM.802 millions were granted under open tenders.*

Raw Materials Credit—Tredefina†

Today import controls are aimed at promoting liberalisation as a means for opening markets to German exports. It was different a few years ago when the chief object was to acquire raw materials for processing and exporting. The Interdepartmental Committee continues to sanction the release of foreign exchange for raw materials credits and for Tredefina transactions. In each case the object is to assure the supply of important raw materials, the foreign supplier granting the credit in the first instance. The raw materials are intended for processing in the country, whereupon they are exported and the proceeds are used to pay off the credit. The intention is to earn the currency in which the raw material credit was originally granted, except where dollars can be procured.

The raw materials credit procedure is based on a Regulation issued in the autumn of 1951. It is complemented by the Tredefina procedure, the beginnings of which go back to the early twenties. At that time the Netherlands granted a credit of 200 million guilders, 140 millions for industrial raw materials and 60 millions for foodstuffs. These transactions were interrupted by the Second World War. Eventually, however, in 1951, it proved possible to resume the Tredefina transactions though on a different basis and on a substantially smaller scale. The present Dutch credits are not State credits, but are granted by Dutch banks and amount only to approximately 40 million guilders. The credits are expressed in dollars as well as in guilders, and thus permit Dutch transit deals in dollar goods. They are revolving credits; a twelve-months' guilder credit can, for example, revolve three times in the case of a textile concern. They are chiefly employed by large enterprises, particularly in the

---

* A certain amount of supervision has still to be exercised, e.g. to keep a check on Mutual Security Agency imports, on imports of strategic materials, etc. In such cases the Federal Authorities have to act. This includes transit business, etc.

† Treuhandgesellschaft für deutsche Finanzierungan: German Finance Trustee Co.

electrical industry, which availed itself of similar credits as early as 1921. Tredefina branches exist in Munich and Düsseldorf. One advantage for the borrower lies in the fact that dollar credits do not necessarily have to be repaid in dollars, but also permit exports into soft currency countries, while the Bank deutscher Länder undertakes repayment in the original currency.

Raw material credits of this kind can be made to play a very constructive part. Tredefina credits, for instance, can be developed beyond the function of permitting imports of raw materials until they amount to genuine working stocks, though admittedly these stocks have to be imported in the form of raw materials. Once this has been done, however, the credit remains available to the German producer as a regular foreign credit, permitting, moreover, the financing of his export business. The duration of Tredefina guilder credits is generally twelve months, and of dollar credits six months; interest is 7–8%. Raw materials and Tredefina credit lines in 1951 permitted the importation of goods worth DM.27 millions, having an export value in the finished state of DM.89 millions with a consequent foreign exchange surplus of DM.62 millions. We imported copper, cotton, zinc and tin chiefly from the dollar or the guilder area and wolfram, kaolin, cotton, jute, manganese and steel rods from the E.P.U. area. We exported cotton and jute tissues and wolfram powder to the E.P.U. area as well as copper goods, fine china, and tubes to the dollar area.

Reciprocal Transactions

Reciprocal transactions proved an important stimulus to German exports in the early stages, and have continued so to some extent, though the progress of liberalisation and normalisation in trade has much restricted their scope. By these transactions we mean deals where imports are reciprocally tied to exports. This sort of business began in 1949. In the first instance it helped to expand the narrow framework of imports and exports laid down by J.E.I.A. though even then it was necessary to overcome strong resistance from the Occupying Powers; later it served to ensure and improve supplies of raw material, as a part of our planned export drive. From 1949 to the beginning of 1952 countries with dollar resources were the leading parties in these transactions, particularly the United States and Canada, with which no trade treaties were in force. Raw materials were exchanged against German exports, with a surplus, payable in foreign exchange, of 25%. The foundation on which these transactions rested lay in the substantial price differential between dollar world market prices and prices in the clearing countries, a difference which at that time was 50% and over, and was only slowly eliminated. The prices payable for raw materials inside Germany were chiefly determined by the raw material prices ruling outside the dollar area. Imports from the dollar area were at that time substantially below German prices and resulted in differentials allowing importers to pay large premiums to exporters. These premiums provided the latter with an incentive to effect exports and thus to earn the dollars needed by the importers. With the help of these premiums it proved possible to lower the prices of German exports in the severely competitive dollar markets.

Transactions of this kind run counter to the clear notions of a market economy, and the Federal Republic was compelled to adopt them partly by the switching practised in the Netherlands. The Dutch bought German goods in the E.P.U. clearing and sold them against dollars. With these dollars they bought cheap raw materials on the free dollar markets and resold them to the Federal Republic at the high prices ruling in the clearing countries. This increased our dollar gap; and it thereupon became necessary to combat this development through the practice of reciprocal transactions. And in fact in the autumn of 1951 approximately 40% of our entire trade in the dollar area was carried through on this basis. The progressive assimilation of dollar world market prices to the prices ruling in the clearing countries towards the end of 1951 and the beginning of 1952 demanded a less rigid system than that provided by the reciprocal transactions, with their separate licensing both of imports and of exports. Accordingly in 1952 they were replaced, so far as the free dollar area was concerned, by the so-called import certificates, which represent a generalised system of reciprocity with a 60% foreign exchange settlement; at the same time they introduced a general liberalisation for our imports of dollar goods from the dollar area. A conspectus of these goods was furnished on appropriate lists. Reciprocal deals were suspended in the autumn of 1951 with countries where special agreements existed, because with them such deals would merely have hampered the full exchange of goods laid down in the existing treaty.

The certificates did not serve to stimulate exports for long. After April, 1952, the date at which the certificates were introduced, the raw materials prices in the clearing countries and consequently the German domestic prices, came to approximate to world market prices to such an extent that the premium commanded by the certificates fell from about 20% to virtually nil.

In the spring of 1953 the prices of the certificates were not even sufficient to meet the banking charges involved. Today they provide no stimulus for export. Supplies of raw materials and foodstuffs, including those from the dollar area, have greatly improved; prices in the countries with which we have trade treaties have come closer to dollar prices; at the same time our resources of O.E.E.C. and of bilateral clearing countries' currencies have grown. Accordingly interest has dwindled in this type of transaction, a development which can be interpreted as a step towards normalcy in world trade. In the summer of 1953 the certificates were abolished, the International Monetary Fund having previously requested member States to abstain from special practices of this kind.

As the network of our trade agreements becomes closer so there is less point in continuing the reciprocal transactions described. The liberalisation of German imports thus makes this type of deal more and more superfluous. They continue to be important in connection with countries where this class of business is permitted or has been agreed upon, e.g. Afghanistan, Ethiopia, and Syria, as well as with countries like Liberia, Saudi Arabia, the Yemen, etc., where it is impossible to exchange goods in any other way; and finally in transactions with countries with which we have only recently resumed business relations, e.g. with the countries of the Eastern bloc with which no trade treaties exist. As things are at present we shall hardly be able to renounce altogether reciprocal deals of this kind. Generally they have a pioneering function; frequently they are necessary to get trade started at all. Presumably this accounts for the fact that in its annual report for 1952, the Federation of German Industries expresses the wish to retain this system as a reserve instrument for trade policy, the reason being that many countries are glad enough to sell to us but are shy about purchasing. This applies specially to countries belonging to the dollar area, but not possessing sufficient dollars.

The process of liberalisation and quasi-liberalisation has now reached such a stage that many individual concerns can establish these linkings of imports and exports on a purely private basis. They are important as an instrument of policy only in those cases where we are forced to compete with State sponsored exports as practised, for instance, by the French Government.

Export Promotion

It is interesting to note that the London conversations in the spring of 1953, when the part to be played by the Federal Republic in the British endeavours to make sterling convertible were discussed, evidently led to the discovery of a common basis for the reduction of export subsidies. The growing recognition of the importance of a free market economy in foreign trade has involved a growing sense of the annoyance caused by export subsidies, and a shift of emphasis to the rational and long-term promotion of exports through market study, information services and the extension of official and private agencies. The root of export subsidies lies undoubtedly in economic nationalism which favours the growth of monetary and currency autarky and is consequently compelled to resort to artificial measures for cutting down imports and stimulating exports. In such a system export subsidies are used, in Heinrich Rittershausen's words,

15

'to push goods into the world market by the use of unrealistic rates of exchange and contrary to the price differential while protectionism is employed at the same time to counteract the artificial differential by which foreign goods are carried into the country'.

Now export subsidies of this sort are supposed to be used merely to correct such artificialities; mostly, however, these corrections have a dynamism of their own and open wide the door to artificial State measures for stimulating exports. At the present moment, for instance, the rate of exchange is such that French industry is hardly able to compete with that of the Federal Republic. However, the State, by practically repaying the greater part of the social security contributions and even of actual wages, by giving guarantees for prices and costs, and by providing an arbitrary financial backing, enables French merchants in countries like South America, where competition at present is particularly severe, to offer up to seven years' credit and to rest content with almost impossibly low prices.

The gradual abolition of export subsidies by a process of negotiated reciprocal concessions is somewhat difficult because subsidies of this sort are either non-existent or low in countries where a free-market economy has been adopted, so that in these cases there is little room for concessions. This could create the impression that countries like France, for instance, were being asked to abolish subsidies without receiving anything in exchange. However, the source of the trouble does not lie ultimately with the subsidy as such, but in its deeper cause, i.e. in economic nationalism and in a policy of artificial rates of exchange. And countries with a free-market economy have something important to offer, viz. a clear, long-term trade policy without the obstacles arising from foreign exchange controls and other arbitrary measures.

We can now appreciate the negotiating strength of countries possessing a free-market economy. These countries cannot repay in like coin the reduction of export subsidies by other countries; what they can do is to offer unhampered trade on a free-market basis. In the background, but only in the background, there may also lie the consideration that countries with a free-market economy may be driven in desperation to have recourse to extreme measures; and in this case they would be able to take steps calculated to neutralise, if not to outdo, the subsidies with which their competitors operate.

At present neither subsidies nor premiums of any sort are used to stimulate exports from the Federal Republic. The measures used to promote exports are confined to the following groups (as in May, 1953):

(1) Tax concessions. All exports from the Federal Republic are free of turnover tax. The rebate of sales tax granted to German exporters amounts to $2\frac{1}{2}\%$ for finished goods, to 1% for semi-finished goods and to $\frac{1}{2}\%$ for other products. With regard to corporation and income tax, a tax-free sum can be set off amounting to 1% of the export proceeds for the trader and to 3% for the producer (4% when imports are processed on behalf of foreign producers). Reliefs also exist for stamp duty and insurance tax.

(2) In transactions with private foreign customers export guarantees are granted by the Hermes Credit Insurance Co. of Hamburg to cover production risks. In the case of State transactions with other countries an export guarantee is also granted relating to the price determined on or to the costs incurred by the manufacturer. Here again the risks of production are covered. In principle Hermes covers, in the case of export guarantees, (a) the economic and political risks and (b) in certain cases, the risk that the amount due may not be paid; it also covers the risks connected with production, conversion and transfers. In the case of export guarantees under (a) the policy holders are required to assume at least 25% of the uncovered monetary risk and at least 15% of the political risk. In the case of (b) the exporter is required to assume a share of the risk which is not guaranteed by the State; this amounts to 5% of the amount covered, plus 10% of the balance. Where risks connected with conversion, transfer and exchange losses are covered, the exporter must also assume a 15% share of the uncovered balance.

(3) Banks undertaking foreign-trade business grant credits of up to ninety days by discounting bills and acceptances to finance exports. Medium- and long-term business to supply foreign

customers has been done since April, 1952 by the A.K.A.*
which deals in two main lines of credit:

(a) It grants its own line of credit in conjunction with the
customer's own bank; these lines run from twelve to
forty-eight months and carry interest at 7%.

(b) A credit line with the Bank deutscher Länder for redis-
counting credits with a duration of either six to twenty-
four, or of twenty-five to forty-eight months. Both lines
of credit are limited.

(4) An export bonus amounting to 4% of the gross proceeds
which is credited to the foreign exchange working fund of the
exporting concern.

Finally, raw material credits can be granted to promote
processing on behalf of foreign producers. These credits are
likely to become less important as the main object of the
Federal Republic's foreign economic policy, viz. convertibility with all its favourable effects on the internationalisation of capital, becomes a reality.

All in all, the Federal Republic's system of promoting
exports, so far as it influences the cost of exports, and the
granting of credit, can be regarded as entirely moderate.
The level of export prices depends solely on the competitive
ability of individual undertakings. Moreover, an official
circular of 1951 urges German exporters to obtain the best
possible prices in the light of world price levels. The essential
point of our trade policy so far as it concerns itself with our
competitive ability, lies in the maximum liberalisation of
imports, which effects a wholesome pressure on the domestic
price level. This in turn is meant to benefit exporters by
enabling them to keep their own prices low and thus to
compete more effectively on world markets.

Much would be gained if the discussions on the reduction
of export subsidies dear to bodies like the International
Monetary Fund, G.A.T.T., etc., were to lead Governments to
confine themselves to the measures listed above. The Federal
Republic will probably be ready to reduce even the remaining measures to a minimum.

* Export Credit Co.

CHAPTER XV

IMPORTS AS AN INSTRUMENT OF EXPORT POLICY. SOME THOUGHTS ON THE WAY

THE growing difficulties encountered by our exports of capital goods make it natural that more attention should be given to the problem of strengthening or prolonging our export credits. The suggestion of an export loan or the hopes one can hear that the World Bank may soon grant a credit are an eloquent expression of such thoughts. At the same time it must be remembered that export credits, if pursued alone, could easily lead to dangers. We cannot neglect capital exports, and for this very reason the speedy reform of our capital markets is desirable. Yet capital exports should not be over-stressed; if, for instance, we were to extend credits of up to ten years, we would be competing with other countries at a point where we are particularly weak and vulnerable. Countries like Switzerland or the United States can always underbid our interest rates and overbid our credit terms. This would be particularly true if American industry were to concentrate still further on international investment. Where the granting of credit is concerned, our chief competitors undoubtedly hold strong cards.

Problems of Foreign Capital

The World Bank and other institutions for employing foreign capital will not entirely solve our problems. On the contrary foreign loans to finance our exports threaten rather to accentuate the problem they are meant to solve. Dollar loans would make it easier for us to buy goods in the United States and would put at a disadvantage the countries whose chief customers and debtors we are. Despite all we have done to liberalise our imports, our visible trade obstinately retains its export surplus. This being so the grant of a foreign loan would not increase the volume of our imports. Our foreign currency surpluses would in any case allow us to import far more than we are at present importing, and a dollar loan would simply increase our export surplus with the clearing countries or the E.P.U. Such loans would thus not help to finance the existing surplus balance, they would simply create further export balances with the non-dollar area; and it is simply these balances which the loan would then cover. It is as though the suggestion were made that the United States should reduce its vast surplus and creditor status in foreign trade by floating a foreign loan. But foreign loans presuppose an import surplus which has to be financed by foreign capital. It is undoubtedly useful, and even essential, that contacts with American capital should exist in this country; but they must have a different purpose, that of providing American capital for the under-developed countries. This is the only way in which the ambitious foreign projects will be brought nearer to realisation. But we cannot hope that our own DM. gap will be closed by such measures.

Increasing Imports

One important way to promote exports in the present situation would therefore be to increase our imports. To secure our exports a regular programme of import promotion is needed. Such a policy would accord with our traditional position as a transit country and as the biggest consumer in Europe. A deliberate stimulation of imports would also be a sound long-term undertaking, and would provide a valuable means for stabilising and strengthening our position as a world trading power. This is all the more true since we have heavily reduced our purchases of raw materials in recent months in view of the declining tendency in the world's raw materials markets. This declining trend may become less important. Its reason is to be found in the tendency towards dearer money which has induced traders to liquidate their stocks and in the reluctance on the part of industry to build up stocks. At the same time the falling tendency has set off a new spiral of stock reduction and buying restraint. Today, however, the question arises whether it might not be wise to increase stocks of raw materials. It is worth asking whether West German undertakings should not be given fiscal induce-ments to increase their imports of raw materials and to build up their stocks rather than to indulge in export credit competition.

The practical question is whether we should raise our imports from the clearing countries and the sterling area. By doing so we would enable our leading potential cus-tomers in overseas capital development to acquire the pur-chasing power, viz. Deutsche Marks, which they need to buy our capital goods for cash. Such a method would avoid the need to grant long-term export credits, with undesirable risks for ourselves leading to an equally undesirable indebted-ness on the part of our customers, whose balance of payments would suffer an unnecessary burden. We would also avoid putting an unnecessary strain on our customers' balance of payments, a strain involved in the purchase of capital goods and in their subsequent servicing. Such a development would be undesirable since it would leave proportionally less money available for the purchase of German consumption goods, chemicals, etc. Important as are our exports of machinery and tools, the list of our exports is also largely made up of consumption goods, intermediate products, etc., the sale of which could be endangered by the one-sided forcing of capital goods exports. The promotion of exports is rational only if it applies to every section, and avoids favouring one at the cost of others.

Better Prices

Other considerations lead to the same conclusion. Coun-tries like Brazil, for example, would certainly be prepared to pay adequate prices for machinery if we were prepared to pay adequate prices for their own produce. By raising our imports we could do something to relax the cut-throat competition in which exporters of machinery in the different countries are now compelled to engage. This alone would do much to counteract the extra cost resulting from the importa-tion of stocks of raw materials. Accordingly if the State were to encourage private purchases of stocks by tax reliefs, the cost would hardly be greater than that which the State would incur by stimulating exports through the grant of cheap long-term credits, through guarantees, etc. Individual concerns, e.g. in the electrical industry, would find it easier to obtain contracts for power stations, telephone systems, etc., and many of the problems they encounter in financing such projects would vanish if they were to resolve, under the prompting of fiscal measures, to increase their imports and stocks of non-ferrous metals, etc. This method is attended by risks; but the same is also true of long-term export credits.

Transit Business

In the transit trade covering raw materials and foodstuffs Germany has always played an important part as between Western and Eastern Europe. Frequently a certain division of labour with the City of London was adopted. Even today, despite the Iron Curtain, there are considerable openings for transactions of this kind. They would offer us substantial opportunities to reduce our overseas creditor status and to increase the absolute volume of world trade. South American products, for instance, could in this way be sold to the countries of the Eastern bloc, our export surplus to Brazil being eliminated at the same time. We could export our machinery to Brazil without raising too many awkward credit questions, and our transit business would allow us to expand trade between East and West in politically unobjectionable goods. Precisely because exports to Eastern Europe are subject to embargo lists, this transit business could do much to finance our higher overseas exports of machinery without causing detriment at the same time to our trade with Eastern Europe. Financial and other methods to promote this class of transit business would thus be an exceedingly effective method to promote our exports generally and would at the same time stimulate our exports of capital goods to the benefit of all. One condition of course would be that we must not have a surplus balance with every country.

Part of our surplus and of the DM. gap is simply an expression of the fact that the multilateral payments and trade systems of the world are not functioning properly. We could partly close this gap by increasing our imports for transit purposes. Excessive capital exports, on the other hand, would merely postpone the problems. Moreover, the fact that we are creditors in visible trade and in our balance of payments should not lead us to the conclusion that we are structurally a creditor and surplus country like the United States. The wide difference in interest rates alone, which would lead to a large flow of capital into Germany if capital movements were free, is enough to refute this view.

Prospects for Raw Material Prices

In forming a judgement of the world raw materials position a clear distinction will have to be made between the day-to-day factors affecting markets and the structural ones. In the May, 1953 issue of *The Banker* Mr. E. H. Stern has made a careful analysis showing that the Western economy is still suffering from a raw materials shortage resulting from the fact that industrial production continues to exceed that of raw materials. Special influences, such as the apparent *détente* between East and West, the dearer money policy, etc., have induced consumers to liquidate some of their stocks of raw materials. But this process merely masks the structural rise in the price of raw materials and of foodstuffs, as compared with pre-war levels, and such falls in price levels as have occurred are unlikely to be permanent.

Trade Policy at the Parting of the Ways

All in all, trade policy and exports have once again reached a parting of the ways, a fact which shows how much we need flexibility in our foreign trade. By adopting the system of open tenders and by going ahead with the process of liberalisation, both within the E.P.U. and with non-participating and with clearing countries, the Federal Government has done much to set our import market free from bureaucratic barriers. But this does not exhaust the possibilities for increasing imports. Besides reducing trade barriers we can also take positive steps to promote imports. Under this heading fall questions regarding our stocks of raw materials, the amplification of transit business, and positive measures in the field of fiscal and credit policy by which our purchasing power could be more fully exploited as an instrument of trade policy. Measures to stimulate domestic consumption, like the recent reductions in the tax on coffee and tobacco, etc., or the reduction in our industrial prices calculated to set free the public's purchasing power for the import of foodstuffs, work in the same direction. Only if imports are deliberately stimulated in this way will it be possible to see in their true light the problems of credit-granting in connection with the export of capital goods. Capital exports would then become less urgent and a rational connection would have been established between imports and exports.

CHAPTER XVI

MACHINERY FOR ENCOURAGING
FOREIGN TRADE

Information Services

If the Government's policy and the private initiative of traders are to meet with success in the markets of the world, they will require an ample supply of information. More than before we require a knowledge of foreign markets in psychological, political and economico-strategic terms. As our foreign trade comes to rely more heavily on capital development and comes to deal with countries which, closely as they have to depend on external markets, have also an economic policy of their own to pursue, so we find increasingly that apart from the day-to-day knowledge of a given market we must also acquire systematic information about future openings and possible supplies. Market research and the collection of economic information are thus confronted with new tasks.

Before the First World War it seemed almost superfluous for Germany, more than for most countries, to maintain abroad its own machinery of information agencies, Chambers of Commerce, etc. The business connections maintained by our overseas merchants seemed to suffice; and their intimate knowledge of foreign markets was a jealously guarded property. When, after the First World War, the Foreign Office and the Reich Ministry of Economics built up an official news-gathering system (as in the later 'Reich Office for Foreign Trade' and its publication, *Information on Foreign Trade*) many conservative traders almost felt that the Government were trespassing on their own ground. Today the position has changed completely. Business connections continue to be valuable and indeed indispensable; they form the foundation for the growing overseas business of our concerns in Hamburg and Bremen. Gradually, however, economic initiative, particularly overseas, has begun to emanate rather from new official bodies; and this change, together with the new emphasis on industrialisation and on capital development, is giving a fresh importance to the unknown factors in the markets of the world, factors which contain both opportunities and risks. Industrial and constructional undertakings are playing a greater part in exports. The nature and technique of gathering economic information abroad have thus undergone a change even relatively to the time before the Second World War. At that time the Reich Office for Foreign Trade tried chiefly to answer business inquiries. At the same time the official missions abroad were supplemented by the network of correspondents maintained by *Information on Foreign Trade*. A routine news-gathering prevailed; market developments were followed passively, though a certain amount of analysis and of forecasting was included.

Looking into the Future

What matters today is not so much to grasp contemporary facts as to look into the future. This means that the official supply of information does not so much consist in answers to inquiries as in an attempt to supply German business-men with facts about new tendencies and opportunities before these become universally obvious. Moreover, a synthetic method of study is being adopted which looks upon economic policy and the general events in a country as a whole. This method supplements the point by point study of a given market. It follows that different conditions must now be fulfilled if a market is to be successfully studied. No single market is today determined by purely internal factors; it is dependent on economic and political factors operating at a world level, on the general trend of development, etc. Even the ablest representative of a private merchant concern can hardly be expected to acquire a knowledge of these factors, which are beyond his real field of interest; yet it is essential that he should somehow acquire it. A sensible division of labour between the scrutiny of market details and the study of the grand outlines of economic development follows more or less logically. Accordingly the Federal Office for Foreign Trade Information in Cologne and the publication, *Information for Foreign Trade* which it brings out, are given a field of operations adapted to the conditions governing modern world trade. Its importance is all the greater since we have still to make good the losses caused by years of isolation. It goes without saying that, side by side with this basic and authoritative information, ample scope is left to the initiative of private bodies, particularly of the Press.

The private representative of German enterprises abroad will have to become more fully aware of his strategic and forward-looking tasks. In this respect he will differ from his predecessor of earlier years. His way will lead him not only to the markets and importers in the country where he works, but to the drawing and planning offices of the new Governments. He will be compelled to familiarise himself thoroughly with general aspects—with sociological, psychological, national and cultural questions, besides many others, relating to the country where he is working. In the activities of the official missions and of the *Information for Foreign Trade* correspondents, he will not see any invasion or supervision of the reports he sends out himself. Private offices and newspapers, e.g. the *Handelsblatt*, the General Economic News Service, etc., will have similar and important spheres of operation.

It was under this new inspiration that the Federal Office for Foreign Trade Information was formed in the spring of 1951 under Dr. Karlrobert Ringel. The principle governing the set-up of the earlier Reich Office for Foreign Trade was adopted, and accordingly the work of supplying news from abroad was left in the hands of a private organisation, the Deutscher Wirtschaftsdienst G.m.b.H. The idea of adopting a constructive and active method of gathering information seemed appropriate if only because the many years of isolation had largely destroyed the ability even to ask the right sort of questions. Genuine pioneering work will therefore have to be done in the field of information gathering; this work can then enter into fruitful partnership with mercantile pioneers.

Dissemination of Information

The isolation just mentioned stresses the importance, from more points of view than one, of the dissemination of information. The steady publication of virtually every type of information is therefore under present conditions an essential method for effective dissemination. The more widely official news is spread in the first instance, the less necessary will it be for individual inquiries to be made, and the more effectively will the minds of German exporters be directed towards the new tendencies prevailing in world markets. Accordingly printed matter of every sort plays a much more important part at present in the work of the Federal Office of Information than it did previously. The various publications are now doing most of the work done earlier by private information services. The Federal Office has deliberately been placed at the head in the German Foreign Trade Information machinery. It works directly only with official bodies, and with industrial organisations. Contact with individual firms is indirect and is carried on through Chambers of Commerce and kindred bodies or by way of the publications brought out by the Federal Office. A great deal of information is made available to the Federal Office for internal use; but the Federal Office regards that sort of information as best which appears in publications which anyone can obtain who is interested. For this purpose the *Notes on Foreign Trade* are available, which represent a current series of information. The leading publication, *Information for Foreign Trade*, has again been appearing daily since the spring of 1953. Monographs are also published on different countries; these are intended to form the basis for further private market study.

The division of work between private undertakings and official market research centres results from the principle that the Federal Institutions are intended to serve the interests of groups but not of individual concerns. 'The chief objective is to assist the large number of medium and small export undertakings which are not in a position to study overseas markets from their own resources.'*

* The Federal Information Office also runs certain special publications, e.g. the Customs Information Service and the loose-leaf series called 'Transpatent' which deals with special legal questions interesting importers and exporters. The Overseas Trade Book, 1952 (that for 1953 is in preparation) is another publication brought out by the Federal Information Office with the help of other bodies.

The problems connected with the collection of economic information from abroad show that it will not suffice to reconstruct the earlier machinery or merely to continue where we left off before the war. Here, as elsewhere, the promotion of foreign trade must meet the requirements of the second half of the twentieth century. The same probably applies to many private market research undertakings. It will not suffice merely to reflect analytically the condition of world markets at any given moment, for in this case the researcher would be assuming the permanence of non-permanent circumstances. The methods of a new market strategy of the type aimed at by the Federal Information Office are gradually becoming effective.

German Chambers of Foreign Trade

The problem of our Chambers of Foreign Trade is not solved by simply restoring the pre-war bodies in various countries of Europe and elsewhere.* In our return to world markets the Chambers of Trade will play a different and presumably far more important part. Admittedly our trade policy gives priority to private initiative and assigns a merely supporting part to State organisations. But private initiative itself will have a special field in overseas capital development. German traders abroad have today to act in manifold roles—as engineers, as advisers to foreign authorities, as organisers, as heads of firms, as traders or as industrialists. Their stature is growing and consequently the stature of the people employed in these Chambers ought also to grow. We know from the early history of German trade in Egypt that an over-riding importance belonged to the German-Egyptian Chamber of Trade in Cairo, especially before any official German mission arrived there. The Chamber provided a platform for high level economic policy and for the discussion of German-Egyptian economic interests in general. Experienced heads of such Chambers will be particularly valuable in the future.

* See Dr. F. von Napolski, 'Chambers of Trade Abroad and the Promotion of Foreign Trade', 'Foreign Trade Book', 1952. See also the same author's: 'Lessons from the Work Done by Chambers of Trade Abroad', published by the German Industrial and Trade Conference, Publication No. 14.

At the same time the question arises where, in Germany, the threads leading back from the different Chambers are to be centralised. At present the Chambers are the prerogative of the German Conference on Industry and Trade, while the Federation of German Industry has little to say in practice. Yet the functions of a modern Chamber of Trade, particularly overseas, embrace the sphere of German industry.

At the beginning of the century German Chambers of Trade hardly existed abroad. The strongest opposition originally came from Hamburg and Bremen. A few half-hearted attempts were made to found such Chambers of Trade, but by 1905 not a single one survived. In the same year twenty-nine French and twenty-one Italian Chambers existed, besides a large number belonging to other countries. A German Chamber was not formed again until 1912, in Switzerland, and it was only after the First World War that the authorities began to see in the Chambers a valuable instrument for opening world markets to Germany. Eventually a wide network was formed.* At the beginning of 1953 altogether fourteen Chambers existed in the following countries: Egypt, Argentina, Belgium, Brazil (in Rio and São Paulo), Chile, Greece, Italy, Mexico, South Africa, Spain, Switzerland, Sweden, the United States and Uruguay. The earliest Chambers were formed in countries where German undertakings had been allowed to set up agencies.

Before the war Chambers tended to be formed on a national basis, the head and the management generally consisting entirely or at least predominantly of German nationals. Since the war the new or reconstituted Chambers have mostly been on a mixed basis, a major part being played by foreign concerns having close trade contacts with the Federal Republic. The reason for this change lies in the fact that most of the German firms abroad were broken up by the war, so that at first it was impossible to find enough German merchants or undertakings to allow the formation

* See Theodor Dieckmann: 'German Overseas Chambers of Trade, A Digest of Earlier Experiences.' Published by the German Industrial and Trade Conference, Publication No. 15.

of national or mixed Chambers. At present with the multiplication of German agencies abroad, Germans are beginning to play a bigger part in the general management of Chambers, and this is probably a natural development. Yet the principle of reciprocity is playing a growing part, a fact doing justice to the new climate of world economy, particularly in the under-developed countries. In these countries the Chambers have an opportunity to act as intermediaries in establishing contacts between private undertakings and to establish relations with the authorities in the young nation States.

Since 1952 the Federal Ministry of Economics has subsidised the Chambers through the intermediacy of the Industrial and Trade Conference, with the object of giving them financial assistance in their difficult pioneering work. The Foreign Office, moreover, has given the Economic Divisions attached to its foreign missions special instructions on the most fruitful co-operation with the German Chambers of Trade abroad.

Fairs and Exhibitions

The Federal Ministry of Economics has given active, including financial, aid to Germans taking part in foreign fairs and exhibitions, as well as to those promoting German export fairs. Efforts have also been made to attract foreign exhibitors and visitors. Attempts to leave these problems to the unaided help of industry failed as early as 1948–9; Federal subsidies were first granted in 1950. The grant of these monies is justified by the fact that industry is bound to run a certain risk without being able immediately to obtain tangible rewards. Thus on the one hand subsidies are given to encourage Germans to take a part in foreign fairs. On the other hand, so-called fair quotas exist to encourage foreigners to patronise German fairs. These quotas are special amounts of foreign exchange which are allowed to foreign exhibitors at German fairs for the import of non-liberalised goods.

At present special attention is being paid to overseas fairs in countries with openings for capital development. During the last few years the natural course has led from European

16

fairs to those in other continents. The Federal Government attached special value to the setting up of so-called information stands and to prestige exhibits, particularly in connection with fairs which might provide a key to new markets. But the most important part in German participation has always been assigned to private industry represented either by individual concerns or by group exhibits. The technical work is done by the Exhibitions and Fairs Committee of German Industries, in which the national federations of trade, industry, etc., are represented. The Committee acts as trustee for Federal subventions. For the more important undertakings abroad a special sub-committee is generally formed which places orders in connection with German participation.

In 1948 private industry financed its own participation in fairs and exhibitions held abroad, and in 1949 the Federal Republic provided *ad hoc* subventions—in that year particularly in Chicago, New York and Milan. Since 1950 regular budgetary subventions have been provided. Since then German exhibits have been arranged at representative fairs in important countries, e.g. those at Bolzano, Chicago, Istanbul, New Delhi, Smyrna, Stockholm, Utrecht and Vienna. In 1951 the Federal Government granted subventions for the Triennale in Milan and financed information stands in Utrecht, Brussels, Stockholm, Paris, Bolzano, Bari, Barcelona and Cape Town. Representative exhibits and information stands were arranged in Milan, Smyrna and Karachi. Further extensions were undertaken in 1952 and for 1953 information stands were planned for Paris, Casablanca, Johannesburg, Barcelona, Luxembourg, etc. It was also intended to arrange representative exhibits and information stands for Toronto, Milan and Smyrna.

The part to be played in future in trade fairs abroad is regarded as pioneering work—work which cannot yet be done in a routine manner. The authorities are aware that the old methods are not necessarily the right ones, and new forms are under consideration. Old problems, e.g. whether special trade fairs or national exhibitions should be specially favoured, and many other problems, are again becoming important.

The Significance of the Machinery Adopted

The activities treated above, extending from the Federal Office of Information and the official economic missions abroad, to questions of market research and to Chambers of Foreign Trade and thence to problems connected with fairs and exhibitions, all constitute part of the machinery of foreign trade, a machinery specially necessary under a regime of free trade and of a free-market economy. Other types of machinery exist elsewhere which seek to replace private initiative and to work in the direction of State foreign trade monopolies, bureaucratic control, etc. The machinery mentioned above, on the other hand, aims at assisting and not replacing private traders. Hence the need to establish a close connection between these bodies and those maintained by private industry in the motherland. Among these are the Advisory Committee on Foreign Trade, the Foreign Trade Committee of the Federation of German Industry, the Foreign Trade Committee of the different national industrial federations, and the Foreign Trade Sections maintained by these national organisations. It is the work of these bodies to remain in constant touch with the Federal Ministry of Economics, the Foreign Office, the Chambers of Foreign Trade, etc. From the organisational point of view we can distinguish three stages by which contact is established with foreign countries. These could be defined as:

(1) Trade follows the flag.
(2) Trade follows the bureaucrat.
(3) Trade follows the engineer.

In the era of 'Trade follows the flag' which virtually ended with the First World War, there was relatively little scope for the sort of machinery which has been described. In the era of 'Trade follows the bureaucrat' it was chiefly an extension of the official bodies existing at home. Today a phase of economic development has been reached in which industrialists, merchants, technicians and pioneers hold the dominant position. But this phase of 'Trade follows the engineer' calls for numerous horizontal connections between technical, mercantile, financial and State initiatives. It is the function of the machinery described above to promote these connections.

On the other hand, we may have to consider setting up special bureaucratic machinery when we come to deal with the countries of the Eastern bloc where trade is handled by State monopolies.

The Foundation: Setting up Establishments Abroad

If our foreign trade is to be given a sound businesslike basis it will require the existence of a really wide network of German establishments. The confiscation and expropriation of German property abroad in the name of reparations has either destroyed or eliminated our former establishments or, alternatively, has put them to different uses. Accordingly the Federal Government began at an early date to make available foreign exchange for the construction of these establishments abroad and for the financing of German participations. A basis was provided in an official circular of January, 1952. Since February, 1952, the Ministry of Economics has had the power, jointly with the Bank deutscher Länder, to sanction the setting up of these establishments and the participation of German undertakings in foreign ones. The enterprise of German concerns, particularly in Hamburg and Bremen, is shown by the fact that the losses they incurred abroad in consequence of the two world wars have not deterred them from risking their money a third time. This is all the more remarkable since it was not exactly encouraging to find the Allies claiming the right to share any information obtained.

The reconstruction of German establishments abroad and the acquisition of shares in foreign undertakings followed a sort of concentric pattern. A beginning was made with the countries neighbouring on the Federal Republic; later the authorities tried to follow in the footsteps of earlier establishments and participations.

The circular mentioned above, No. 15/52, was specially designed to economise foreign exchange. The first objective for exports is to bring in goods, services or claims. Expenditure on the acquisition of legal rights and of special information is sanctioned only where no danger exists that German exports may be jeopardised. Moreover, any establishment set up abroad has to be economically self-supporting. A point to be noted is that countries still exist in which discrimination against German property has not yet been formally abolished. Another difficulty lies in the fact that we have not yet concluded any trade treaties settling the right to set up establishments in the countries concerned. (A preliminary agreement on the conclusion of a long-term agreement with the United States was reached on June 3, 1953.) In some of our trade agreements this point is dealt with, but this is exceptional. Meanwhile the rehabilitation of our trade has reached a stage which makes it desirable to conclude comprehensive treaties of trade, navigation and friendship as soon as possible.

Other questions are thus raised, chief among them the problem of double taxation, which urgently demands an early and comprehensive settlement by treaty. For the rest, the re-forming of German establishments provides an opening for the export of German specialised knowledge and of German patents. It is relevant to note that our balance of payments for patents and licences continues adverse, particularly with the dollar area.

'The resuscitation of our system of establishments and participations abroad offers us opportunities of increasing our exports of special knowledge, and thus of tapping a further source of foreign exchange. Ultimately the problem is closely connected with the question of German capital exports. Here again the attainment of convertibility may reasonably be expected substantially to ease matters. The construction of German establishments abroad could form an appropriate object for international financing.

Apart from the formation of new establishments abroad for the support of our foreign trade, the urgent task remains of saving what can be saved of the pre-war assets, among which are the claims of German creditors. This is all the more important now that the financial obligations of the Federal Government and of West German nationals towards their foreign creditors have been settled by the London Debt Agreement. The consequent liquidations have not yet been completed, and the proceeds have not been withdrawn in their entirety. The treatment of questions connected with German property abroad is still reserved to the Occupying Power, and the Federal Government will not be able to conduct international negotiations until the transitional treaty leading to a general treaty of peace enters into force. In a number of States German property has been released, either in part or in full, and we may now hope that an understanding of the economic and political situation will gradually predominate and enable settlements to be reached. According to the stage which has been attained, different methods of treatment may be necessary; release may be complete or partial, applying either to the existing properties or to the proceeds; settlements may be made, or finally the proceeds may be set off against debts. So far only one overall settlement has proved possible with another country, viz. Switzerland (August 26, 1952). In this instance one-third of the property was renounced; the rest was restored.*

The Instrument: Patents and Trade-Marks

The development of our foreign trade was grievously hampered by the confiscation of the existing trade-marks and patents. Moreover no possibility existed of acquiring protection for new German patents. The legal position was thus insecure, with the result that the exports of goods manufactured in accordance with German inventions and bearing German trade-marks was either of questionable value, or else entirely impracticable. It was not until August 20, 1949, that J.E.I.A. Directive No. 24 made it possible to secure the foreign exchange needed to acquire new patent rights. The Directive permitted the transfer of the money needed to pay the dues for establishing and maintaining rights of this kind abroad. The number of the countries which were prepared at that time to guarantee protection to German inventions and trade-marks was

---

* Questions of German Property have been dealt with effectively (this includes propagandist treatment) by the Study Group for Private Interests Abroad, Bremen.

barely twenty. Since then the number has been nearly trebled in the course of trade treaty negotiations. In this way German patents enjoy legal protection in all civilised countries.

It has proved much more difficult to recover the use of pre-war trade-marks and protections, whether through trade treaties or in other ways. With regard to patents, German industry has largely been compelled to write off the loss. It proved impossible to obtain what the Federal Republic had been compelled to grant by Law No. 8 of the Allied High Commissioners (October 20, 1949). By this instrument the Federal Republic had been compelled to restore to these Powers their patent rights in full within the Federal Republic, and in doing so had been compelled to exclude the war and post-war periods from the ultimate expiration date of the patents. Thus while foreign patents have a life of approximately ten years more than the normal in the Federal Republic, the Federal Republic for its part was compelled to accept the premature expiration of German patents abroad. This obvious inequity proved supportable only because, in the great majority of cases, the war-time measures confined themselves to destroying a monopoly based on the existence of the patent without depriving the German inventor of the ability to export the goods manufactured under it. Where the latter procedure was nevertheless adopted, it proved possible to counteract it in the course of trade treaty negotiations with different countries. The most potent counter-measure, however, was that adopted by German inventors in making new inventions. These, thanks to the work already done by the Federal Government, again enjoy full protection in all civilised countries.

In the case of trade-marks, where the period of protection differs from that given by patents in that it can be prolonged indefinitely, it did not prove possible to arrange for protection for registrations which had not been in effect before the end of the war. Eighty per cent of the goods protected by trade-mark which are exported at present bear marks which were protected at home and abroad before the end of the war. The Federal Government, recognising that a trade-mark is the permanent expression of the quality of the products covered in this way, did all it could in the course of its trade treaty negotiations to have all trade-marks freed and restored to German hands. This practice was adopted from the moment in 1949 that the Federal Government was again allowed to conduct international negotiations. These endeavours met with a good measure of success. In Turkey, Egypt, Greece, Italy, Iceland, Luxembourg, Belgium, the Netherlands, Denmark, Norway, Great Britain, the United States, Australia, Cyprus, Yugoslavia, Pakistan, India, Siam, Iran, Chile, Uruguay, Argentina, Colombia, Paraguay, Peru, Venezuela, Bolivia, Nicaragua, Salvador, Cuba and in other States the German proprietors are again in a position more or less completely to enjoy the benefit of the old trade-marks.

These achievements do not alter the fact that much remains to be done in this field. The export losses arising from the fact that the trade-marks question has not yet been fully solved cannot amount to less than DM.800 millions a year. France (differing therein from Britain and the United States) obstinately refuses to recognise that trade-marks are not reparations goods and that their restoration is an obligation under the Marshall Plan as well as a recognition of their character as an element of protection for the consumer at home and abroad. In a number of countries the Governments have not yet made up their minds to restore trade-marks which were taken over and transferred to other parties in isolation or in connection with the transfer of expropriated establishments abroad. It is entirely improper to set up a distinction between the trade-marks relating to establishments abroad on the one hand, and the parent concern on the other. The trade-marks ultimately embody the parent concern's real efficiency, and the distinction is improper even where the subsidiary establishment was confiscated, since ultimately it is the consumer who pays. It is satisfactory that Argentina, by restoring such trade-marks, has opened the way to a wider recognition of these facts.

Progress has also been made in the acquisition of manufacturing licences. As late as the end of 1948 it was virtually impossible for any firm to transfer money abroad to pay for the use of foreign skills or inventions. The old treaties had been superseded and new ones could not be concluded. Yet it is a matter of the greatest importance for the Federal Republic to establish contact with foreign research. At first sanctions had laboriously to be obtained from J.E.I.A. for each major treaty. Eventually Directive No. 31 of August 20, 1949, transferred the entire sector of invisible imports to the German authorities. The principles laid down at that time permitted payment to be made for foreign licences, etc., provided they were calculated to assist German exports. Today such questions are treated on uniform lines by the Federal Trade Office.

The Federal Republic has a strong adverse balance in the payments for such licences. Revenue in 1952 came to DM.31·5 millions and expenditure to DM.115 millions, the chief items being payments to the United States, the sterling area and the E.P.U. area.

Exports of German Films

A further adverse item clearly reflecting the results of losing the war is to be found in film exports and imports. At first the Allies had ensured a large influx of foreign films; since then this has been somewhat reduced in the interests of building up competitive German entertainment films. According to the schedule in force at present two hundred such films can be imported annually from the United States, thirty each from France, Great Britain and Italy, and twenty from Austria. The earnings from American films continue to be paid into a blocked account, whereas transfer arrangements exist for payments to E.P.U. countries. The Federal Government is working hard at present to foster joint inter-European productions in the hope of integrating the European film industry. Useful beginnings have been made in this connection with France and Italy, and everything has been done in the way of facilitating transfers to help the conclusion of contracts for joint film production. In 1951 DM.16 millions were transferred abroad for hire, of which DM.7 millions went to Austria, DM.3·4 millions to

Great Britain, and DM.2 millions each to France and Italy.

At present our exports of films are small. In 1952 they brought in DM.5·4 millions, most of this sum coming from Austria. In 1951 our exports brought in no more than DM.1·7 millions. The Federal Ministry of Economics publishes the *German Trade Archives* (a conspectus of trade agreements, tariffs, and other regulations covering international trade) which furnishes a German version of all foreign legislation covering tariffs and foreign trade. It is a valuable aid for all interested in foreign trade and for the official bodies concerned with trade policy.

CHAPTER XVII

SETTLEMENT OF FOREIGN DEBTS

The London Debt Agreement

Our return to world markets cannot be effected solely through the visible exchange of goods. It demands an atmosphere of trust, fostering credit transactions on both sides, and particularly those in which we obtain credit from foreign sources. Before this can happen our public and private debts abroad must be settled. This was attempted and, so far as it goes, done in the so-called London Debt Agreement under the prudent but energetic leadership of Herr H. J. Abs, who was in charge of the London negotiations from 1951 to 1953. In this way important work was done to develop the hoped-for influx of foreign capital. The Agreement came into force on September 16, 1953 for the Federal Republic and for France, Great Britain, the United States, Sweden and Egypt. Other countries will shortly join.

The Agreement provides a basis for the restoration of German credit. It will provide the necessary conditions for settling the still outstanding obligations and capital questions.

Course of the Negotiations

In the first instance our creditors were offered the annual transfer of DM.500 millions which was later to be raised to DM.600 millions. This offer was rejected by the creditors under four heads:

(1) The obligation was to be determined not by the debtor's ability to transfer the money, but by his ability to raise it.

(2) The offer of DM.500 millions was inadequate and must be substantially raised.

(3) The offer must not be made in the form of an overall settlement; it must cover each class of debt separately.

(4) The offer must be conditional; it must not be made to depend on considerations of trade, economic or monetary policy.

The Agreement did justice to most of these objections. The Germans, however, stuck to their view that the repayment of debt must depend on the Republic's ability to transfer the debt, in the sense that, with few clearly defined exceptions, no payments were to be made into a blocked account; the transfer must exhaust the entire payment. The amount to be paid in this way over the first five years was fixed at DM.567 millions a year. During the first year approximately DM.110 millions fall to be added towards settlement of the DM.1,000 millions arising out of the clearing with Switzerland and towards the preferential settlement of old trade debts. From 1958 onwards, when private pre-war debts and obligations arising out of American post-war aid begin to fall due, the average amount will rise to DM.765 millions.

As a result of these negotiations our debts and their service underwent a substantial reduction. The American post-war claims arising, for instance, from goods supplied under G.A.R.I.O.A. and the Marshall Plan, amounted to approximately $3·2 milliards. They were reduced to $1·2 milliards. Analogous British claims were reduced from £200 to £150 millions, and French ones from $16 to $12 millions. Pre-war debts were reduced from DM.8·3 to DM.6·2 milliards for the capital amount, and from DM.4·4 to DM.1·4 milliards for interest, so that the total obligation was reduced from DM.29·3 to DM.14·5 milliards.

The Agreement lays down details for each class of debt. An important point lies in the fact that a consultative clause has been introduced which makes it possible to suspend or reduce the service of the indebtedness if considerations of payment or the general condition of trade make this necessary. Article 34 of the Agreement allows consultations to be held at the request of one of the parties. It is expressly stated that such consultations can cover difficulties experienced by the Federal Republic in meeting its obligations.

In the consultations all relevant economic, financial and monetary considerations bearing on the Federal Republic's ability to effect transfers (as influenced by internal and external circumstances) and on the constant fulfilment of these obligations, must be taken into consideration.

The Agreement of February 27, 1953 contains a passage, in Annex B, Paragraph 21 (the Annex is an official report on the Conference) declaring that the Conference has recognised the principle that the transfer of the payments provided for under the Plan presupposes the attainment and maintenance of a balance of payments in which these payments and others for current transactions can be covered by earnings of foreign exchange arising out of exports and invisible transactions so that currency reserves will not be drawn upon for other than brief periods. The Conference has therefore recognised that the attainment and maintenance of this balance of payments would be facilitated by further international co-operation in the sense of a liberalised trade policy, an expansion of world trade and the restoration of free convertibility of currencies. The Conference accordingly recommends the parties concerned to give due weight to the principles mentioned in this paragraph. Moreover, the Federal Republic can request that the advice of appropriate international organisations or of other independent experts shall be sought. The preamble to the Agreement expressly refers to the recommendations contained in the Annex.

These points require special stressing because they assure that the Agreement shall fit into a dynamic conception of the Federal Republic's economic policy and of that of the West in general. Justice is done to this principle by the proviso that the debt service is to figure as a current transaction in any payments and trade agreements. The fulfilment of these obligations presupposes a substantial export surplus on our part, and such a surplus does in fact exist at present with the E.P.U. area and the clearing countries. The Agreement does not cover any political obligations like those connected with the problem of reparations. Moreover, in the many addresses he has delivered, Dr. Abs has consistently pointed out that in the important final session the

German delegation declared in the plainest terms that the Federal Republic would be unable to fulfil the Agreement if further claims were raised against it under the heading of reparations.

FOREIGN DEBTS OF THE FEDERAL REPUBLIC UNDER
THE LONDON DEBT AGREEMENT
(in millions of Deutsche Marks)

	Indebtedness		Annual Payments		
	Capital	Arrears of Interest	1953	1954–7	1958–62
Total	13,125	1,356	675	585	734
Of which pre-war debts					
Public	3,606	490	203	195	202
Private	2,556	866	252	169	197
Post-war debts					
Public	6,963	—	220	221	335
Indebtedness by Areas					
Dollar Area	6,893	496	240	238	368
E.P.U. Area	5,910	749	400	323	336
of which Great Britain	2,764	333	162	141	149
of which Switzerland	1,688	226	133	95	89

The obligations assumed under the Agreement must moreover be considered in the light of the fact that much of our foreign property has been lost, partly for instance under the 19-Power Paris Reparations Agreement of 1946. Under this Agreement the debts caused by the war—which were reflected chiefly in the clearings accounts—were supposed to be discharged.

The Federal Republic's Debt Service

Of our total obligations 52·5% relate to the dollar area, and 45% to the E.P.U. area. Of the annual payments, on the other hand, 59·2% go to the E.P.U. area during the first five-year period and 35·6% to the dollar area. From 1958 onwards each of these two areas gets rather less than half of the total payment.

A general agreement has been reached for the leading categories of indebtedness. Of interest in arrears two-thirds are to be paid, of contractual interest payable until the indebtedness is discharged, three-quarters, and of amortisation, two-thirds. The interest payable varies between 4% and 5¼%; the amortisation rate is generally 1% to 2%. The Agreement does not cover the remaining debts as they fall due, since the main objective was to lay down in clear terms the obligations existing over a fairly lengthy period. The stand-still agreement which affects leading foreign banks whose claims in 1939 amounted to RM.7 milliards, is particularly important because the discharge of these debts as covered in the Agreement makes it possible at the same time for new short-term credits to be granted to German import and export houses.

The London Debt Agreements admittedly do not cover more than part of our foreign indebtedness which falls under the following heads:

(1) The pre-war debts covered by the Agreement, amounting to approximately DM.7 milliards, to which must be added (2) another DM.7 milliards of post-war debts, settled under the Agreement. There are further (3) DM.3·5 milliards under the ten-year agreement with Israel and (4) approximately DM.5·4 milliards under individual restitution obligations. Finally there are (5) certain other foreign obligations relating to investment in property, to capital debts in German currency, and to blocked accounts in connection with which interest, rents, dividends, etc., have to be paid.

Politically the Agreements are important, because the Federal Government in its basic declaration of March, 1951, acknowledged its responsibility for the entire foreign indebtedness—not merely for a part—of the German Reich. With the full agreement of the Opposition it has stated that in its view the Federal Republic is identical with the German Reich. It has thus assumed responsibility for public debts relating to the ceded territories and to the Eastern Zone and has thereby made clear its view that Germany is a single unit for whose entire financial obligations it has assumed liability.

The question now arises whether these obligations will prove bearable. As far as the E.P.U. area is concerned, our present creditor position makes this probable; our payments to the dollar area on the other hand will constitute a severe burden so long as our balance of trade with this area remains adverse.

Prospects

Regarded in the light of general trade policy, the importance of the Debt Agreement lies in the fact that it also meets the chief condition for the settlement of the debts not covered in this Agreement. These amount to considerable sums. The object must obviously be completely to liberalise all current payments relating to capital transactions as soon as possible, and for all the different currency areas. The attainment of this aim is an essential condition for achieving the convertibility of the Deutsche Mark and for establishing normal relations with foreign countries; and these conditions must be fulfilled if these countries are to grant us new credits and to invest again in the Federal Republic. A further growth of blocked accounts must be prevented.

O.E.E.C. Obligations

We have bound ourselves to liberalise, and the O.E.E.C. and several of its members are asking with growing impatience that we shall live up to this obligation. Accordingly it will become desirable for us to take further steps to clear up our indebtedness. The O.E.E.C.'s liberalisation code binds us to liberalise all the most important current payments arising out of capital transactions. The statutes of the International Monetary Fund lay down a similar obligation.

The London Agreement thus represents a first step towards the liberalisation of these current capital transactions, and the relevant questions will have to be settled before we can argue that our current payments with other countries must not be distorted by the absence of substantial debit items. The rational settlement of these remaining debts and capital items would however mean a large additional strain on our balance of payments, of which three-quarters would relate to the E.P.U. area and approximately a third to the dollar area.

It may reasonably be argued that, by the spirit of the London Agreement, the obligations it imposes must not conflict with those arising out of the O.E.E.C.'s liberalisation code; and indeed the German delegation at the London Debt Conference consistently stressed the point that a certain margin must be left for meeting other foreign obligations, the chief point they had in mind being the transfer of sums arising from property investments. It would not therefore be proper to invoke the London settlement in order to evade the O.E.E.C. obligations. The guiding consideration must surely be that we cannot hope to obtain the use of foreign capital so long as the proceeds of old capital investments remain blocked. Ultimately, after all, there is a harmony between the principles of non-discrimination which are common to the liberalisation code and to the London Agreement. From all this it follows that a comprehensive settlement assigning a place to all our obligations must be reached. To harmonise these different interests will be a difficult task demanding a careful but comprehensive solution within the limits imposed by our ability to transfer sums abroad.

CHAPTER XVIII

ENTRANCE INTO WORLD FINANCE

The World Bank and the International Monetary Fund

The Bretton Woods Institutions, i.e. the International Monetary Fund and the World Bank, afford us a new approach to participate in world-wide economic developments. They were opened in due course to the Federal Republic, and we made our entry in the autumn of 1952. The World Bank is of special topical importance: this institution has now carried its studies of German creditworthiness and of the openings we offer for investment to a successful conclusion. The World Bank is a joint foundation with fifty-four member States. Its resources are derived from contributions made by the members and from flotations which are made on the capital markets of different countries. At present the Bank's task is to finance, after thorough investigation, development projects in every part of the world, which it does by granting credits to the Governments of the member States or to concerns whose indebtedness must then be guaranteed by the country's government. In principle the World Bank finances projects for which it has proved impossible to mobilise domestic finance or the foreign exchange needed for the requisite imports. It is a condition that these projects must bring about a vigorous expansion in the country's economy, calculated to contribute largely to the growth of production, to a rise in the standard of living, and to the foundation of undertakings based upon the original one. Under this heading credits have been granted to India for opening up the densely populated Damodar Valley, to certain Latin-American countries for the construction of hydro-electric projects and communications, and to Australia for the improvement of farming and for the importation of earth-moving machinery. The Bank finances the import component of the project, and in doing so usually mobilises credits amounting to several times the money it finds itself by inducing governments to finance that part which can be dealt with by local labour and local materials.

Since the autumn of 1952 the Federal Republic has been represented by a Governor (Ludwig Erhard) and by an alternate Governor (Fritz Schäffer). The Governors constitute the general meeting as representatives of the 'shareholders'; they normally meet once a year. Most of their rights and voting powers have been transferred to the sixteen executive directors, among whom the Düsseldorf banker, Dr. J. Zahn, represents the Federal Republic and also Jugoslavia. Within the directorate the Americans, as the biggest subscribers—subscribers, moreover, of dollars—have the greatest weight. The votes of the United States, Great Britain, Nationalist China, France and India suffice for an absolute majority. The German share in the Bank's authorised capital of nominally $10 milliards amounts to $330 millions, of which 2% have to be made available in gold or dollars, and 18% in Deutsche Marks. The latter quota can be utilised by the Bank only with our assent. The remaining 80% are our conditional liability as a member country, and can be mobilised only if the Bank needs them to meet obligations arising out of loans taken over from other parties or guaranteed by the Bank itself.

The Federal Republic has thus paid in $6·6 millions in gold or American dollars. Of the 18% (amounting to $59·4 millions) of its contribution only $3·1 millions have so far been placed at the Bank's disposal in cash; this amount represents the German share in the Bank's loan to Jugoslavia. The remaining $56·3 millions which at present have been subscribed in the form of a bond can still be made available in cash. We thus have an opportunity for sharing without undue risk in the Bank's development plans, particularly in those outside Europe.

It is interesting to note that member States have recently been making available a growing part of their 18% quota in local currencies. By the beginning of May, 1953, thirty-one out of the fifty-four member States had in this way made available amounts totalling $1,031 millions. It is a sign of the growing buyers' market abroad that members are

17*

becoming anxious to get easier control of their quotas, because they obtain in this way an opportunity for taking part in certain fairly ambitious projects. In this way Great Britain, for instance, has made available 77% of its quota, i.e. approximately $180 millions for projects within the Commonwealth. The Bank's capital derived from member States' subscriptions amounted to $1,807 millions in the spring of 1953. To this must be added reserves and the proceeds of the Bank's flotations amounting to $556 millions.

The Bank's securities have been placed in the capital markets of the United States, Canada, Switzerland and Great Britain: with the sums thus realised the Bank has been financing its projects. An important aspect of its procedure lies in the fact that the repayment of the credits provides a steadily replenished fund for new transactions. The Bank is anxious not only to raise capital from hard currency countries, but also tries to finance deals against goods in soft currencies, for which purpose the above-mentioned quotas are utilised. Repayment is facilitated in this way for the debtors and at the same time a contribution is made towards overcoming the structural dollar shortage. The Bank thus offers the Federal Republic an opportunity of borrowing capital and also, what is even more important, of contributing its exports towards ambitious joint projects, particularly in the under-developed countries. The directorate and staff of the World Bank have at their disposal a number of experts trained in business and banking; and these planning experts do much to provide an economically and financially wholesome free-market climate in different overseas regions. Two ways lie open to us at the same time. We can play our part as lenders, and we can also borrow to catch up with our own reconstruction. The 18% quota is also a valuable reserve to maintain the exporters' market. Moreover, the possibility of selling Deutsche Marks to the World Bank against dollars (as was done, for instance, in the case of the Jugoslav loan) offers us an additional opportunity for acquiring dollars. The fact that the Federal Republic is represented on the directorate naturally does not mean that decisions on the granting of credits to the Federal Republic rest with the

German director alone. Such credits are decided upon by the directorate as a whole.

The International Monetary Fund, where we are represented by Dr. Vocke as Governor, by Dr. von Mangold as alternate Governor and by Dr. Otto Donner as ordinary member, has still to play its full part. Its statutes are drafted in a way which is bound to prevent the Fund from becoming fully effective before its leading members have gone over to convertibility and are thus enabled to use their transitional quotas within an intrinsically sound balance of payments. Statements made by representatives of the Fund, e.g. at the Vienna Conference of the International Chamber of Trade in the spring of 1953, suggest that the Fund is prepared to show greater readiness in assisting the transition to convertibility. Nevertheless, it cannot become really effective until currency restrictions have been overcome; and these it cannot eliminate by its own activities. To bridge the gap the Fund can utilise members' contributions (the so-called 'quotas') of which in principle 25% is payable in gold. Those countries whose reserves of gold or convertible currencies are somewhat low have at present to pay a subscription in gold amounting merely to 10% of the individual country's monetary reserves, the rest being payable in the domestic currency. The total contributions of all the member countries amount to approximately $8·7 milliards, of which at present approximately $3·25 milliards are in gold and convertible currencies, the latter consisting almost entirely of United States and Canadian dollars.

Members can buy other currencies from the Fund against their own, but only to remove temporary difficulties in their balance of payment and subject to clearly determined rules. All in all, such transactions must not exceed 200% of the member's quota in the aggregate, or 25% within any one year. Under this rule the Federal Republic cannot acquire more than $82·5 millions' worth of other currencies within a year. In the aggregate, since it has so far paid in gold only 10% of its quota, it can obtain no more than 110% of the quota, i.e. $363 millions. The Fund's work is governed by a statute providing for supervision of and joint consultation regarding changes in the par of exchange. A first variation of 10% in any country's rate has to be sanctioned automatically; wider variations are subject to sanction by the Fund. Non-observation of this rule can be penalised by withholding drawing rights on the Fund. The fact that most currencies are not yet convertible has powerfully restricted the Fund's efficacy, as is apparent from the low volume of its turnover. Some change may have to be introduced in the Statutes resulting from our improved knowledge of the way in which currencies can be made convertible. The formation of the Fund, like that of the World Bank, was the outcome of the Bretton Woods negotiations in 1944; at that time it was impossible to form a clear picture of the post-war condition of the world's economy.

The occupation statute of May 12, 1949, made the observance of the Fund's basic principles—this was even before the Republic became a member—mandatory upon the Federal Republic. And indeed all the means of entry into world markets here described—O.E.E.C., G.A.T.T., the Bretton Woods institutions, and the Havana Charter—constitute not so much an offer as an obligation to share in the integration of the West.

CHAPTER XIX

LOOKING AHEAD

AT the stage reached in the spring of 1953 the main lines of our trade policy seemed to meet at a point marking the end of one phase of our return to world markets, and opening a new phase for our trade problems and trade policy. A close network of trade and payments agreements has been constructed on a foundation which, though it contained elements of legal uncertainty and indeed of a more general insecurity, was yet steadily gaining in strength. This process was accompanied by our closer participation in new organisations aiming at world-wide economic co-operation. With the exception of hard currency countries our trade and payments are now covered by businesslike agreements. These mostly have a fairly short term, so that we are able to adapt ourselves rapidly to the existing payments and foreign exchange problems; a large margin also exists for the reciprocal grant of quotas. While this development was going on the formation of E.P.U. and the adoption of liberalisation have provided the basis for large-scale and multilateral trade within Western Europe. Through a system of clearing agreements and the adoption of swings we have also assured ourselves of close contacts abroad to the full extent that such contacts can be assured by the type of agreement prevalent today.

Despite all this, our trade policy remains largely provisional. We have succeeded in adapting our foreign trade so that it benefits by the impulses affecting the trade of the world; but we still have to create a system of long-term trade treaties. This is indeed the most important task still awaiting our trade policy.

The pre-war system of trade treaties has today been largely eliminated. The restoration of the German-American trade treaty of 1923 (it came into force again in June, 1953) denotes the beginning of this new phase. Apart from this treaty the number of pre-war treaties still in force is small indeed. The exceptions are provided by a few non-belligerent countries, e.g. Eire; with certain other neutrals, e.g. Portugal, it has proved possible to reach arrangements in which the pre-war system is treated as still in force. With the former belligerents we have not yet succeeded in putting into force trade treaties of the classical type.

But even the old treaties which in fact or by convention are regarded as still in force, require almost without exception discussions to introduce modifications. The structure of trade and the legal requirements have changed almost everywhere. New ideas have prevailed, and there is a general demand for a new version of the old classical trade treaty. To construct a new network of this kind may well form the centre of our trade policy during the coming ten years. It follows that a large number of provisional arrangements which have been introduced into the existing trade agreements will have to be introduced into the new standard treaties. Naturally enough, the arrangements in force at present are formally subject to doubt and insecurity. Matters have to be settled executively which generally require ratification by Parliament. Precisely because such arrangements have generally been formulated somewhat cautiously, their binding force is not strikingly great. This applies also to certain governmental utterances the effect of which is that of a 'statement of policy', but not of a 'commitment'. This also applies to the conclusion of the preliminary trade treaties, even when these were later placed before the appropriate Legislature for ratification. Agreements of this kind have been concluded with Pakistan, Iraq and Ceylon.

Ensuring Most-Favoured-Nation Treatment

On the other hand, the most important item in every classical trade treaty, viz. unconditional most-favoured-nation treatment, has to a large extent been successfully realised. This is the effect of the G.A.T.T. treaty system. G.A.T.T. provides a long-term and evidently solid contractual basis for trade, ensuring us of the chief advantages which would result from an extensive network of classical treaties, although this network does not yet in fact exist. Special arrangements regarding most-favoured-nation treatment are required only with non-members of G.A.T.T. Such special arrangements have naturally a certain importance also because they assure us of most-favoured-nation treatment by a bilateral approach; the most-favoured-nation treatment therefore will remain even though the other country should decide to leave G.A.T.T. The new considerations to which justice would have to be done in a future system of trade treaties can here only be sketched. They relate partly to questions of exemption from military service, to special provisos for questions of immigration and emigration, to legal guarantees for the security of international investments, to the assurance of non-discrimination in questions of property, and to the problems of regional groupings and the exceptional position which such groupings might enjoy under a most-favoured-nation system. The special relationship to the United Nations might also find expression in the trade treaties.

Convertible Currencies

The conclusion of classical trade treaties will become more urgent as convertible currencies are more freely adopted and as trade and payments agreements accordingly lose in importance. The search for convertibility is sure to become a central problem in the settlement of world trade. If convertibility is one day achieved, the present type of trade agreement will largely become superfluous since import quotas will largely disappear with the disappearance of foreign exchange control. Any surviving quotas would have to be settled under the new trade treaties. The provisional character of the current trade agreements emerges also from the fact that we have not yet concluded any treaties with the more important countries of the dollar area, e.g. with the United States (until the middle of 1953), with Canada or with Venezuela. Our existing agreements have not done justice to the real problems relating to a healthy world-wide trade, a condition resulting from the half-baked state of the soft currency countries. The absence of special treaties with many of the dollar countries is, of course, also due to the fact that these countries hitherto have not troubled to secure openings for themselves with the soft currency countries. The Americans have abandoned their original attitude and in practice have never raised any objections against discrimination resulting from their own hard currency status. They have never, for instance, asked the Federal Republic to conclude a special trade agreement—though this in itself would have been logical—in order to secure their own position *vis-à-vis* bilateral soft currency countries. Conversely, the Federal Republic has never felt the need for a trade agreement with the dollar countries simply because our exports were never subjected to any currency restrictions. The sole exception is that of Cuba, whose exports so strongly reflect the country's reliance on a single product. This circumstance prevents Cuba from being as liberal as the other dollar countries. For this reason the Cubans have demanded a guaranteed market for rather large quantities of sugar in return for which certain preferences were granted on a most-favoured-nation basis.

Visible Trade Surpluses

The temporary nature of our system of treaties with the soft currency countries appears from our current account surpluses, which grew strikingly until the summer of 1953. New trading and currency problems arise from this development, problems which will have to be solved partly by the further expansion of capital development business overseas. Our surpluses within the E.P.U. and those existing with the clearing countries pose widely different problems. The E.P.U. surpluses constitute a convertibility problem in the sense that we would like to use the resulting balances to finance our purchases from the dollar area, or possibly to export capital overseas. This being so, the difficulty of converting the E.P.U. balances is an obstacle to our overseas trade. Our surpluses in Latin America and in other clearing countries, on the other hand, are a symptom of the lack of an efficient international capital market and of our overseas debtors' failure to settle their currency and financial problems. Our overseas balances indicate that we are exporting capital on current account and within the limits of the agreed swings, although in fact this export ought to be carried through altogether outside the system of current trade and current payments. Under-developed countries are structurally countries with high adverse balances because they are compelled to import capital in the form of machinery, etc. On the other hand, our export surpluses on current account wrongly suggest that we are in a position to export capital whereas in fact we are simply relying on advances made by the central bank of issue. We are endangering our own currency and interfering with our export of consumption goods. The problems arising out of our creditor position can be summed up by saying that we are exporting capital which we do not possess to the clearing countries and that we are exporting capital to the E.P.U. area which those countries do not really want. Our export surpluses with the clearing countries mask the capital shortage from which the under-developed countries suffer, while our E.P.U. surpluses mask the shortage of convertible currencies. In each case some of our circulating capital is fixed, capital which is waiting to be unfrozen by the formation of an effective capital market and the attainment of all-round convertibility.

A Dynamic Trade Policy

These developments indicate the beginning of a new phase in our trade policy. Its main difference from the preceding one will probably lie in one special point. Hitherto the task has been to harmonise economic impulses coming from abroad with our internal ones; in future an active programme will be needed to overcome the limiting factors which have meanwhile become visible. In detail the task will be as follows:

(1) In dealing with the E.P.U. area, i.e. with our European trade partners, visible trade will have to be simultaneously expanded and brought nearer to balancing. In other words, we shall have to increase our imports so as to permit the

other E.P.U. countries to continue in turn to import freely from the Federal Republic. An active programme of dollar saving operating through higher imports from the E.P.U. area and the subsidiary currency areas overseas, the sterling area in particular, will be one important task. Already this joint interest in an increased international division of labour has become more important than the occasional friction arising out of Anglo-German competition. It thus becomes clear that if the European currencies and sterling are to be made convertible simultaneously, much will first have to be done by British and Continental initiative in the way of dollar-saving. New openings for a vigorous German trade policy thus appear. It will be at a later stage, possibly in 1954, when it may be hoped that American trade policy has become clearer, that the United States could begin to play their part by granting stabilisation credits and similar measures. When this stage has been reached the entire payments system of the world could be merged in the mechanism of the International Monetary Fund.

(2) In dealing with the clearing countries overseas, i.e. with the under-developed regions, we shall have to adopt a new policy of stimulating visible imports and capital exports. Here again we shall have to overcome by constructive measures the limitations which are becoming visible in the present phase of adopting foreign impulses to domestic ones, and vice versa. The problem relates particularly to the under-developed countries still outside the multilateral system of payments. On the other hand, the problem of financing, e.g. for India or Pakistan, mainly concerns the London capital market, whence the problem of London's contact with other capital markets also arises. A country like India, for instance, can at present borrow in London and immediately use the capital raised to buy machinery in the Federal Republic. The problems arising from its capital imports are consequently reflected in our E.P.U. surplus and thus reduce themselves to a simple question of convertibility. The case is different with countries like Brazil, Argentina, Egypt, etc. Here new ways must be found to enable us to invest our capital. This also implies a vigorous import policy,

not only raising our present imports from those countries to a still higher level, but also opening future markets for the raw materials which may be produced as a consequence of these capital investments. The task thus arises automatically of making the creation of new outlets for our exports of consumption goods an essential part in these overseas deals. This further involves the freeing of international capital transactions. And this in turn may involve a reform of our own money market and our own fiscal system; at the same time international measures will be needed to overcome the currency control in force overseas.

Overseas Transactions

However much we avail ourselves of every opportunity, the uncertainties of any future trade with the East are such as to make it essential for the Federal Republic to play a larger part in capital developments overseas. Moreover, a more vigorous expansion of capital development in the overseas possessions of our E.P.U. partners is one essential if we are to continue a dynamic expansion of our foreign trade within the E.P.U. system. It would take us too far to describe in detail the deeper reasons affecting overseas development opportunities. The dynamism which may be expected to prevail in the overseas regions is partly due to their growing political independence and their consequential striving after industrialisation. This overseas trade will be capable of supporting heavy stresses—a consequence of the structural change undergone by the terms of trade as between raw materials and industrial goods since before the war. In agricultural as well as in industrial countries a growing industrial superstructure is based upon an output of raw materials which is being progressively subjected to the law of diminishing returns, which means rising costs per unit output. The Paley Report of 1952, as well as other analyses of the long-term trend for the output of foodstuffs and raw materials, suggests that the purchasing power inherent in raw materials in the widest sense has improved as against industrial products, despite all that can be done by chemical substitutes. Accordingly the risks attaching to overseas capital development tend to diminish as the opportunities increase. But if this type of business is to be given free play we shall need a trade policy ensuring currency convertibility, growing imports into the Federal Republic and stronger capital development for our exporting industries. Taken as a whole these tasks demand a long-term system of trade treaties of the kind indicated above.

Hitherto our trade policy has been confronted by a large number of open doors giving access to world markets. The strength derived by our economy from the existence of vigorous private enterprise and of industrious workers enabled us to pass through these doors with ease. In future we shall be confronted by new doors, and though these are not bolted we shall have to use special keys to open them. This will require thought and action on a large scale in terms both of space and of time, as well as a realistic view about the economic policy to adopt at home and for world trade. The satisfactory results obtained hitherto are encouraging and justify the hope that those in charge of our trade policy possess the equipment needed, jointly with private enterprise, successfully to enter upon this new phase.

EDITOR'S POSTSCRIPT

THE present work was produced in the Foreign Trade Section of the Federal Ministry of Economics. It is based on official papers and on the expressed views of those concerned in its production. It was easy to draw a clear and consistent picture: the notion of a free market economy which the Minister has infused into his Department was strongly reflected in the actual trade policy pursued. It remained to indicate the sources, to exchange views with members of the Ministry, to analyse the material available, and thus to provide a full description of our return to world markets.

In doing this the standpoint of the Foreign Trade Section was deliberately adopted. We then attempted as far as possible to establish co-ordination with other sections, including the Trade Policy Section of the Foreign Office. At present our trade policy is the joint product of Section V of the Ministry of Economics under Dr. Reinhardt, and of the Trade Policy Section of the Foreign Office under Dr. von Maltzan.

The picture we have drawn may appear imperfect in some respects. Some details might have been given more fully, others more tersely. If we had gone more into detail the years preceding the currency reform would have appeared even more full of incident. Subsidiary subjects like the growth of our mercantile fleet, the question of restaffing, etc., have been omitted, perhaps wrongly, and our trade with certain individual countries should perhaps have been described more fully. But we were not trying to provide an encyclopædia of trade policy since the war if only because time was short. Our object was to draw some of the main outlines, to point ahead and thus to show that new problems arise as the old ones are solved. Trade policy in this light becomes a dynamic process. It lives on change and on a proper understanding of this changing environment. The present work tries to catch some of the everyday ideas and problems, particularly those of the last few months.

It would take us too far to thank the many people who gave help in this work. All had a lively sense of their duty towards the public, an attitude showing a genuine sense of public relations. To play a part in producing this work was thus a pleasure for myself in the human and personal as well as in the practical sense.

Düsseldorf, Summer of 1953. HERBERT GROSS

INDEX

Abs, Herr H. J., 251, 253
Afghanistan, 185, 224
Agricultural Union, 148, 153
Agriculture, Ministry of, 36
Albania, 192, 196
Anglo-German Monetary Agreement, 140
Angola, 131
Annecy Conference, 198, 199, 205 sq.
Argentina, 159, 162, 168 sqq., 171, 248, 268
Assuan Dam, 185 sqq.
Australia, 137, 139, 143, 161
Austria, 63, 68, 76, 87, 100 sq., 104, 111, 249 sq., 258

Bank deutscher Länder, 107, 113, 129, 162, 169, 188, 217 sq., 222, 228, 244
Bank for International Settlements, 98
Belgian Congo, 123, 139, 146
Belgium, 77 sqq., 85, 87, 98, 100 sq., 103 sq., 106, 110, 123, 139, 146, 158
Belgo-Luxembourg Union, 123
Benelux Plan, 207 sq.
Benelux States, 121, 206
Beyen Plan, 213
Bipartite Economic Control Group, 62
Bismarck-Osten, F. von, 25
Bolivia, 171
Brazil, 68, 84, 159, 162, 164 sqq., 171, 231 sq., 268
Brazil, foreign exchange regulations in, 165 sqq.
Bulgaria, 192
Bullock, R. J., 67
Buy American Act, 178
Byrnes, Mr. J., 20, 70

Cairncross, Professor A. K., 107
Canada, 134, 178 sqq., 207, 223, 260, 265
Ceylon, 142, 264
Chambers of Foreign Trade, 239 sq.
Chile, 159, 162, 168 sqq.
Clay, General L., 81
Clearing area, 182
Clearing countries, 155, 178, 223, 230, 233, 266
Coal and Steel Community, 148, 150 sq., 153 sq.
Colombia, 160, 162, 171 sq.
Common List, 112
Control Council, Allied, 51 sq.
Convertibility, 27, 30 sq., 140, 146 sq., 265, 270
Council of Europe, 46, 204, 211, 213
Council of Länder, 57, 59 sq., 63
Counterpart Funds, 94 sq.
Cuba, 160, 172 sq., 175, 180, 266
Cuba, Agreement with, 27
Currency Reform, 82 sqq., 199
Czechoslovakia, 63, 68, 76, 88, 192

Damodar Project, 143, 187, 258
Dawes Loan, 107
Dawes Plan, 45
Deliberalisation, 137 sq., 145
Denmark, 36, 63, 81 sq., 124, 126 sq., 129, 192
Deutsche Mark, 23 sqq., 145
Deutsche Mark gap, 35, 99, 158 sq., 230, 232
Dietrich, Miss E., 62
Dollar area, 40, 140, 146, 176 sqq., 219, 223 sq., 254, 256 sq.
Dollar gap, 20, 23 sq., 31, 38, 41, 47, 140, 145, 157, 181, 191 sq.

Donner, Dr. O., 261
Draper, Col. W., 55, 62
Drawing Rights, 100 sq., 103
Dutch East Indies, 122

Eastern Committee of German
Industrialists, 196
E.C.A., 95, 99
E.C.E., 38 sq., 41 sqq., 47, 191,
196
Economic Council, 64, 71
Economics, Administration for,
55, 82
Economics, Ministry of (Federal
and Land), 35 sqq., 53 sqq.,
58 sqq., 73, 80, 175, 194, 216,
241, 243 sq., 250
Economics, Office of, 71
Ecuador, 160, 172
Eder Valley Barrage, 187
Egypt, 184 sqq., 239, 251, 268
Eire, 264
E.P.U., 6, 22 sq., 26 sq., 29 sqq.,
82, 104 sqq., 108 sqq., 113 sq.,
118, 120, 124, 130 sq., 134, 136,
138 sq., 145 sqq., 178, 188, 206,
223, 230, 233, 253, 263, 266 sqq.
Erhard, Professor L., 56, 83 sq.,
202, 259
E.R.P., 91 sqq., 95
Ethiopia, 185, 224
European Customs Union, 203
Export Insurance, 227
Export-Import Bank, 165 sq.

Fairs and Exhibitions, 242 sq.
Far East, 188
Federation of German Industry,
240, 243
Finance, Ministry of, 37
Finland, 127, 130, 153, 192
Foreign Office, 37, 194
Foreign Trade Advisory Council,
55, 83 sq.

Foreign Trade Division, 56
Foreign Trade Information Office,
236 sqq., 243
Foreign Trade Offices, 54 sq.,
67 sqq., 80, 90
France, 43, 52, 68, 76, 88, 98,
100 sq., 103, 111, 115, 120 sqq.,
139, 158, 195, 226, 249 sqq.
Franco-German Treaty, of 1927,
46

G.A.R.I.O.A., 5, 91 sqq., 106, 252
G.A.T.T., 17, 46, 49, 85, 89, 119,
131, 147, 177, 179, 201, 204 sqq.,
209, 211 sqq., 228, 262, 264 sqq.
German-American Trade Association, 179
Great Britain, 43, 63, 68, 73, 98,
100 sq., 104, 110 sq., 120, 127,
135, 139, 157 sq., 178, 194 sq.,
203, 249 sqq., 260
Greece, 79, 85, 100, 104, 111, 153

Harms, B., 45
Havana Charter, 17, 147, 201,
205, 262
Health Pool, 148, 152
Hermes Credit Insurance Co., 227
Hungary, 192

Iceland, 130
Imhoff, Herr L., 156
Imperial Preference, 211
Imports, Category A, 21 sq.
India, 84, 139, 141 sqq., 268
Indonesia, 146, 188 sqq.
International Monetary Fund, 17,
46, 89, 166, 206, 228, 256, 258,
261 sq., 268
Iran, 184, 187
Iraq, 184, 264
Israel, 187
Italy, 76, 82, 87, 98, 101, 103, 106,
111 sq., 115 sqq., 145, 249 sq.

Jacobssen, Hr. Peer, 107
Japan, 189 sq.
J.E.I.A., 20 sq., 49, 53, 55, 71 sqq., 84 sqq., 88, 97, 116, 136, 161, 215 sqq., 222, 246, 249
Jordan, 185
Jugoslavia, 132 sq., 259

Kastl, Dr. L., 56
Kerber, S. E., 148
Korean boom, 24, 106, 110, 113, 117, 125, 206, 218
Kroll, Dr., 194

Labrador, 180
Layton, Lord, 211
Lebanon, 184 sq.
Liberalisation, 22, 26, 43, 104, 106, 108, 110, 112 sqq., 117 sq., 120, 124 sq., 143, 148 sq., 198, 201 sq., 218, 256, 263
Liberalisation Code, 111
Liberia, 180, 224
Little Marshall Plan, 100 sqq.
Logan, Mr. W. J., 80, 86
London Debt Agreement, 135, 145, 246, 251 sqq.
Lupin, Herr von, 127
Luxembourg, 123

Maltzan, Freiherr von, 37, 53, 55, 62, 71, 81, 87, 126, 155, 199, 271
Manchuria, 189
Mangold, Dr. von, 261
Marshall Plan, 23, 30, 41, 46, 79, 81, 85, 87, 91 sq., 94 sq., 97 sqq., 102, 105 sq., 116, 147, 149, 153, 191, 203, 248, 252
Meinhold, Professor H., 150
Mexico, 159, 175, 180
Meyer, Professor F., 150
Middle East, 183 sqq., 187

Military Government Law No. 53, 51, 73
Military Government Law No. 61, 51
Military Government Law, No. 161, 73
Monnet, M. J., 154
Most-favoured-nation treatment, treaties, clause, 17, 50, 85, 89, 131, 163, 174, 176, 185, 198 sq., 211, 213, 264 sq.
Mueller, Dr. R., 71 sq.
Mutual Security Agency, 46, 92

Napolski, Dr. F. von, 239
Near East, 183 sqq.
Netherlands, 36, 63, 65, 81 sq., 85 sqq., 100 sq., 103 sq., 106, 110, 115, 118, 122 sq., 146, 188, 223
Newfoundland, 180 sq.
New Zealand, 143, 161
Norway, 81, 87, 101, 103 sq., 124, 126 sq.

Occupation Statute, 33, 47
O.E.E.C., 29, 49, 87, 95, 99, 106, 108, 112 sqq., 119, 135 sqq., 145, 201, 204, 206, 218, 224, 256, 262
Office de Commerce Extérieur, 52 sq., 66, 70, 85
Ohlin Plan, 210 sqq.
Oslo Conference, 211
Ottawa Tariffs, 212
Ouchy Conference, 211

Pakistan, 136, 139, 141 sqq., 187, 264, 268
Paley Report, 269
Panhorst, K. H., 156
Paris Convention (April 16, 1948), 147

Patents, 247
Peru, 172
Peso Rates, management of, 170
Pflimlin Plan, 154, 208 sqq.
Philippines, 190
Poland, 192, 194
Portugal, 100, 264

Regional Economic Offices, 68
Reich Office for Foreign Trade, 235 sq.
Reinhardt, H., 37, 56, 271
Remington, Mr., 75
Reparations Agreement, 254
Reuter, Dr. H., 196
Ringel, Dr. K., 237
Rittershausen, H., 197, 225
Roumania, 192, 196
Russia, 191 sq., 194, 196

Saudi Arabia, 184 sq., 187, 224
Scandinavia, 124 sqq., 128, 139, 206
Schacht, Dr. H., 108
Schäffer, Herr F., 259
Scherpenberg, Dr. van, 56
Schlepegrell, A. F. K., 81 sq.
Schmid, Professor Carlo, 48
Schmitt, Dr. M., 179
Schöne, Dr., 71
Schuman Plan, 46, 148, 150
Seeliger, Dr., 169
Semler, Herr, 212
Society for the Promotion of German-American Trade, 179
Spain, 130 sqq., 153, 180
Sperl, F., 56
Steinkopf, Herr, 56
Sterling area, 109, 134 sqq., 140, 145 sq., 182, 268
Stern, E. H., 233
Sudan, 185
Sweden, 36, 68, 86 sq., 101, 104, 124, 126, 128 sq., 192, 251
Swings, 85, 156, 162 sqq., 168, 171, 185, 189, 193, 263, 267

Switzerland, 68, 70, 76, 86 sq., 98, 100 sq., 103, 106, 110, 115, 139, 206 sq., 211, 229, 246, 252, 260
Syria, 185, 224

Tenders, tendering procedure, 219 sq.
Thailand, 190
Torquay Conference, 200 sq., 205 sqq.
Trade-marks, 247 sq.
Trade Policy Section (of Foreign Office), 34 sq., 37
Transferable Sterling, 138 sq.
Tredefina, 221 sq.
Trendelenburg, Dr., 204
Trieste, 153
Turkey, 88, 101, 104, 153, 184 sq., 187

Union of South Africa, 143
United States, 38, 40, 63, 68, 78, 85, 96, 105, 120, 134, 136, 139, 147, 157 sq., 161, 165, 167, 170, 172, 176 sqq., 207, 212 sq., 223, 229, 233, 245, 249, 251, 260, 265, 268
Uruguay, 84, 156, 162 sq., 168

Venezuela, 172 sqq., 265
Versailles, Treaty of, 45 sq., 50 sq., 198
Vocke, Dr., 261

Wapenheusch, J., 51
War Damage Assessment Commission, 53
Weir, Sir Cecil, 55
World Bank, 17, 46, 132, 143, 163, 186, 229, 258 sq.

Yemen, 185, 224

Zahn, Dr. J., 259
Zottschew, T. D., 25

THE END